THE STRUCTURE OF COORDINATION

Studies in Natural Language and Linguistic Theory

VOLUME 57

Managing Editors

Marcel den Dikken, *City University of New York*
Liliane Haegeman, *University of Lille*
Joan Maling, *Brandeis University*

Editorial Board

Guglielmo Cinque, *University of Venice*
Carol Georgopoulos, *University of Utah*
Jane Grimshaw, *Rutgers University*
Michael Kenstowicz, *Massachusetts Institute of Technology*
Hilda Koopman, *University of California, Los Angeles*
Howard Lasnik, *University of Connecticut at Storrs*
Alec Marantz, *Massachusetts Institute of Technology*
John J. McCarthy, *University of Massachusetts, Amherst*
Ian Roberts, *University of Cambridge*

The titles published in this series are listed at the end of this volume.

THE STRUCTURE OF COORDINATION

Conjunction and Agreement Phenomena in Spanish and Other Languages

by

JOSÉ CAMACHO

*Rutgers University,
New Brunswick, U.S.A.*

KLUWER ACADEMIC PUBLISHERS
DORDRECHT / BOSTON / LONDON

A C.I.P. Catalogue record for this book is available from the Library of Congress.

ISBN 1-4020-1510-0

Published by Kluwer Academic Publishers,
P.O. Box 17, 3300 AA Dordrecht, The Netherlands.

Sold and distributed in North, Central and South America
by Kluwer Academic Publishers,
101 Philip Drive, Norwell, MA 02061, U.S.A.

In all other countries, sold and distributed
by Kluwer Academic Publishers,
P.O. Box 322, 3300 AH Dordrecht, The Netherlands.

Printed on acid-free paper

All Rights Reserved
© 2003 Kluwer Academic Publishers
No part of this work may be reproduced, stored in a retrieval system, or transmitted
in any form or by any means, electronic, mechanical, photocopying, microfilming, recording
or otherwise, without written permission from the Publisher, with the exception
of any material supplied specifically for the purpose of being entered
and executed on a computer system, for exclusive use by the purchaser of the work.

Printed in the Netherlands.

CONTENTS

Acknowledgements	vii
Preface	ix
Introduction	1
What are the Properties of Coordination?	3
The Structure of Coordination	33
Coordination and Agreement	91
Coordination of Larger Phrases	151
References	173
Index	179

ACKNOWLEDGEMENTS

This book stems from work for my dissertation (Camacho 1997). Many people have been very generous with their time and support. Their names are scattered throughout the book, but here I will highlight some of them: for help with difficult judgements, ideas, references, comments: Pablo Albizu, Alfredo Arnaiz, Lina Choueiri, Mary Dalrymple, Arantzazu Elordieta, Gorka Elordieta, Jane Grimshaw, Marcello Modesto, Liliana Paredes, Liliana Sánchez, Roger Schwarzschild, Barry Schein, Germán Westphal and two anonymous reviewers. For all kinds of support: Mercedes Orosco, Laura Reiter, Liliana Sánchez. The Kluwer staff and series editor: Jacqueline Bergsma, Iris Klug and Liliane Haegeman. This book is dedicated to Liliana, Yésica and Lucía.

PREFACE

This book analyzes the structure of coordination from two perspectives: the symmetrical properties the construction imposes on its conjuncts, and how conjuncts interact with other categories outside coordination with respect to agreement and other grammatical phenomena. A substantial amount of data represented in this book are taken from varieties of Spanish. Unlike English, Spanish has a rich pattern of overt agreement between the subject and the verb, between nouns and adjectives, and also between clitics and lexical DP objects and indirect objects. Spanish agreement paradigms reveal very interesting patterns of agreement mismatch that provide important theoretical insights. Unless otherwise specified, it can be assumed that non-English examples are from Spanish.

CHAPTER #1

INTRODUCTION

Although coordination has figured more or less steadily in the Generative tradition beginning with Chomsky's (1957) Conjunction Transformation (later known as Conjunction Reduction), until recently, the two prevailing areas of research had been ellipsis (see, for example, Van Oirsouw 1987) and the semantic interpretation of conjuncts.[1] The internal structure of coordination was usually left unanalyzed, or assumed to be ternary branching, as in (1).

(1)

Beginning in the 1990s, the situation started to change. Several analyses began to address issues regarding the internal structure of coordination. In this book, I will review the most important contributions from recent analyses of coordination, and I will make a proposal that builds on important insights provided by those analyses, but which departs from them in several respects. The proposal claims that coordination should satisfy two basic properties, presented in chapter 2: *c-command asymmetry* and *licensing symmetry*. The first property argues that one of the conjuncts c-commands the other(s), as argued by several researchers (cf., for example, Munn (1993)). Most recent proposals on the structure of coordination capture this property (cf. Munn 1993, Johannessen 1993, 1998 Zoerner 1995, Camacho 1997). However, unlike those proposals, I will argue that coordination must be symmetric with respect to a licensing head. In simple terms, each conjunct should reflect the same structural properties as if it were in a simplex sentence. Thus, if a conjoined constituent can be the subject of a sentence, each of the conjuncts can usually also appear as a subject of a sentence without coordination.[2] Whatever structural property licenses a constituent in a simplex sentence should also license each of the conjuncts in the corresponding coordinated sentence. In some sense, this is the simplest theory, although with important consequences.

In addition to satisfying these two properties, my proposal for the structure of conjunction accepts the underlying idea behind Chomsky's Conjunction Reduction: I will claim that conjunction always involves a set of sentential functional projections

---

[1] Some of the substantive issues surrounding coordination are quite old, as Lasersohn (1995) documents.
[2] This property is not true for what Johannessen (1998) calls unbalanced coordination, see chapt. 2 and 3.

(cf. also Schein 1997, 2001 for a semantic proposal that shares the same assumptions).

In the second chapter I will review the different proposals concerning the structure of coordination, and suggest what aspects of them should be maintained and accounted for and which need to be modified. The third chapter presents the bulk of my proposal. On the one hand, I will support the contention that coordination is propositional in nature; on the other, I will present evidence for the structural properties of conjoined constituents. Together, these two sets of evidence will lead to a proposal for the structure of coordination where conjuncts are always either specifiers of or complements to sentential functional (propositional) projections.

Chapter 4 will analyze the consequences of my proposal for agreement systems. Particular attention will be paid to languages that display partial agreement systems with conjunction. Chapter 5 will present cases where conjunction involves larger structures, in particular cases with gapping.

Throughout the book, I take "propositional" and "sentential" to be different sides of the same coin.

CHAPTER #2

WHAT ARE THE PROPERTIES OF COORDINATION?

Analyses of coordination did not consider the internal configuration of coordinated constituents until the mid 80s (with the notable exception of Dik 1968), when research into the internal structure of coordination began to yield important insights. One of the areas of discussion in the literature had to do with the relationship between conjuncts and heads that license them. In particular, when conjuncts have conflicting features (i.e. sets of features that together do not match those of an outside head with which they agree), which one prevails? What are the conditions for cases where only one of the conjuncts triggers agreement or matches case, etc.? Some of these issues, in turn, have direct impact on the structural representation of coordination: a binary-branching representation may provide a more principled explanation than a ternary structure as to why only one of the conjuncts triggers agreement. In a ternary structure, both conjuncts have the same structural position, whereas in a binary structure it is possible to define one conjunct as structurally closer to a head than the other. Another important issue discussed is whether coordination displays some kind of structural asymmetry: is one of the conjuncts structurally higher than the other? Finally, an important issue in the background of the discussions about the status of coordination involves how the interpretation of conjoined phrases provides evidence for their structural representation, etc. In this chapter, I will review each of these topics, presenting the relevant proposals in turn. First, I will deal with peripherality, next I will turn to structural symmetry, and finally I will present some general properties of coordination.

1. LICENSING SYMMETRY

Some of the issues regarding licensing of conjuncts by an outside head include the following: do conjuncts behave in the same way they would if they were in simplex sentences? In what sense is a conjoined subject a subject? How is this reflected by the structural representation? How are conjuncts licensed? I will frame the issue of conjunct licensing by introducing the notion of *licensing symmetry*: a representation complies with licensing symmetry if each conjunct is licensed in the same way as they would be if they were not conjoined. Consider the following representation: the Coordination Phrase is the one licensed with respect to I^0, so each conjunct is licensed in a way that is different from the non-conjoined counterpart. Conj1 is the specifier of a different functional projection (CoordP vs. IP in the non-conjoined counterpart); Conj2 is the complement of a different projection.

(1)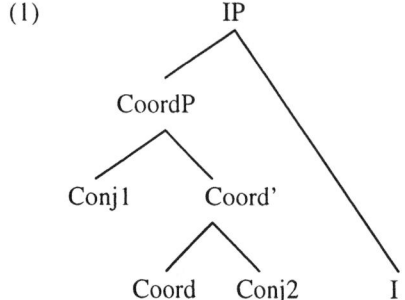

Given that in the general case (see below for exceptions), a conjunct can appear in the same position as it could appear if it were not conjoined, licensing symmetry should be respected as much as possible. Thus, each of the subject conjuncts in (2)a can independently appear as subjects, as in (2)b, c, from Spanish.

(2) a. Los perros y   los gatos son animales domésticos.
       the dogs   and the cats are animals   domestic
       'Dogs and cats are domestic animals.'
    b. Los perros son animales domésticos.
       the dogs   are animals   domestic
       'Dogs are domestic animals.'
    c. Los gatos son animales domésticos.
       the cats are animals   domestic
       'Cats are domestic animals.'

Pullum and Zwicky (1986)[3] formalize this intuition in a generalization, slightly reformulated in below:[4]

(3) *Law of Coordination of Likes* (Wasow's generalization). If a coordinate structure occurs in some position in a syntactic representation, each of its conjuncts must have syntactic feature values that would allow it to occur individually in that position and those feature values must be the same for each conjunct.

(2) illustrates the first part of Wasow's generalization: a conjunction of subjects can appear in the same configuration as a simplex subject can.(4), on the other hand, illustrates a case where Wasow's generalization is violated: (4) a is ungrammatical as a coordination of subjects because (4)b is ungrammatical as a simplex sentence. Presumably, both sentences are ungrammatical because subjects must be nominative in English, and in (4)a, the second conjunct is not, in (4)b, the only subject is not.

---

[3] This section is based on Camacho (2000a).

[4] Wasow's generalization is related to Williams' (1986) Across-the-Board Extraction rule, in the sense that Williams' cases also require structural parallelism. See also Dalrymple and Kaplan (2000).

Following Pullum and Zwicky, I will call the element with which the conjuncts agree (or check case, etc.) *the factor*. In (4), the verb (or inflection) is the factor that checks the case features of the conjuncts.

(4) a. *The men and to the women left the room.
  b. *To the women left the room.

The second part of Wasow's generalization (the requirement for symmetry among conjuncts) can be seen in (5). Although each conjunct could independently appear with the factor (as shown in (5)b-c), when they are conjoined, they cannot receive different thematic roles (see also Godard 1989 and Lasersohn 1995 for similar assumptions). I will call cases of conjuncts that have similar features, *symmetric* or *balanced coordination*.

(5) a. *Juan y el cuchillo cortaron el pan.
   Juan and the knife   cut   the bread
  b. Juan cortó el pan.
   Juan cut the bread
   'Juan cut the bread.'
  c. El cuchillo cortó el pan.
   the knife cut the bread
   'The knife cut the bread.'

Since Wasow's generalization seems to be fairly pervasive (although exceptions exist, see below), theories of coordination should be compatible with it. There are two logical ways for analyses of coordination to comply with it. On the one hand, it could be proposed that each conjunct should be licensed separately as if it were in isolation (i.e. licensing symmetry). Thus, if nominative case is checked in spec-head configuration with Infl, then, each subject in (4)a must be checked in a spec-head configuration with Infl. Goodall (1987), Camacho (1997, 2000a) take this path, as we will see immediately below.

On the other hand, one could claim that conjoined phrases form a conjunction phrase (of the same type as the conjuncts), and this higher phrase is licensed. Versions of this solution underlie proposals by Gazdar et al (1985), Munn (1993), Johannessen (1993, 1998), Zoerner (1995), Thiersch (1994), Kaplan and Maxwell (1995), Progovac (1997), Arnaiz and Camacho (1999). Note that in this solution there is no obvious reason why conjuncts should respect Wasow's generalization. Such solution must derive Wasow's generalization from on constraints imposed on the relationship between conjuncts and the higher conjunction node. Such constraints are not always explicitly formulated.

1.1 Goodall (1987) and Kaplan and Maxwell (1995)

Goodall (1987) and Kaplan and Maxwell (1995) represent two different solutions to the issue of licensing symmetry. Goodall proposes a tridimensional structure for coordination, which he argues should be extended to other cases like causatives, Kaplan and Maxwell take advantage of LFG's division of labor between c-structures (tree markers) and f-structures (functional relations) by imposing constraints on the shape f-structures can take. I will briefly review both solutions. Goodall's proposal is described as a solution "wherein coordination is represented as a union of phrase markers ... it will suffice to think of it in tree terms as a 'pasting together,' one on top of the other, of two trees, with any identical nodes merging together (p. 20)." In a representation such as (6), where *Jane* and *Alice* are in separate planes (represented by the dotted lines), it is possible to define relationships of precedence and dominance between each element in the sentence and every other element, except for the coordinated elements *Jane* and *Alice*. Since these two elements are not ordered with respect to each other, Goodall has a Linearization Principle that insures the correct word order.

(6)
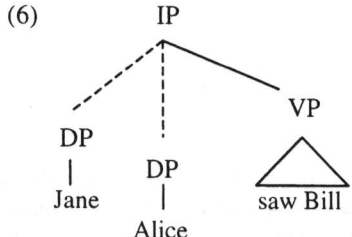

Goodall's proposal clearly respects licensing symmetry, since each conjunct is licensed in the same way.[5] Johannessen (1998) points out a potential problem for Goodall's theory. Consider (7)a and (7)b. According to Johannessen, in the first sentence, the total number of cars sold is ten, whereas in the second one, it is twenty. The reason why this might be a problem is that presumably, both sentences have the same representation. Note, however, that both interpretations are available in both sentences (as an anonymous reviewer points out), although the one in which the total number of cars sold is twenty is preferred in (7)b, whereas the one where the total number of cars sold is ten is the most natural one in (7)a. When adverbs like *respectively* or *each* appear, the twenty-car reading surfaces for (7)a, as shown in (8)a. Conversely, it is possible to get the reading where only ten cars are bought with the two full clauses, as shown in (8)b. This shows that the preference for a given reading with a sentence does not entail the ungrammaticality of the other reading.

---

[5] It also maintains the intuition behind the Conjunction Reduction analysis of ` (1957), namely, that *Jane and Alice saw Bill* is, in some sense, a conjunction of clauses. Chomsky's original proposal required some additional mechanism to delete the parts of the conjoined sentence that do not appear overtly (cf., for example, Gleitman 1965 for a detailed approach to deletion), in Goodall's account deletion is no longer necessary.

Rather, the source of the preference may be due to the operation of Gricean principles.

(7) a. Tom and Carol bought ten cars.
  b. Tom bought ten cars and Carol bought ten cars.

(8) a. Tom and Carol bought ten cars each.
  b. Tom bought ten cars and Carol bought ten cars, and they turned out to be the same cars.

Johannessen (1998) presents a final objection to Goodall's analysis. In Norwegian, anaphors and pronominals share the same form in the third person. However, when they are conjoined, as in (9) (from Johannessen), only the pronominal interpretation is possible.

(9) Per og Kari så seg/selv   og en ku.
  Per and Kari saw him/himself and a cow
  'Per and Kari saw themselves/*himself and a cow'

The reason why this is problematic for Goodall's analysis is that the uncoordinated sources for (9) are presumably ambiguous with respect to the anaphoric or pronominal status of *selv* 'self,' but the conjoined one is not ambiguous. Johannessen suggests this same contrast holds in English, as illustrated in (10). However, (10) c is given as fully grammatical by Goodall. His original contention was that this example can be derived only in the *respectively* reading, whose sources would be *John saw himself* and *Mary saw a cow*. In the other reading, there would be *Mary saw himself* in addition to *John saw himself* as a source, violating the requirement that *himself* have a singular antecedent. Hence, the unique reading of (10)c is predicted in Goodall's theory.

(10) a. John saw himself.
   b. Mary saw a cow.
   c. ??John and Mary saw himself and a cow (respectively).

Goodall's (1987) analysis represents the narrowest interpretation of licensing symmetry: in his representation of coordination, each conjunct always behaves as if it were not a conjunct. The cost of maintaining this conceptual simplicity is introducing tridimensional structures in the grammar. Kaplan and Maxwell (1995), on the other hand, solve the issue of licensing symmetry in a different way. As I mentioned, they take advantage of Lexical-Functional Grammar's two different levels of syntactic representation for a sentence: c-structure, which represents structural relations, and f-structure, which encodes functional relations, such as subject, predicate, object, agreement, etc. These two levels of representation are related by a function that maps nodes in the c-structure to f-structure units. In order to see how licensing symmetry is dealt with, I will present an example of how conjoined constituents are analyzed.

The c-structure of conjoined items involves an n-ary branching constituent (cf. (11) b, and the f-structure constitutes a set of f-structures, one for each conjunct (cf. (12)), from Kaplan and Maxwell (1995).

(11) a. John bought apples and John ate apples.
     b.

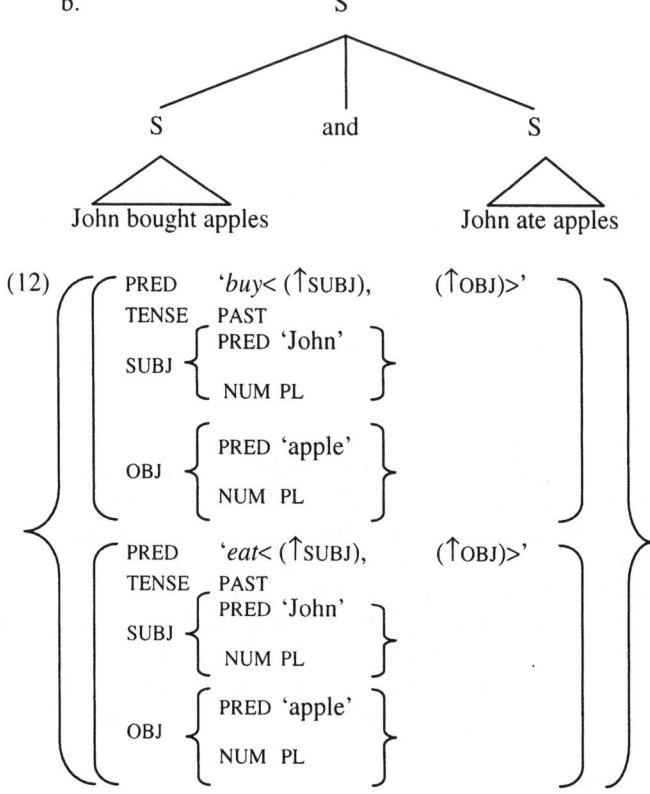

For the case of coordination of items that share a constituent, as in (13)a, the c-structure is (13)b and the f-structure,(14).

(13) a. John bought and ate apples.

b.

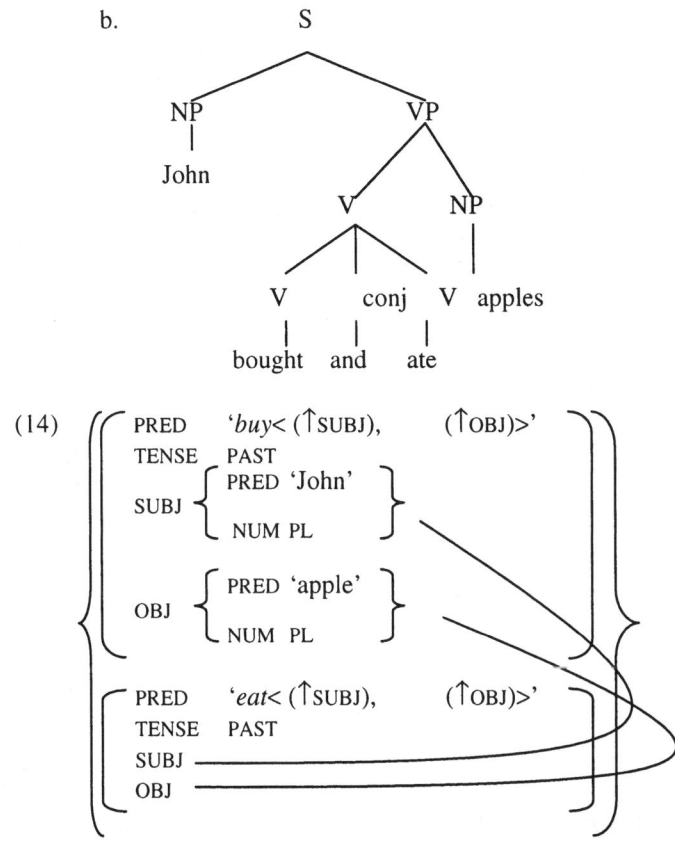

The subjects and objects of *buy* and *eat* are linked by allowing function application to operate on sets of functions (cf. Kaplan and Maxwell 1995, following Bresnan, Kaplan and Peterson 1985). By virtue of defining linking this way, the properties asserted on a set as a whole must be distributed across all of the elements of the set. This explains why the subject and object of (13)a are distributed across verbs. Linking allows each conjunct to individually satisfy the requirements that it would satisfy if it were not a conjunct (i.e. to be licensing symmetric). The crucial difference with respect to Goodall's approach is that licensing symmetry is enforced on f-structures, not on the structural representation (the c-structure). This, in turn, is going to be a weakness of the analysis, as it will be shown that there are c-command asymmetries among conjuncts that cannot be stated in terms of f-structure.

1.2 Systematic Violations of Wasow's Generalization

In most languages, conjuncts satisfy Wasow's generalization, as shown earlier. In certain languages, however, this is not the case. There are two systematic types of violations of the generalization. The first one involves cases in which only one of the conjuncts satisfies the requirements of the factor. Thus, in some languages, only one of the subjects agrees with the verb (see Corbett 1983, Johannessen 1993, 1996, 1998 in particular, Aoun, Benmamoun and Sportiche 1994, 1999, Munn 1999, among many other references). This type of coordination is called *unbalanced* or *asymmetric coordination*. For example, in Norwegian (cf. (15) from Johannessen 1998, p. 18), the first pronoun has nominative case, but the second one has accusative (a case otherwise not licensed in subject position). Johannessen also observes the following correlation: head-initial languages allow the last conjunct to be unbalanced, head-final languages allow the first conjunct to be unbalanced.[6]

(15) Han   og meg   var   sammen om det.
     he(NOM) and me(ACC) were together about it
     'He and I were in it together.'

These facts and the directionality correlation lead Johannessen to propose the following structure for head-initial languages (head-final languages would be symmetrical).

(16)

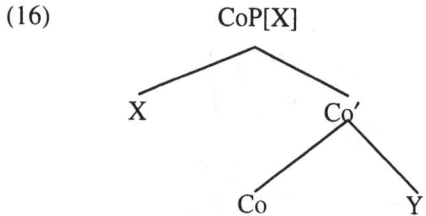

The conjunction is the head of the structure, hence it is a Conjunction Phrase. However, CoP "inherits the syntactic category features from its specifier conjunct by spec-head agreement (Johannessen 1998, p. 110). Since the second conjunct is in complement position, its features will not be inherited by the maximal phrase.[7] One of the problems this solution raises is that in general, spec-head agreement does not allow features to percolate randomly to the maximal phrase. In particular, categorial features never percolate by spec-head agreement. Otherwise, a subject in spec, IP, would turn IP into a nominal projection. Johannessen's analysis is oriented towards accounting for cases of unbalanced coordination. In effect, it could be argued that this proposal makes unbalanced coordination the default coordination pattern.

For a subset of languages that have asymmetric coordination, a further generalization holds: partial agreement (i.e. agreement with one of the conjuncts only) can only happen between the factor and the closest conjunct. For example, in the structure V [DP$_1$ and DP$_2$], the verb agrees with DP$_1$. Furthermore, partial

---

[6] As an anonymous reviewer points out, this property does not hold for English. The unexpected accusative/oblique case in (i) is first in a head-initial language:

(i.) Me and John are going home.

[7] This solution is very similar to the one proposed in Arnaiz and Camacho 1999.

agreement exists in the typologically marked order for that language. Thus, in an SVO language, partial agreement would only occur in the order VS. These two observations are true of Spanish, Portuguese, Arabic, among other languages. See chapter 4.

The second type of exception to Wasow's generalization involves cases in which the features of the conjuncts do not exactly match those of the factor, but they can be considered a proper subset of the features of the factor. Consider the following example:

(17) Juan y yo comimos tortilla.
　　　Juan and I ate(1p.PL) omelette
　　　'Juan and I ate omelette.'

In this example, the factor, *comimos* is 1st person plural, but the first conjunct is 3rd person singular, and the second one is 1st person singular. Thus, neither one of the conjuncts can indidually match those of the factor. In these cases, generally know as *feature resolution* (see Corbett 1983) the features of the factor include, in some intuitive manner, those of each of the conjuncts.

A slightly different case, *feature indeterminacy,* is described an analysed by Dalrymple and Kaplan (2000), and can be illustrated with the following example, from Polish. In this example, each of the verbs has different case requirements: genitive and accusative, yet *kogo* can satisfy both of them.

(18) kogo Janek lubi a Jerzy nienawidzi?
　　　who Janek likes and Jerzy hates
　　　'Who does Janek like and Jerzy hate?'

The core of Dalrymple and Kaplan's analysis assumes that feature values can be sets of items in addition to individual items. For the case of feature indeterminacy, the word *kogo* will take as its CASE values {GEN, ACC}, which will satisfy each verb. In the case of feature resolution, the feature representation of the conjoined set will include {1P, SG} {2P, SG} and the features for the coordinate structure {1P, PL}. The latter set of features satisfies the verb's requirements. Notice that implicit in this latter statement is the idea that {1P, SG} + {2P, SG} = {1P, PL}, it is not explicitly stated which what the possible combinations of features are.

Feature resolution typically affects φ-feaures (person, number, gender), but tend not to be possible with other types of features. In the next section, I will show how explore the question whether feature resolution operates with other kinds of features besides case and agreement, such as temporal, aspectual, etc. In previous work (cf. Camacho 1999, 2000a), I have found that temporal and aspectual features in Spanish are not subject to feature resolution rules. I will summarize and extend those results in the following section.

1.2.1 Conjunction of Temporal and Aspectual Categories

At first sight, verbal coordination violates Wasow's generalization with respect to tense as shown in common examples like (19) from Spanish: each verb can have different temporal values. The issue, however, is not as clear, since that sentence can have at least two possible structures: (20)a or (20) b. Temporal feature parallelism will only be relevant for structure (20)a, and only in that case will Wasow's generalization be violated. If the structure of (19)a is (20)b, then temporal feature parallelism will not be relevant because temporal feature specification operates at the level of TP, not at the level of XP.

(19) [Subió   y   va   a traerlo]
went(PAST) up and is-going to bring-it
'S/he went upstairs and is going to bring it'

(20) a. [$_{TP}$ subió] y [$_{TP}$ va a traerlo]
b. [$_{XP}$[$_{TP}$ subió]] y [$_{XP}$[$_{TP}$ va a traerlo]]

In what follows, I will argue that a conjunction of two verbal projections like (19) may be ambiguous between the two structures in (20). It can be shown that whenever the structure is (20)a, tenses must be identical. The way to force a structure like (20)a is by using adverbs that modify inflection (temporal and aspectual adverbs, as well as negation). If they take scope over both conjuncts, temporal identity becomes obligatory, as shown in Camacho (1999, 2000). Negation can have scope over both conjuncts or over one of them. Thus, a sentence like (21)a can have the interpretations in (21)b, with negative scope over both conjuncts, or the one in (21)c, with negative scope over the first one. The latter reading is less preferred, for pragmatic reasons, but nonetheless available.

(21) a. Pepa no llegó y   pidió   un café
Pepa not arrived and ordered a coffee
b. Pepa didn't arrive and order (a cup of) coffee (she arrived and ordered three cups)
c. Pepa didn't arrive, and she ordered (a cup of) coffee

However, when negation has scope over both conjuncts, the tenses cannot be different, as shown in (22)a. If tenses are different, as in (22)b, negation cannot have scope over both conjuncts. It is also possible to have negative scope over both conjuncts and to have different tenses, but then there must be two negations, as in (22)c (see Johnson 2000 on the scope of negation and quantified phrases over two conjuncts).

(22) a. *Pepa no [llegó   y   va   a pedir café]
Pepa not arrived(PAST) and goes to order coffee
'Pepa did not arrive and is going to order coffee'

b. Pepa [no llegó] y [va a pedir café]
   Pepa not arrived(PAST) and goes to order coffee
   'Pepa did not arrive and she is going to order coffee'
c. Pepa [no llegó] y [no va a pedir café].
   Pepa not arrived(PAST) and not goes to order coffee
   'Pepa did not arrive and is not going to order coffee'

The same paradigm can be observed with other adverbs, as illustrated in (23) and (24). Temporal/aspectual adverbs with scope over both conjuncts require temporal/aspectual parallelism.[8]

(23) a. Este jugador siempre [se cae   y   pierde la pelota]
       this player   always   CL falls and loses the ball
       'This player always falls and loses the ball'
   b. *Este jugador siempre [se cae y va   a perder la pelota]
       this player   always   CL falls and is-going to lose the ball

(24) a. El gato casi   [se sube a la escalera y se cae]
       the cat almost CL climbs to the ladder and CL falls
       'The cat almost climbs on the ladder and falls'
   b. ??El gato casi [se sube a la escalera y se cayó]
       the cat almost CL climbs to the ladder and CL fell
       'The cat almost climbs on the ladder and fell'

These paradigms argue for the idea that temporal features are also subject to Wasow's generalization.[9] Furthermore, at least in Spanish, there is no feature resolution with respect to tense. That is to say, it is not possible to have a temporal feature specification that includes the feature specifications of both conjuncts, even though the temporal features of some tenses overlap.

To summarize so far, the examples presented in these sections show that, in the general case, features in conjuncts must be parallel; these features are the ones that appear in the corresponding simplex sentences, and only person, number, gender and case are subject (at least in Spanish), to resolution rules.

1.3   Asymmetric Coordination in German

---

[8]Conversely, if an adverb does not modify tense or aspect, then the prediction is that temporal features will need not be identical (because coordination will be higher than TP). The following example shows such a case (this observation is due to Elena Herburger, p.c.):

(i.)   Lamentablemente, se subió   a la escalera y   se va a caer.
       regretfully   CL climbed to the ladder and CL goes to fall
       'Regretfully, he/she climbed the ladder and is going to fall down'

[9] The adverb *casi* modifies the aspectual structure of the VP, see Camacho (2000a) for a full analysis of its distribution.

German presents a different type of asymmetry, one in which the conjoined categories are different, as in (25)a, due to Höhle (1990), quoted in Thiersch (1994). This sentence involves a coordination in which the first conjunct has a verb-final clause, typical of embedded clauses; and the second conjunct has a root-like, verb-second clause. The structure is schematically shown in (25)b. However, this combination is not possible in normal circumstances, as shown in (26)c-d:

(25) a. Wenn jemand   nach Hause kommt und da   steht der
       If   someone to   house comes and there stands the
       Gerichtsvollzieher der Tür
       bailiff   the door
       'If someone comes home and the bailiff is standing there in front of the door.'
    b. C [$_{IP}$ ...V] and [$_{CP}$ V [$_{IP}$ ...]]

(26) a. Er meint, Karl sei schon hier.
       he thinks Karl is already here
       'He thinks Karl is already here.'
    b. Er meint, dass Frieda die Kartoffeln geschält   habe.
       he thinks that Frieda the potatoes   peeled   has
       'He thinks that Frieda has peeled the potatoes.'
    c. *Karl sei schon hier und dass Frieda die Kartoffeln geschält habe, meinte Fritz.
    d. ??dass Frieda die Kartoffeln geschält habe und Karl sei schon hier, meinte Fritz.

As Thiersch (1994) points out, Höhle notes the fact that extraction from the second conjunct is possible in these asymmetric constructions, but not from the first one, as shown in below:

(27) a. Seine Bücher$_i$ verkaufte er e_i unde wandte sich   der   Malerei zu.
       his   books   sold   he   and   turned himself the(DAT) painting to
       'He sold his books and turned to painting.'
    b. *Seine Bücher$_i$ wandte er sich   der   Malerei zu und verkaufte e_i
       his   books   turned he himself the(DAT) painting to and sold
       'His books, he turned to painting and sold.'

Höhle's proposal is based on the idea that the relevant criteria for coordination is the level of saturation of the predicates. In (25)a, there is a coordination of a saturated V^{MAX} and a saturated I^{MAX}.[10] Thiersch assumes this basic intuition and tries to account for the fact that only the second conjunct allows for extraction by

---

[10] Notice that this solution preserves licensing symmetry by switching the criteria for symmetry from category to level of saturation.

suggesting that the first conjunct is an adjunct. Thiersch's proposed structure is the following[11]:

(28)
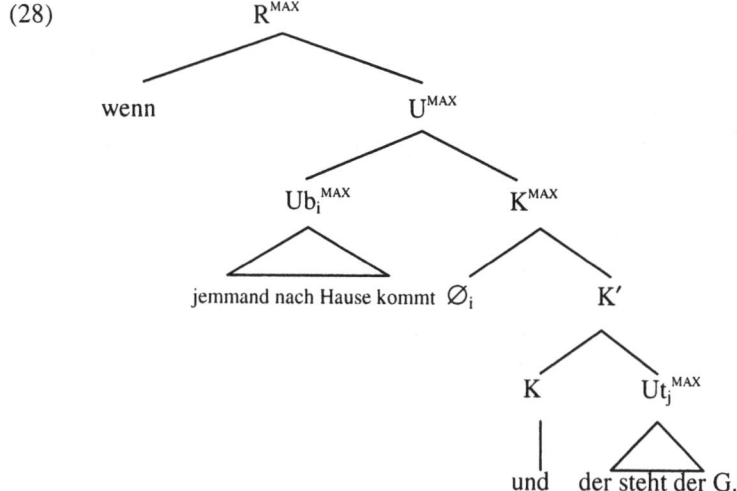

Thiersch's notation requires some elaboration. In his system, there are three types of COMP: argument COMP, labelled G (e.g. *dass*), a relative-like COMP, labelled R (e.g. Bavarian *wo* and *wenn* above), and an assertion COMP, labelled U, the landing site for the verb in V-2 clauses. The assertion COMP (U) appears in a basic word order (SV), which Thiersch calls Ub, and in inverted word order (Ut). Both G and R can take U as a complement. The verb moves to U if and only if it is not governed by a lexical G. Finally, intermediate projections (X') only exist if licensed.

Licensing of the adjunct in (28) is done in the same way other adjuncts are licensed in this system: by coindexation with the empty specifier of K^{MAX}. Since adjuncts are islands, it is expected that the second conjunct, an adjunct in this analysis, will also be an island. This explains why extraction from the first conjunct is impossible. The features of the two conjuncts are resolved at the level of the conjunction node K^{MAX} by computing the features of the empty head in the specifier of K, which is coindexed with the first conjunct; and the features of the complement of K, Ut.[12]

---

[11] It should also be noted that in addition to this asymmetric conjunction structure, Thiersch also proposes a different type of asymmetric structure where one of the conjuncts is the specifier and the other one is the complement of a conjunction head.

[12] The spirit of this analysis is similar to that of Rigau (1989, 1990) for comitatives in Spanish and Catalan.

1.4   Summary

To summarize this section, we have seen two important properties of coordination: first, in the default case, conjuncts operate as in the same as their non-conjoined counterparts. This property was formalized as Wasow's generalization. Second, exception to this constraint are fairly limited in scope: they involve 1) cases where conjuncts resolve their features, yielding a value that includes them in some intuitive way and 2) cases where only one of the conjunct matches its features with the factor. I have also suggested that feature resolution tends to operate in two realms; φ-features (agreement, gender, number, case), and category. In the latter case, resolution make take the form of the same level of saturation. Finally, we have seen two ways in which proposals tend to account for conjunct symmetry: one is by postulating that each conjunct occupies the same position as the others (Goodall's 1987 proposal), another by transferring the licensing requirements from the conjuncts to a higher coordination constituent, an issue I will return to below.

2. C-COMMAND ASYMMETRY

In addition to the different issues presented under the heading of licensing symmetry, research in the past decade, particularly within the generative tradition, has also focused on the internal structure of conjoined phrases. The discussions focused on two perspectives: from a theory-internal point of view, if one assumes Kayne's (1994) Linear Correspondence Axiom (LCA) hypothesis, by which linear precedence is a direct consequence of c-command relations, conjuncts cannot be mutually c-commanding. From an empirical perspective, Munn (1992, 1993) and Progovac (1997) have debated whether there is evidence to argue for asymmetric c-command among conjuncts. Munn, for example, points to examples such as (29) as evidence of asymmetric c-command. As (29)a shows, a proper noun or a quantifier in the first conjunct can be coindexed with a pronoun in the second, but a pronoun in the first conjunct cannot be coindexed with a proper noun or a quantifier in the second one (cf. (29)b). If the first conjunct c-commands the second one, the explanation for the contrasts in (29) would fall under Principle-C of the Binding Theory.

(29) a. John$_i$'s dog and he$_i$ went for a walk.
   b. *He$_i$ and John$_i$'s dog went for a walk.

Based on these examples and other types of evidence, Munn (1993) proposes the structure in (30), in which BP, or Boolean Phrase is adjoined to DP$_1$.

(30)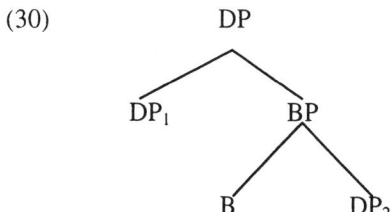

One of the features of Munn's structure is that the higher BP node is the one licensed, hence, there has to be some kind of transmission mechanism between the conjuncts and the higher BP node. This, in turn, leads to the claim that the conjunction phrase behaves like a plural entity of some kind. Thus, Munn's analysis, as well as many others, rests on the apparent similarity in distribution between conjoined DPs and plurals, as illustrated in (31): conjoined DPs trigger plural agreement, as do plural DPs. I will return to this parallelism in section 3.

(31) a. Jairo y Rosita llegaron.
Jairo and Rosita arrived(PL.)
'Jairo and Rosita arrived.'
b. Ellos llegaron.
they arrived(PL.)
'They arrived.'

Progovac (1997) has questioned the paradigm in (29) as evidence for c-command. She points out that the same contrast can be observed across sentences (cf. (32)a vs. (32)b). In this case, the explanation cannot be c-command, since c-command relations are clause-bound. Instead, Progovac argues that a pragmatic principle could account for the contrasts in (32) and that same explanation would extend to (29), avoiding the need to postulate c-command asymmetries.

(32) a. John$_i$ finally arrived. His$_i$ dog went for a walk.
b. *He$_i$ finally arrived. John$_i$'s dog went for a walk.

Progovac's objection also holds for Spanish, as illustrated in (33). Here too, the observation that the unacceptability of sentences like (33)b is a pragmatic effect seems correct. As is usually the case when restrictions are pragmatic in nature, a change in the pragmatic conditions for the configuration *pronoun--R-expression* renders coreference possible. In a sentence like (34), the pronominal *su* can bear the same reference as the subject in the preceding and the following sentences. The availability of coreference between *su* and the subject of the third clause is due to the fact that the discourse structure signals a change of topic between the first and the second clause, and then a return to the first topic in the third clause.

(33) a. Juan$_i$ llegó al fin. Su$_i$ perro salió a pasear.
Juan arrived finally. His dog went out to walk
'Juan finally arrived. His dog went for a walk.'

b. *pro_i llegó al fin. El perro de Juan_i salió a pasear.
      pro arrived finally. The dog of Juan went out to walk

(34) María_i entró en la casa. Su_i perro se quedó afuera pasando frío.
     Maria entered in the house. Her dog CL remained outside undergoing cold
     María_i, en cambio, estaba en el calor de la casa.
     Maria, on the other hand, was in the heat of the house.
     'Maria went into the house. Her dog remained outside in the cold. Maria, on the other hand, was warm inside the house.'

Thus, the conclusion when comparing (33)b and (34) is that a change in pragmatic context alters the coreference possibilities between nominals. However in the case of coreference relations within a coordination of DPs, no change in pragmatic context alters the possibilities of coreference. Consider (35): in this sentence, *María* is contrastively focused (which introduces the presupposition that someone has assumed that only the dog went for a walk); it is well known that contrastive focus can alter the coreferential possibilities, as illustrated in (36). However, in the case of (35), coreference is still not possible.

   (35) *Su_i perro, pero también María_i, salieron/salió a pasear.
        her dog, but also Maria, went out(PL.)/went out(SG.) to walk
        'Her dog, but also Maria, went out for a walk.'

   (36) Everybody likes John. Even JOHN likes John.

The following pair of sentences also suggest that the contrasts just observed are syntactic, not pragmatic (as pointed out by an anonymous reviewer). It is not clear that the pragmatic conditions of (37)a and b are very different, yet the possibility of having the antecedent of *his* in the second conjunct is restricted in the case of conjoined DPs.

   (37) a. His dog, not to mention John himself, is outside freezing.
        b. *His dog and John himself are outside freezing.

The preceding discussion suggests that Progovac's objections to c-command based on examples like (29) is unfounded. Whatever the source of the unacceptability of the cross-sentential orders *pronoun--R-expression* is, the ungrammaticality of cases like (29)b is syntactic, and its most likely source is the Binding Theory, hence the first conjunct c-commands the second one.

Progovac also objects that a c-command asymmetry analysis predicts that both (38)a and b should be equally bad, but they are not. This issue will be taken up in chapter 4.

   (38) a. John and John's wife are certainly invited.
        b. ?*John certainly likes John's wife.

Quantifer binding provides a second kind of argument in favor of c-command (cf. Munn 1993). A quantifier in the first conjunct can bind a pronoun in the second conjunct, as illustrated in (39)a, but a quantifier in the second conjunct cannot bind a pronoun first one (cf. (39)b).

(39) a. Every dog$_i$ and its$_i$ owner paraded down the lane.
   b. *Its$_i$ owner and every dog$_i$ paraded down the lane.

Progovac (1997) argues that this contrast is not due to c-command, but rather to the *Leftness Condition* (cf. Chomsky (1973)), which states that a variable cannot have a pronoun coindexed with it to its left. Thus, when the quantified phrase in (38)b raises at LF, it will leave a variable that will have *its* to its left, as in (40).

(40) *Every dog$_i$ its$_i$ owner and t$_i$ paraded down the lane.

Although evidence in favor of c-command and against the *Leftness Condition* is hard to find in coordination, I think the following contrast argues in favor of c-command, as pointed out in Camacho (2000a). Recall from section 1.2.1 that temporal features are subject to parallelism, provided the structure is properly delimited through the use of an adverb with scope over both conjuncts, as illustrated in (41). In the first sentence, negation cannot have scope over both conjuncts, because the temporal values of each verb are different. In the second one, on the other hand, it can, since the temporal features of each verb are the same.

(41) a. *Pepa no [llegó   y va   a pedir café]
       Pepa not arrived(PAST) and goes to order coffee
       'Pepa did not arrive and is going to order coffee'
   b. Pepa no [llegó   y pidió   café]
       Pepa not arrived(PAST) and ordered(PAST) coffee
       'Pepa did not arrive and did not order coffee'

In this context, a quantified phrase in the first conjunct can bind a pronoun in the second conjunct (cf. (42)a), as in Progovac and Munn's examples, and the pronoun cannot be bound if it is in the first conjunct (cf. (42)b). Assuming that the quantifier raises at LF, the configuration for these two sentences would be the one in (43). Up to this point, the contrast between these two sentences can be explained either by binding or by the *Leftness condition*.[13] However, in (44)a, with the LF configuration in (44)b, there is a pronoun coindexed with the variable to its left, yet the sentence

---

[13] Judgements on this sentence are very subtle. In particular, it is possible to have a pause between both conjuncts, and the sentence becomes grammatical. However, with a pause, the adverb no longer has scope over the second conjunct, suggesting conjunction is higher than VP, and therefore, the clitic will not c-command the trace of the quantifier. This in itself suggests that c-command is at stake.

is grammatical, suggesting that the *Leftness condition* is not at stake here, or in (43). Notice that the pronoun in this case is within the direct object DP.[14]

(42) a. Mi amigo siempre limpia cada plato$_i$ y lo$_i$ guarda cuidadosamente.
my friend always cleans each plate and CL puts away carefully
'My friend always cleans each plate and carefully puts it away.'
b. *Mi amigo siempre lo$_i$ limpia y guarda cada plato$_i$ cuidadosamente.
my friend always CL cleans and puts away each plate carefully
'My friend always cleans it and carefully puts away each plate'

(43) a. cada plato$_i$ [mi amigo siempre limpia t$_i$ y lo$_i$ guarda cuidadosamente]
b. *cada plato$_i$ [mi amigo siempre lo$_i$ limpia y guarda t$_i$ cuidadosamente]

(44) a. Mi amigo siempre limpia su$_i$ borde y guarda cada plato$_i$
my friend always cleans its edge and puts away each plate
cuidadosamente.
carefully
'My friend always cleans its edge and carefully puts each plate away'
b. Cada plato$_i$ [mi amigo siempre limpia su$_i$ borde y guarda t$_i$ cuidadosamente]

The facts illustrated in (42)-(44) argue against the *Leftness Condition*, in particular because (44)a is grammatical but violates the *Leftness Condition*. An explanation of these paradigms based on c-command, on the other hand, makes the correct predictions. Progovac presents one final argument against c-command: a negative polarity item (NPI) in the first conjunct cannot licence another NPI in the second conjunct, as illustrated in the following examples from Progovac 1997, p. 208. As is well-known, NPI licensing involves c-command, if the first conjunct c-commanded the second one, we would expect *nobody* to license *any* in (45)a, just as it does in (45)b. However, example (46), suggested by Barry Schein, shows a case where the negative word in the first conjunct licenses an NPI in the second one.

(45) a. *He chased nobody and/or any dogs.
b. Nobody chased any dogs.

(46) He chased no warm-blooded creatures or any cold-blooded ones either.

In Spanish, the NPI licensing facts are more complicated. The restrictions observed by Progovac also hold. However, in object coordination, an NPI in the second conjunct cannot be licensed by another NPI in subject position, as shown in (47)a, although licensing is possible in the non-conjoined counterpart (47)b. If the NPI is in the first conjunct, the sentence is grammatical, as seen in (48). In this sentence, the NPI is in the first conjunct and the interpretation of the conjoined

---

[14] The ungrammaticality of (42)b suggests that the clitic c-commands outside its conjunct, if this explanation is correct.

constituents must be collective: the sentence means that nobody saw pairs formed by Juan and each of the women.[15] Thus, it is possible that the reason why (47)a is ungrammatical is that the coordination cannot be interpreted collectively.

(47) a. *Nadie vio a Juan y ninguna mujer.
nobody saw to Juan and no woman
b. Nadie vio a ninguna mujer.
nobody saw to no woman
'Nobody saw any woman.'

(48) Nadie vio a ninguna mujer y Juan.
nobody saw to no woman and Juan
'Nobody saw any woman and Juan.'

If the conjunction *y* is replaced by a comitative in (48)a, the sentence becomes perfectly grammatical. Comitatives are known to force a collective reading (cf. McNally 1993, Camacho 1997, 2000b, among others), as shown in (49).

(49) Nadie vio a Juan con ninguna mujer.
nobody saw to Juan with no woman
'Nobody saw Juan with no woman'

The generalization for examples (47)-(49) seems to be that only NPIs in coordinations interpreted collectively can be licensed.[16] It would follow that Progovac's examples cannot be interpreted collectively for some unknown reason. In gapping structures, NPIs within the first conjunct can license an NPI in the second conjunct, as shown in (50). The NPI *tampoco* 'neither' can be licensed by the NPI *nadie* 'no one', as shown in (50)a. The fact that it is *nadie* licensing *tampoco* can be shown by the ungrammaticality of (50)b-c. In the first sentence, there is no negation, in the second one, there is an overt negation in the second conjunct, which is ungrammatical because negation must gap with the verb.

(50) a. Nadie vino y Miguel tampoco.
no-one came and Miguel neither
'No one came, and neither did Miguel.'

---

[15] An anonymous reviewer points out that (48)a should be ungrammatical if *a* appears before the second conjunct, because it forces a distributive reading, as illustrated in (i). The judgements are not clear, since the so-called personal *a* does not necessarily force a distributive reading, at least in my judgement. However, to the extent that (i) is grammatical, it must be interpreted collectively.

(i.) ??Nadie vio a ninguna mujer y a Juan.
nobody saw to no woman and to Juan

[16] Aoun, Benmamoun and Sportiche (1999) make the same observation with respect to pronominal binding in Arabic.

b. *Juan vino y Miguel tampoco.
   Juan came and Miguel neither
c. *Juan vino y Miguel no tampoco.
   Juan came and Miguel not neither

The fact that *tampoco* is an NPI can be seen in the classical NPI word order asymmetry: a preverbal NPI cannot surface with negation (cf. (51)c) vs. (51)d).[17] On the other hand, postverbal *tampoco* must appear with negation, as seen in (51)a vs. b (cf. Bosque 1980).

(51) a. Marta no vino tampoco.
       Marta not came neither
       'Marta didn't come either.'
    b. *Marta vino tampoco.
       Marta came neither
       'Marta came neither'
    c. Tampoco vino Marta.
       neither came Marta
       'Marta didn't come either.'
    d. *Tampoco no vino Marta.
       neither not came Marta

2.1 Summary

To summarize this section, I have reviewed Munn's evidence for asymmetric c-command between conjuncts. I have argued that Progovac's objections to that evidence are unfounded, and therefore, the structural representation of conjoined constituents should be structurally asymmetric, namely one of the conjuncts should be structurally higher than the other.

3. ON THE INTERPRETATION OF COORDINATION

Proposals on the structure of coordination are closely tied with the way in which conjoined phrases are interpreted. To see why, consider Chomsky's (1965) Conjunction Reduction analysis, according to which all cases of NP coordination are interpreted propositionally, hence the syntactic representation of coordination involves clauses that are reduced by deletion of some material to yield the surface string. Among those researchers that favor a clausal/propositional analysis of coordination, we can count Gleitman 1965, Goodall 1987, Schein 1992, 2001, Camacho 2000a, among others). Conversely, analyses of coordination that postulate a Conjunction Phrase of some kind usually tend to favor treating conjunction as a group forming operator that behaves like plurals (cf. Link 1983, Munn 1993). Finally, some postulate both types of analyses: some instances of coordination are

---

[17] (51)d is grammatical in non-standard Peruvian Spanish, where I believe *tampoco* is not an NPI.

propositional/clausal, some are group-forming, plural-like (cf. Partee and Rooth 1983, Johannessen 1998, for example). The three analyses can be illustrated using a sentence like (52)a. This sentence is ambiguous between the reading in (52)b and the reading in (52) c. For the first group, coordination is always like (52)b, for the second group, it is always like (52)c, for the third group, it is ambiguous between both readings.

(52) a. La madre y el padre visitaron a sus padres.
   the mother and the father visited to his/her parents
   'The mother and the father visited his/her parents.'
   b. La madre visitó a sus padres y el padre visitó a sus padres.
   the mother visited to her parents and the father visited to his/her parents
   'The mother visited her parents and the father visited her parents.'
   c. La madre y el padre juntos visitaron a sus padres.
   the mother and the father together visited to his/her parents
   'The mother and the father visited his/her parents together.'

Each of the analyses has different consequences. The first one must explain how inherently collective predicates such as *John and Mary met* are interpreted, since this sentence is not equivalent in meaning to the coordination of its fully clausal counterparts. The second type of analysis must deal with coordination of other categories, where the idea of group formation is much less obvious. Additionally, it must account for the differences in distribution between group-like entities such as plurals and group-like entities such as conjoined DPs, as we will see below. The third type of analysis must account for the fact that no language seems to distinguish overtly between a collective, group-like conjunction and a distributive, proposition-like conjunction. The most natural semantic counterpart for syntactic analyses that propose a single Conjunction Phrase constituent is that they form plurals. This connection is made explicit in Munn (1993). For expository purposes, I will begin with this line of analysis. I will provide evidence against the idea that conjoined DPs are exactly like plurals, based on differences in distribution. Then, I will argue that even if the plural analysis were a good idea for DP coordination, it certainly has a much harder time for coordination of other categories. Finally, I will present evidence that argues for the analysis where all coordination, even the one that involves DPs is interpreted propositionally.

3.1 How Plurals and Conjunction Differ

Example (53) illustrates the first case where conjoined DPs differ from regular plurals (cf. Longobardi 1994 for similar cases in Italian). Spanish does not allow singular or plural bare DPs in preverbal subject position, as shown in (53)b, c (see Contreras 1996, and references in Bosque 1996, among others). Conjoined bare DPs, on the other hand, are possible, as shown in (53)a. If conjunction behaves exactly like a plural, this contrast is unexpected.

(53) a. Perro y gato andaban suelto-s.
dog and cat roamed loose-PL.
'The dog and the cat roamed freely'
b. *Perro andaba suelto.
dog roamed loose(SG.)
c. *Perros andaban suelto-s.
dogs roamed loose-PL

It could be argued that (53) only shows that conjunction is equivalent to D, and not that it is different from a plural (as an anonymous reviewer points out). Even if it is correct that conjunction is like a D, the contrast in (53) still shows a contrast between conjunction and plurals: whatever plurals are, they are not D of the type that can be licensed in subject position.

Another difference between plurals and coordination is that a conjunction of subject nouns entails participation of each of the conjuncts, but a plural noun does not (cf. Camacho 2000a). For example, suppose Juan, Pedro, María and Irma are the only relevant people in the discourse. In such a context, (54)a entails that each of them participated in cooking, whereas (54)b does not. Some of the individuals may have been bystanders, while others did the cooking.

(54) a. Juan, Pedro, Irma y María cocinaron.
Juan, Pedro, Irma and Maria cooked
'Juan, Pedro, Irma and Maria cooked.'
b. Los muchachos cocinaron.
the young-people cooked
'The young people cooked.'

Distributionally, conjoined DPs and plurals display another difference. As Schein (2001) points out, in Lebanese Arabic, VS word order supports singular agreement with coordination, but not with plurals, as shown below.

(55) a. ddəhḥak alia w Marwaan
laughed(3P.FEM.SG.) Alia and Marwan
'Alia and Marwan laughed.'
b. *ddəhḥk-o t-tleemiz
laughed(3P. SG.) the students

A final set of differences between plurals and conjoined DPs has to do with propositional adverbs, to which we will turn next.

3.2 *Propositional Adverbs and Conjunction*

Collins (1988a, b) observes that certain adverbs (the ones which modify the propositional content of a sentence) cannot modify DPs in English, but they do become possible if the DP is conjoined, as the following example from his work shows (judgements are his):

(56) a. ???John kicked [evidently his daughter(s)]
b. Perhaps John and maybe Mary will come.

Given that *evidently* and *maybe* cannot modify a DP, as shown above, Collins argues that they must modify the conjunction. Since there can be two adverbs, then there must be two conjunctions, one of them null (in Collins' structure, the first conjunct is null). Schein (1992), on the other hand, gives these facts a different interpretation. Strictly speaking, the contrast between conjoined and non-conjoined DPs only shows that there is propositional content in conjunction. The fact that the conjoined version allows a propositional adverb is explained because conjunction is propositional.

Spanish also argues in favor of Schein's conclusion. In this language, propositional adverbs can appear in several positions in the sentence:

(57) a. Los niños *siempre* traen un regalo.
b. Los niños traen *siempre* un regalo.

c. Los niños traen un regalo *siempre*.
the boys bring a gift always
'The children always bring a gift.'

Given the availability of these three positions for adverbs in Spanish, it is harder to prove that they cannot modify the DP. There are two indications that this is in fact true. If one gives these sentences an intonation that groups together the DP and the adverb, the sentence becomes considerably degraded. More importantly, the DP and the adverb cannot undergo syntactic operations that traditionally have been argued to require constituenthood, such as Clefting (cf. (58)) or Right Node Raising (RNR) (cf. (59)). (58)a is a clefted subject with a propositional adverb, and it is ungrammatical; (58)b is the corresponding object cleft, and it is also ungrammatical.

(58) a. *Son [los niños   siempre] los que traen un regalo.
       are   the children always   the that bring a gift
       'It is the children always who bring the gift.'
b. *Es [siempre un regalo] lo que traen los niños.
   is always   a gift   that bring the children
   'It was always a present what the boys bring.'

Although RNR structures are not very natural in Spanish, and in particular (59)a is not very good, there is a sharp contrast between (59)a and (59)b.

(59) a. ?Los niños   traen e_i, y entregan siempre, [un regalo]$_i$
        the children bring   and deliver always   a present
        'The children bring, and always deliver, a present.'

b. *Los niños   traen e_i, y   entregan, [siempre un regalo]$_i$
   the children bring   and deliver   always a gift
   'The children bring, and deliver, always a gift.'

These examples argue in favor of the idea that propositional adverbs do not modify simplex DPs in Spanish. Let us now introduce conjunction.[18] As (60) shows, propositional adverbs can modify either the second conjunct (cf. (60)b and (60)c)) or both conjuncts (cf. (60)b), but they cannot modify the first conjunct only, as (60)d exemplifies.

(60) a. Daniel siempre, y   Lucía a veces,   llegan   tarde.
       Daniel always   and Lucia sometimes, arrive(3P.PL.) late
       'Daniel always and Lucia sometimes, arrive late.'
   b. Daniel, y   Lucía siempre, llegan   tarde.
       Daniel and Lucia always,   arrive(3P.PL.) late
       'Daniel and Lucia always arrive late.'
   c. Daniel, y   siempre Lucía, llegan   tarde.
       Daniel and always Lucia,   arrive(3P.PL) late
       'Daniel and always Lucia arrive late.'
   d. *[Siempre Daniel],   y   Lucía llegan   tarde.
       always   Daniel and Lucia arrive(3P.PL) late
       'Always Daniel and Lucia arrive late.'

It is also possible to have propositional adverbs with conjunction in non-subject positions, as illustrated below.

(61) Marcela trae   siempre libros y   a veces   revistas.
    Marcela brings always   books and sometimes magazines
    'Marcela brings always books and sometimes magazines'

In this case, the asymmetry between first and second conjuncts also seems to hold, although it is more subtle, since it is hard to tell apart true DP coordination from gapping.[19]

(62) a. ??Marcela trae   siempre libros, y   revistas.
       Marcela   brings always   books and magazines
       'Marcela brings always books and magazines.'
   b. Marcela trae   libros y   siempre revistas.
       Marcela brings books and always   magazines
       'Marcela brings books and always magazines.'

---

[18] Several speakers don't share the judgements in (58)b-d. They become much better if both conjuncts have an adverb, a fact that can be seen as part of Wasow's generalization discussed earlier.

[19] Sentence (62) a is grammatical if the adverb has scope over both conjuncts.

These facts are consistent with Collins' observation that propositional adverbs can modify conjoined DPs but not non-conjoined DPs. In particular, it strongly suggests that conjunctions are propositional heads. On the other hand, it also argues against treating ConjP as a plural, since plurals cannot be modified by propositional adverbs.[20]

One final objection to treating coordination as plurals is the following: if conjoined DPs are plurals interpreted as sets, it is not clear what the reference of *possibly the Harvard students* is in (63) (from Schein 1992), as Schein points out. The modal adverb cannot scope out of the conjunction, because that would yield the incorrect interpretation: "the set of people possibly formed by Harvard students and Columbia students." One of the situations in which (63) is true is the one where the Columbia students formed the chain by themselves.

(63) The Columbia students and possibly the Harvard students formed an unbroken chain around the Pentagon.

In the following section, I will extend the adverbial test proposed by Collins to other syntactic environments. The data that will emerge suggest that conjunctions are propositional even in other cases.

3.3   *Adjectives and Propositional Adverbs*

There is another instance in which propositional adverbs can appear: modifying adjectives, as shown in (64). However, not all adjectives can be modified by a sentential adverb: only extensional adjectives can, as shown by the ungrammaticality of (65).

(64) Daniel trajo   un juguete seguramente nuevo.
     Daniel brought a toy   probably   new
     'Daniel brought a probably new toy.'
(65) *Hoy descubrí   la seguramente principal razón.
     today discovered the probably   main   reason
     'Today, I discovered the probably main reason.'

It has been proposed on independent grounds (cf. Sánchez 1995), that extensional adjectives (but not intensional ones) involve a predication projection. Sánchez gives at least two types of arguments for this distinction. One of them is that extensional adjectives, but not intensional adjectives, can appear with copular verbs:

(66) a. El juguete es nuevo.
        the toy   is new
        'The toy is new.'

---

[20] The true generalization regarding propositional adverbs goes beyond conjunction: adverbs like *siempre* can also modify focused DPs, as shown in Munn (1993) and Camacho (1997, 2001).

b. *La razón es principal.
   the reason is main
   'The reason is main.'

If the copular verb is simply a dummy category which supports verbal inflection markers, but the true predicational force of the sentence comes from the adjective, the contrast between (66)a and b follows: the extensional adjective, but not the intentional one can appear with *ser* 'be', because the first one is predicational. Syntactically, the predicational nature of extensional adjectives is projected in a Predicational Phrase. The second argument in favor of distinguishing extensional from intensional adjectives is the possibility of licensing null nominals:

(67) a. El *juguete$_i$* nuevo y el *e$_i$* viejo
        the toy   new   and the old
        'The new toy and the old.'
     b. *La *razón$_i$* principal y la *e$_i$* supuesta
        the reason main   and the   alleged
        'The main reason and the alleged.'

Sánchez (1995b) argues that the licensing of null categories inside DPs involves a functional category. Since the presence or absence of the null category correlates to a certain extent (see below) with the extensional vs. intensional partition, postulating a Predication Phrase would account for both differences.

As Ignacio Bosque (p.c) points out, these two properties do not coincide all the time, however. Relational adjectives can license a null nominal but cannot appear in copular constructions. Thus, for example, *musical* 'musical' can either be relational or predicational. In the latter sense, it can be used in a phrase like *una melodía musical* 'a musical melody' which says something about the musical quality of the melody. In the former sense, it can be used in a phrase like *la crítica musical* 'musical criticism', which says nothing about the musical quality of the criticism (cf. Bosque 1996 for an analysis of these two types of adjectives). Given this distinction, we have the following contrast:

(68) a. La *crítica$_i$* de cine y la *e$_i$* musical
        the criticism of film and the musical
        'Film and music criticism'
     b. *Esta crítica es musical.
        this criticism is musical

This contrast shows that null nominal licensing is a necessary but not sufficient condition for an adjective to appear in copular constructions. Semantically, the existence of a predicational projection inside a DP in the case of extensional adjectives also makes sense, given that the meaning of these adjectives is 'the X is Y': 'the toy is new', whereas intensional adjectives have a different meaning: 'the alleged reason' is not 'the reason is alleged' (with a copular meaning for *is*, not a passive auxiliary meaning). If extensional adjectives involve a predication projection, then Collins' observations should be extended to cover predication projections, including among them conjunction, sentential inflection and certain kinds of adjectives.

Before ending this section, I will present one final piece of evidence that conjunction may target propositional content in the absence of an overt proposition. In many varieties of Spanish, the conjunction *y* 'and' can appear by itself with two meanings: as the equivalent of *what's new?* and as the equivalent of *so what?* For example, suppose that in the context of a conversation about why school funding is so low, someone says (69)a. Someone else could answer (69)b, which would reflect that the second speaker does not consider the first speaker's statement a justifiable reason:

(69) a. A los republicanos no les gusta pagar impuestos.
    to the republicans not CL like pay   taxes
    'Republicans don't like to pay taxes.'
  b. ¿Y?
    and
    'So what?'

The precise analysis of this use of *y* is not obvious. The presupposition speaker B holds is the sentence uttered by speaker A, but speaker B seems to request further information about this utterance. In some sense, the first sentence is interpreted by speaker A as focus, and *y* requests further (more relevant) information about A's proposition. The interesting point is that *y* here targets as focus the whole proposition, not a subpart.[21] Notice that this example is not a case of conjunction of two clauses with the second one null (as an anonymous reviewer suggests). Speaker B is denying the relevance of speaker B's utterance, not just assuming it as background information.

To summarize this section, I have presented evidence showing that conjoined DPs have a different distribution from plurals. Furthermore, I have reviewed the distribution of propositional adverbs, and shown it includes conjunction and extensional adjectives in addition to sentential inflection. I have argued that all three categories share a common feature: propositional content, syntactically manifested in a functional projection.

3.4 Verbal Pluralities

Postulating that conjoined DPs are pluralities of some kind is intuitively appealing because they have a fairly similar (although not identical) distribution to truly plural DPs: they both trigger plural agreement on different kinds of factors (verbs, adjectives, etc.), they both satisfy selectional restrictions for verbs (cf. (70)), they can both be antecedent to plural anaphors (cf. (71)), etc. Furthermore, this

---

[21] As an anonymous reviewer points out, this exchange suggests that *y* can have propositional content, although this does not mean that it always has propositional content.

parallelism is pervasive across languages: whenever there is an overt form of plurality, its distribution is similar to that of conjoined DPs.

(70) a. The girls met.
   b. Jane and Jill met.
   c. *Jane met.

(71) a. We talked to each other.
   b. She and I talked to each other.
   c. *She talked to each other.

If all conjunction were group-forming, however, we would expect similar parallelisms when coordinating other categories: we should find equivalents to "plural" VPs (the counterpart to conjoined Vs), "plural" PPs (the counterpart to conjoined Ps) and "plural" APs (the counterpart to conjoined As). The fact is, however, that such cases seem to be systematically absent cross-linguistically. Although it is perfectly conceivable to have a "plural" event formed by two sub-events like *sing* and *dance*, this new event, suppose we call it *act*, this new event does not form a separate item with different syntactic properties from *sing* and *dance*. A seemingly good candidate for "plural" events are collective verbs. However, a collective predicate like *meet* or *being dense in the middle of the forest* entails that there is more than one participant, but the event itself is not plural: if there is one participant, we don't say that the event of meeting or the event of being dense in the middle of the forest is a singular event, it just does not make sense. In this sense, collective predicates are more like mass nouns than pluralities. The fact that we don't find plural-like categories corresponding to conjoined verbs, prepositions and adjectives makes the analysis of coordination as plural formation less plausible.

4. CHAPTER SUMMARY

This chapter has presented evidence for two properties of coordination: first, it must be c-command asymmetric, namely, one conjunct must c-command the other(s). Second, it must be licensing-symmetric in the general case, namely, each of the conjuncts must license the same set of features as the other(s). Given a restricted theory of grammatical licensing, this means either that they must all appear in the same positions (specifiers or complements), or that there must be a constituent (ConjP) that is licensed, whose features are inherited from the conjuncts. I have argued that postulating this constituent leads to two kinds of problems: first, it forces one to treat conjoined structures as groups/plurals. I have argued against this solution based on two facts: the distribution of plurals is not exactly the same as that of conjoined DPs, and there is no syntactic equivalent of plurals for other conjoined categories. Finally, I have argued that certain kinds of evidence suggest conjunction is always propositional.

The proposal to be presented in the following chapter has the following features: it is c-command asymmetric, it allows each conjunct to be licensed independently (this is also the intuition behind Goodall's (1987) proposal, and also behind Zoerner's (1995) analysis, in particular of gapping), it treats conjunctions as heads and it assumes, following Sag et al.'s (1985) idea, that conjoined structures are as underspecified as possible.

CHAPTER #3

THE STRUCTURE OF COORDINATION

In the previous chapter, I established the main features that conjoined structures must have: they must be c-command asymmetric, namely, one conjunct must c-command the others, and they must be licensing symmetric, namely, each conjunct must be licensed in a similar way as the other. I also provided evidence about the propositional nature of coordination.

In this chapter, I will begin by proposing a structure for coordinated constituents that complies with the conditions summarized in the preceding paragraph, and I will provide a set of facts that can best be explained if coordination is propositional. These facts involve the distribution of switch-reference markers, which, in many languages, have properties of coordination, but only target verbal inflection projections.

1. CONJUNCTION AS A HEAD

The status of conjunctions as heads is hard to establish. Johannessen (1998) explores certain criteria for being a head, and conjunction does not conclusively comply with most of them. To take an example, heads determine subcategorization properties of phrases. However, a conjunction like *and* in English does not subcategorize for any category. Certain conjunctions are more restricted; in Spanish, for example, the conjunction *pero* 'but' cannot conjoin two DPs (cf. Camacho 1999):

(1) a. [IP Vinieron] pero [IP no entraron]
         came   but   not entered
        'They came but they did not go in.'
    b. *[DP Marta] pero [DP María] no saben.
          Marta   but   Maria   not know

Likewise, in Norwegian, the conjunction *for* 'for' can only coordinate finite clauses without a complementizer (cf. Johannessen 1998, p. 78). Notice, however, that the more specific the subcategorization requirements the conjunction has, the more semantically specialized it is. Thus, the all-purpose coordination *and* tends not be specialized in meaning beyond an additive meaning, and it accepts any category as conjunct.

Another criterion Johannessen discusses is obligatoriness. Here again, everything depends on one's analysis. For example, certain languages systematically use juxtaposition as a means of coordination. Whether this means that there is no conjunction or that the conjunction is null, is a matter of analysis. In a language like English, at least one conjunction must surface, as Kayne (1994) points out:

(2) a. The girl and the boy were discussing Linguistics.
    b. *The girl the boy were discussing Linguistics.

What does not seem to exist, to my knowledge, is languages where only null coordination is used. This, together with the similarity in distribution between null conjunction structures and lexical conjunction structures (cf. Johannessen 1998) argues in favor of considering conjunctions obligatory.

In addition to these arguments, there is other evidence in favor of treating conjunction as a head. First, it blocks case assignment. It is well-known, for example, that the case a DP receives in a case position can be altered if the DP is conjoined, as in the following examples from Spanish (due to Goodall 1987)[22]:

(3) a. Para mí
       for me(OBL)
       'For me'
    b. *Para yo
       for   I(NOM)
       'For me'
    c. Para él   y   yo
       for   him(NOM/OBL) and I(NOM)
       'For him and me'
    d. *Para yo   y   él
       for   I(NOM) and him(NOM/OBL)
       'For him and me'
    e. *Para él   y   mí
       for   him(NOM/OBL) and me(OBL)
       'For him and me'

The paradigm in (3) shows that in isolation, the preposition *para* assigns oblique case, as shown by (3)a *mí* vs. (3) b *yo*. However, if two pronouns are conjoined, the second one must be non-oblique, as in (3)c vs. e. Zoerner (1995, p. 66) points out similar examples for English:

(4) a. *Me left.
    b. Robin and me left.
    c. Me and Robin left.
    d. *Kim saw I.
    e. Kim saw Robin and I.

---

[22] The paradigm of prepositional case marking has changed throughout the history of Spanish, as Cuervo (1973), §123 illustrates.

If case is assigned by heads (or checked by heads), and heads are subject to minimality, the contrasts above would follow if the conjunction head blocks case assignment.[23]

1.1 Negative Polarity Conjunction

Bosque (1992) notes that Spanish has a Negative Polarity Item (NPI) which is closely related to conjunction:

(5) a. Juana y Pedro no vinieron.
   Juana and Pedro not came
   'Juana and Pedro didn't come'
 b. Ni Juana ni Pedro vinieron.
   neither Juana nor Pedro came
   'Neither Juana nor Pedro came.'
 c. *Ni Juana ni Pedro no vinieron.
   neither Juana nor Pedro not came
 d. No vinieron ni Juana ni Pedro.
   not came neither Juana nor Pedro
   'Neither Juana nor Pedro came.'

As other NPIs, *ni* shows the preverbal/postverbal asymmetry (cf.(5)): preverbal *ni* cannot appear with negation (cf. (5)c), postverbal *ni* must appear with negation (cf. (5)d). On the other hand, *ni* shows a subject/object asymmetry: if it is in subject position, two instances of *ni* must appear: one before each conjunct. In object position, on the other hand, the first *ni* is optional:

(6) a. *Juana ni Pedro (no) vinieron.
   Juana nor Pedro (not) came
   'Juana nor Pedro did(n't) come'
 b. Pedro no conoce (ni) a Juana ni a Miguel.
   Peter not knows (neither) to Juana nor to Miguel
   'Peter doesn't know Juana nor Miguel.'

In Bosque's (1992) analysis, which follows Bosque (1980) and Laka (1990), NPIs in Spanish need to be licensed by covert movement to the specifier of a Negation Phrase. In the case of preverbal NPIs the head of NegP is empty, whereas

---

[23] Needless to say, not all the contrasts follow from the assumption that conjunction is a head, in particular the contrast between (4)e and (i).

(i.) *Kim saw I and Robin.

it must be full for a postverbal NPI.[24] For Bosque, the structure of *ni NP ni NP* is the following:

(7) Bosque's Structure for [ni NP ni NP]

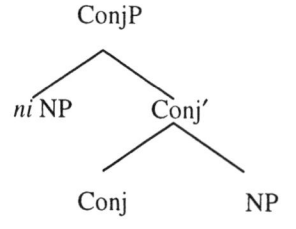

```
           ConjP
          /     \
       ni NP    Conj'
               /    \
             Conj    NP
```

As with other NPIs, this ConjP must be licensed by movement to the spec of NegP either overtly or covertly. The asymmetry between subjects and objects is due, according to Bosque, to proper government of an empty *ni* in the spec of ConjP: in object position, this empty *ni* is properly bound by the verb, whereas in subject position it is not. Since the empty *ni* is not licensed in the spec of ConjP in subject position, it cannot identify the whole ConjP as an NPI, and therefore it cannot be licensed. In a sense, this empty *ni* acts as an agreement (or scope) marker.

Bosque's analysis creates an asymmetry in the status of each *ni*. The second *ni* is a head, but the first one (the one that is optional in object position but obligatory in subject position), is an agreement marker of some sort. Note that in object position, only the higher *ni* can be optional, in subject position, both are obligatory, as we have seen:

(8) a. *Ni   Juan y/o   Marta vinieron.
       neither Juan and/or Marta came
       'Neither Juan nor marta came.'
    b. *No vimos ni   a Juan y/o   (a) Marta.
       not saw neither to Juan and/or (to) Marta
       'We didn't see neither Juan and/or Marta.'

If the first *ni* is just an agreement marker, it should be enough to indicate the negative scope of the whole conjoined phrase, but this is not the case. This contrast indicates that both *ni* must be licensed. Although I will return to the facts of NPI *ni*, for the time being, I will take them to indicate that conjunction is a head, since it interacts with other heads like negation.

1.2   On How Conjunction Is not a Quantificational Head

One would be tempted to treat conjunction as a quantificational head, given its additive meaning. However, the evidence suggests it does not interact with other quantifiers, as it should if it were quantificational. This can be seen in the following paradigms from Spanish. In this language, it is possible to conjoin the same verb

---

[24] On NPI licensing in Spanish, see also Arnaiz (1996), among others. For most dialects of Spanish, except Basque Spanish, the negative item must be null when the NPI precedes the verb.

several times, as shown in (9). The two examples are interpreted in different ways, given that the subject is definite in (9)a but indefinite in (9)b. The first example is ambiguous: it could be different sets of people or the same people who arrived repeatedly. (9)b, on the other hand, is unambiguous. It must be the same group of people that arrived several times.

(9) a. La gente llegó y llegó y llegó.
the people arrived and arrived and arrived
'People arrived, and arrived and arrived.'
b. Un grupo de gente llegó y llegó y llegó.
a group of people arrived and arrived and arrived
'A group of people arrived and arrived and arrived.'

Contrast this behavior with that of a truly quantified phrase, such as *cada cinco minutos* 'every five minutes' in (10)[25]:

(10) a. La gente llegaba cada cinco minutos.
the people arrived each five minutes 'People arrived every five minutes'
b. Un grupo de gente llegó cada cinco minutos.
a group of people arrived each five minutes
'A group of people arrived every five minutes'

Unlike the conjoined cases, both examples in (10) are ambiguous: it can be the same people arriving every five minutes or different people. (10)b, in particular can mean that there were groups of people arriving every five minutes all night. Both examples show scopal interactions, unlike coordinated VPs. Hence, we can conclude that conjunction is not quantificational.

1.3 Underspecification of Conjunction

Gazdar et al. (1985) propose that coordinated structures are drastically underspecified. The only relevant information present is that conjuncts are heads. A conjunction, in turn, is not a head but a feature (CONJ) that can have the value *and, but, neither, empty*, etc. This idea is consistent with the treatment of general-purpose conjunctions like *y* 'and' in Spanish or *and* in English. As I already mentioned, these conjunctions can coordinate any category and can appear in any structural position, as illustrated in (11).

(11) a. Las gaviotas y los patos emigraron ya.
the seagulls and the ducks migrated already
'Ducks and seagulls already migrated.'

---

[25] These examples were suggested to me by Liliana Sánchez.

b. Nos dieron de comer ayer   y   hoy.
   CL   gave to eat   yesterday and today
   'They gave us something to eat yesterday and today.'
b. Compraron una camisa azul y roja.
   bought a shirt blue and red
   'They bought a blue and red shirt.'

2. THE STRUCTURE OF COORDINATION

The two main constraints discussed in chapter 2 were licensing of conjuncts and structural asymmetry. One additional important question to be answered is how is the conjunction licensed? It cannot be licensed by virtue of being a lexical item, since it has no unique meaning of its own. *And*, for example, seems to have a basic meaning of addition, but this is not always the case: for example, *and* can have a causal meaning, as in *I pushed it and it fell*. In this case, there doesn't seem to be additive meaning of any kind. In other cases, *and* is sometimes interpreted collectively (*John and Mary met*) and sometimes distributively (*Pat Metheny and Charlie Haden are from Missouri*). Thus, there is no unique lexical meaning to it. Furthermore, conjunctions belong to a closed class, as functional categories do. What kind of functional head is it? Based on the evidence from propositional adverbs presented in chapter 2, which pointed to the propositional content of conjunction, I will assume that conjunction is a sentential functional head that has propositional content. Its subcategorization requirements are minimum in the general case of *and*, but can be more specific for other conjunctions. I will take this to suggest that the minimum feature content of conjunction is limited to +PROP, propositional. The minimal specification for the lexical entry of *and* will be, where only +PROP is specified, and the remaining items (category and any other features) are left unspecified:

(12)   and

$$\begin{bmatrix} +\text{PROP} \\ \ldots \end{bmatrix}$$

It is clear, however, that a conjunction of DPs has the distribution of a DP, a conjunction of VPs has the distribution of a VP and so forth. How is this information represented? I will argue that the way this is achieved is by copying features from another functional category. Thus, a conjunction will copy all of the features from another functional category present in the numeration. Depending on the position of the conjunction, a different licensing head with different feature specifications will give the conjunction content. In this sense, the distribution of conjoined elements will depend on their licensing position in the tree. Let us see how this proposal works for subject coordination. Since subjects are usually licensed by INFL (or Agr_s, depending on whether Agr projects or not), this head will license the conjunction. Hence, the conjunction will copy the features of INFL.

(13) a. Daniel y yo llegamos.
Daniel(3.SG.) and I(1.SG.) arrived(1.PL.)
'Daniel and I arrived'
b.
```
            IP
           /  \
         DP    I'
         |    /  \
       Daniel    
                I      IP
                |     /  \
                y   DP    I'
            {tns, φ,...} |   /  \
                        yo  I    VP
                            |
                         llegamos
                         {tns, φ,...}
```

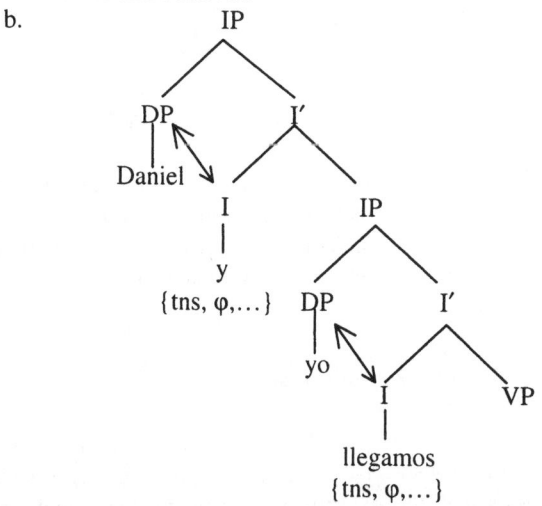

One issue that I will address later is how agreement and case checking are computed in this system. Given the representation in (13)b, the property of licensing symmetry argued for in chapter 3 can be captured in a simple way: each conjunct is in the same structural position as it would be in a simplex sentence. Hence, if a subject in a simplex sentence is licensed as a specifier of INFL, each conjunct in a conjunction of subjects will be licensed as a specifier of an INFL-like propositional projection.

Another immediate advantage that follows from this structure is that it allows us to capture the intuition behind Chomsky's Conjunction Reduction, resurfaced in Goodall's proposal, namely that a conjunction of subjects is, in some sense propositional. This is because each conjunct is a specifier of a sentential projection.

However, in this particular case, it just happens that both sentential projections are identical by virtue of the way coordination is derived.

For the case of conjoined objects, the structure would be the one in.[26]

(14) Object coordination

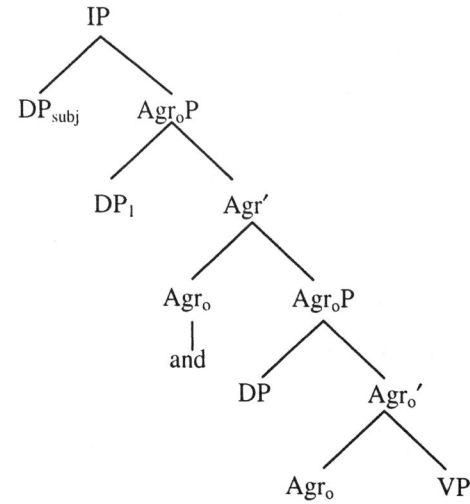

```
                IP
               /  \
         DP_subj   Agr_oP
                  /    \
                DP_1    Agr'
                       /    \
                    Agr_o    Agr_oP
                     |       /   \
                    and    DP    Agr_o'
                                 /    \
                              Agr_o    VP
```

Before explaining how other parts of a sentence are conjoined, I will present some evidence in favor of the idea that conjunction is a functional projection intrinsically linked to sentential inflection. This evidence comes from certain switch-reference languages, where conjunction is intimately linked to inflection and it joins sentences only.

2.1 Switch-reference as Inflectional Coordination

In certain languages, coordination is closely related to switch-reference affixes which are otherwise related to inflectional projections of the verb. If this correlation is not accidental, it suggests that coordination is part of the functional structure of sentences.

2.1.1 Switch-reference Systems

Several languages of different families display switch-reference systems (cf. Munro (1980), Haiman and Munro (1983), Finer (1985), Stirling (1993) for references). These systems involve morphological markers that signal the

---

[26] Throughout the book, I will use both split INFL structures that include Agr_s and collapsed INFL structures, with IP. Nothing in the analysis depends on this choice, so long as there is a case-checking functional position for subjects and for objects.

coreference relations between arguments (usually subjects) of a main clause and a subordinate clause. For example, Mojave indicates subject coreference (SS) with the morpheme -*k* and disjoint reference (DS) with the morpheme -*m*, as seen in the following examples from Munro (1980):

(15) a. '-isay-**k**   '-suupaw-pch.
     1-be=fat-SS 1-know-perfective
     'I know that I am fat.'
  b. 'iipa-ny-ch isay-**m**   '-suupaw-pch.
     man-dem-subj be=fat-DS 1-know-perfective
     'I know that the man is fat.'

Most researchers who work on switch-reference make the point that it is not always possible to tell which of the clauses is adjoined to which. In Munro's (1980) words (p. 147): "Many SR clauses have no argument relationship to the main clause, and, indeed an 'adverbial' or conjoined paraphrase is always available for these sentences." Thus, there is in principle a possible connection between switch reference markers and coordination. This connection has been explicitly suggested by Hale and Jeanne (1976), Munro (1980), Haiman (1983), Stirling (1993). In particular, Haiman (1983) observes that SR marking is consistent with the typological properties of languages: in languages with suffixal SR markers the sentence with the markers precedes the reference sentence, whereas in languages with prefixal SR markers, the sentence with the SR markers follows the reference sentence. This distribution is parallel to the one found with conjunctions, which always appear between conjuncts.

The second observation Haiman makes is that SR has properties similar to gapping in some SR languages. If one assumes that SR involves null categories in the clause marked for SR, two of the properties of switch-reference are similar to gapping, according to Haiman. First, null categories are typical of conjoined structures, not of adjoined structures:

(16) a. Mary likes coffee, and Sam *e* tea.
  b. *Although Mary likes coffee, Sam *e* tea.

Second, deleted elements must be identical to other elements present in the structure (deletion under identity), as in gapping.

Haiman also argues that certain instances of SS marking are best analyzed as gapping of inflection. In a group of SR languages, there is a pattern in which SS marking verbs are morphologically less complex than DS marking verbs. In some of these languages, DS marking involves a verb stem and a person affix, whereas the SS marking involves just a bare verbal root. For example, consider the following paradigm from Ono, a Papuan language from the Finisterre-Huon Superstock (SR marking appears in the first clause):

(17) a. ngauk   ne-ki   ari-mai-ke.   (DS)
       tobacco smoke-3P.SG. go-prog-3P.SG.
       'He had a smoke and (she) went.'
    b. ngak   ne ari-mai-ke.   (SS)
       tobacco smoke go-prog-3P.SG.
       'He had a smoke and went.'

In (17)b, SS is marked with. Haiman argues that the SS structures involve a common inflection for both verbs, whereas the DS structures involve different inflections for each verbal head, as represented in (18). These examples are similar to the English counterparts in (19).

(18) a. [I V] + [I V]   (DS)
    b. I [V and V]   (SS)

(19) a. Mary did arrive and Peter did leave.
    b. John did arrive and leave.

Note that the Ono paradigm above is not the same as the one found in pro-drop languages of the Spanish type, where the following, deceivingly similar pattern occurs:

(20) a. Marta vino   y   yo salí.
       Marta came(3.SG.) and I left(1.SG.)
       'Marta came and I left.'
    b. Marta vino   y   salió.
       Marta came(3.SG.) and left(3.SG.)
       'Marta came and (she/he) left.'

In these examples, the SS case does not involve a bare V root in the second clause, as the Ono example does. (20)a, the Spanish equivalent of the DS case, could be analyzed as a coordination of IPs if the subject is located in the spec of IP, but (20)b cannot be analyzed as I [V + V], since both verbs have inflection.[27]

---

[27] An anonymous reviewer points out that Haiman's arguments could be used to support the claim that SR resembles complementation. Compare (i) and (ii) below. In (i), the "SS" clause, there is deletion under identity, reduced inflection and a null category in the second clause.

(i.)   Juan quiere salir.
        Juan wants go-out
        'Juan wants to go out.'
(ii.)   *Juan quiere María salir.
        Juan wants Maria go-out
(iii.) Juan quiere que María salga.
        Juan wants that Maria go-out
        'Juan wants that Maria go out.'

Summarizing this section, I have presented Haiman's arguments in favor of treating switch-reference as coordination.

2.1.2 Switch-Reference and Coordination in Hopi

A second illustration of the connection between coordination and switch-reference is Hopi. Hale and Jeanne (1976) present the following paradigm (no glosses are given):

(21) a. 'Itana ni-**q** 'ita u tumala'yta.
 'Our father and-DS our mother are working.'
 b. 'Itam ni-**q** 'ima totimho'yam qaavo maqwisni.
 'We and- DS these boys will go hunting tomorrow.'
 c. Nu' mit tiyo'yat ni-**t** mit manaw'yat tuwi'yta.
 'I know that boy and-SS that girl.'
 d. Nu' 'it taavot ni-**t** 'it sowit niina.
 'I killed this jackrabbit and-SS this cottontail.'

In sentences (21)a-b, the conjunction used to coordinate subjects has an ending which "is reminiscent of the obviative (...) conjunction" in Hale and Jeanne's words, whereas in sentences (21)c-d, the object is coordinated with the SS marker. According to these authors, the switch-reference paradigm of Hopi is the one illustrated in (22):

(22) a. 'I-pava paki-**t** puu'pam qatuptu.
 'When my brother$_i$ entered-SS, he$_i$ sat down' or 'My brother entered and sat down.'
 b. 'I-pava paki-**q** puu'pam qatuptu.
 'When my brother$_i$ came in, he$_k$/she sat down' or 'My brother came in and he$_k$/she sat down.'

As these examples show, the switch-reference marker (**-t** in (22)a and **-q** in (22)b) is always adjoined to the verb. We can take this generalization to mean that SR markers are inflectional. As shown earlier, these SR markers are the same as the ones used for coordination.

A natural analysis for the contrasts between SR marking in conjoined subjects vs. conjoined objects, Hale and Jeanne argue, would be to say that coordination is derived by Conjunction Reduction: if the source for these examples is clausal coordination, it follows that two conjoined clauses with the same subject and different objects (as in (23)a) will yield, after transformations, a conjoined subject with DS-marking, as shown in (23).[28]

I agree that Haiman's arguments are not particularly compelling. For additional arguments on the conjoined status of SR, see Camacho and Elías Ulloa (2001).
[28] Hale and Jeanne actually posit a two step transformation, the first one involves backwards gapping, the second one "*ni*-support".

44   CHAPTER #3

(23) a. I know that boy and I know that girl.
     b. I know that boy and=SS that girl.

Two conjoined subjects will derive from an underlying coordination of sentences with different subjects and the same object, as shown in (24). As expected, the S-structure form will be marked with DS. Hale and Jeanne point out that in these sentences the final verb agrees in number with the second of the two DPs.[29]

(24) a. Our father is working and our mother is working.
     b. Our father and=DS our mother are working.

Their main objection against the Conjunction Reduction analysis I have just summarized is an old one: a sentence like (25)a ould have to be derived from (25)b, even though the meaning of the former is different from that of the latter:

(25) a. Mit manaw'yat nit mit tiyo'yat po'ko'at mooki.
        'That girl's and the boy's dog died.'
     b. Mit manaw'yat po'ko'at mooki-t mit tiyo'yat po'ko'at mooki.
        'That girl's dog died and the boy's dog died.'

The first sentence involves one dog possessed by both children, the second one involves two dogs. Additionally, reflexives cannot derive from two underlying sentences. The first objection, based on possessives is only a true objection if one assumes that interpretation is read from D-Structure. Furthermore, if the relationship between both sentences is not strictly transformational, then the objection does not stand. Suppose, for example, that the source for both sentences were something like *that girl's pro died and that boy's dog died*. In (25)a, pro is anaphoric to the second *dog*, and hence it must be the same, whereas in (25)b the first pro would have independent reference.[30]

Beyond the particular analysis of the contrasts just shown, the important point to note is that the SR-markers, which are inflectional in nature and adjoin to the verb, also adjoin to conjunction. This follows naturally if conjunction is a sentential functional projection, as proposed earlier. In the following section, I will formalize the details of this analysis.

2.1.3 The Analysis of Switch-Reference in Hopi.

Recall the basic distribution of Hopi conjunction presented in the preceding section, and repeated below:

---

[29] They do not provide detailed glosses of the verbs to illustrate this point, however.
[30] The underlying reasoning here is that null categories need not have exactly the same properties as their full counterparts, as suggested by Montalbetti (1984).

(26) a. 'Itana ni-**q** 'ita u tumala'yta.
  'Our father and-**DS** our mother are working.'
 b. 'Itam ni-**q** 'ima totimho'yam qaavo maqwisni.
  'We and-**DS** these boys will go hunting tomorrow.'
 c. Nu' mit tiyo'yat ni-**t** mit manaw'yat tuwi'yta.
  'I know that boy and-**SS** that girl.'
 d. Nu' 'it taavot ni-**t** 'it sowit niina.
  'I killed this jackrabbit and-**SS** this cottontail.'

Subject coordination is marked with DS and object coordination is marked with SS. Switch-reference markers are inflectional projections, as such, they can adjoin to the verb or to conjunction (which by assumption is also a sentential functional projection).

Given these assumptions and my proposal for conjunction, subject coordination is a conjunction of Agr_sP nodes (alternatively, IP nodes, if Agr_s does not project), as in (27). Since the verb agrees with the second conjunct, as mentioned above, this suggests that the verb does not raise to the second Agr_sP projection, but rather stays in the first projection. There may be an additional step of covert agreement with the top Agr_s head.

(27) Subject Coordination

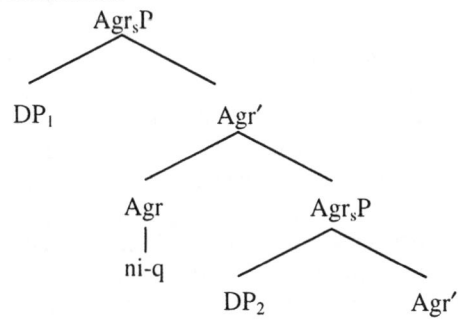

```
              Agr_sP
             /      \
          DP_1      Agr'
                   /    \
                 Agr    Agr_sP
                  |    /      \
                ni-q DP_2     Agr'
```

Object conjunction entails a coordination of object agreement nodes, as follows:

(28)   Object Coordination

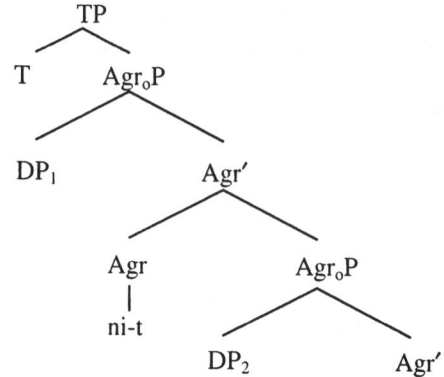

```
            TP
           /  \
          T   Agr₀P
              /   \
            DP₁   Agr'
                  /  \
                Agr   Agr₀P
                 |    /   \
                ni-t DP₂   Agr'
```

Recall that the evidence from propositional adverbs suggests conjunction is a propositional head. Given the representation in (28), Agr₀ must be propositional, a suggestion for which I believe there is independent evidence, as suggested in Camacho (2000b). In that work, I argue for a theory of how event structure is mapped on to syntactic structure. In particular, I assume (following Pustejovsky 1991 and Higginbotham 1995) that the event of a sentence can be decomposed into subevents. Furthermore, there is evidence that these subevents (e, e') can be mapped to specific syntactic arguments in certain cases. Thus, for example, Dowty's (1979:69) observation that intransitive verbs cannot be accomplishments can be explained in a principled way if the events in the argument structure (e, e') must be associated with unique arguments in the sentence. Thus, the first event (the process part) will typically be associated with the subject; the second one, which represents the result, will be associated with a direct object (although the result may be associated with other constituents, as Tenny 1987 has argued). If this is correct, lacking an object or any other constituent associated with the second event position (the result) entails that the result part of the VP cannot be licensed, hence, intransitives cannot be accomplishments because part of the argument structure required for an accomplishment is not licensed.

To summarize, I have adapted Hale and Jeanne's (1975) original suggestion that conjunction in Hopi is best analyzed as a propositional connective because switch-reference markers, which generally adjoin to propositional projections such as INFL, also adjoin to the conjunction.

2.1.4 Comitative Conjunction in Mojave

Mojave, a Yuman language, has a slightly different pattern of interaction between coordination and switch-reference.[31] Making sense of this pattern provides striking

---

[31] The data in this section and much of the analysis of comitative coordination in Mojave are due to Munro (1980).

confirmation for the analysis of coordination proposed here. Munro (1980) gives the following paradigm for the Mojave switch-reference system: -*m* indicates different subject and -*k* indicates same subject (examples from Munro 1980):

(29) a. pap   '-akchoor-**k**   '-salyii-k.
       potato 1-peel-SS   1-fry-TNS
       'After I peeled the potatoes I fried them' or 'I peeled the potatoes and then I fried them.'
   b. 'inyech pap   '-akchoor-**m** Judy-ch salyii-k.
       I   potato 1-peel-DS   Judy-SUBJ fry-TNS
       'After I peeled the potatoes Judy fried them' or 'I peeled the potatoes and then Judy fried them.'

According to Munro, the most common way to express coordination in all the Yuman languages is by using a complex comitative construction, illustrated in (30).

(30) a. 'iipa-ny-ch   thinya'aak-ny-m   havik-**k** hakoloth tayem-m.
       man-DEM-SUBJ woman-DEM-with two-SS Needles go(PL.TNS)
       'The man and the woman went to Needles' or 'The man went to Needles with the woman.'
   b. 'inyech 'iipa-ny   thinya'aak-ny-m   havik-**m** '-iyuu-pch.
       I   man-DEM woman-DEM-with   two-DS   1-see-perf
       'I saw the man and the woman' or 'I saw the man with the woman.'

There are three relevant properties of coordination in Mojave: first, it is done with a comitative marker, second it has an additional pluralizing verb (see below) and it involves SR-marking. The comitative case marker -*m* appears on the second DP in (30). The first DP is marked with the regular case marker: subject -*ch* in (30)a and object ∅ in (30)b.

The verb *havik* also appears in (30). This verb has the meaning 'two', and follows the second DP in both sentences. The SR markers are attached to it. There is little question that numbers in Yuman carry the typical verbal inflections, such as person agreement:

(31) '-havik-k.
     1-two-TNS
     'There are two of us.'

Havik is not the only verb used in Yuman for conjunction, other verbs with a similar, collectivizing meaning, are also used (cf. Munro 1980). Munro points out the similarity between comitative coordination and switch-reference. A sentence like (30)a an be paraphrased as 'the man went to Needles, being two with the woman' (cf. Munro 1980, p. 149), which resembles a regular SR sentence. However, there are are some differences. Ordinary SR sentences can use a prefix *nya-* 'when' on the subordinate verb, as in:

(32) nya-isvar-k   iima-k.
     when-sing-SS dance-TNS
     'when he_i sang, he_i danced.'

This is not possible in the case of comitatives, even though the meaning of a sentence like (30)a would allow for such a prefix.

Munro provides several arguments in favor of considering comitative SR a case of coordination. The first one, not surprisingly, is that agreement on the verb is plural. In sentence (30)a, the verb *tayem-m* is plural, which is an indication that the subject of the sentence is also plural. Since the only candidates for being a plural subject are *the man and the woman*, it seems reasonable to argue they are the subject.[32]

Yuman comitatives appear with objects, and there is an optional plural object marker, as seen in (30)b , repeated below:

(33) 'inyech 'iipa-ny   thinya'aak-ny-m   havik-m ny-'-iyuu-pch.
     I   man-DEM woman-DEM-with   two-DS PL.OBJ-1-see-PERF
     'I saw the man and the woman.'

Although the subjects that SS morphemes relate to need not be identical (there may be inclusion of one of the subject referents in the other), in the case of comitatives, this is never the case: SS indicates same subjects, DS always indicates different objects.

Person agreement also suggests that comitatives are conjoined structures: if a first person noun is conjoined with a third person noun, the main verb is first person, regardless of whether the comitative marker is on the first person noun or on the third person noun:

(34)   a. 'iipa-ny-ch   'inyep-m 'ny-havik-k Parker '-tayem-m.
          man-DEM-SUBJ me-with   me-two-SS Parker 1-go-PL-TNS
          'That man and I went to Parker' or 'That man went to Parker with me.'
       b. 'inyech 'iipa-ny-m   '-havik-k hakoloth '-tayem-m.
          I   man-DEM-with   1-two-SS Needles 1-go-PL-TNS
          'I and that man went to Needles' or 'I went to Needles with the man.'

Munro gives another argument for considering comitatives coordinate structures. Yuman has headless relative clauses, as shown in the following example:

(35) [tunay   iipa   i-uuyuu-ny-ch]   'ahot-taahan-m.
     [yesterday man   1-see-NOM-DEM-SUBJ] good-very-TNS
     'The man I saw yesterday was very nice.'

---

[32] In effect, Munro argues that *'iipanych thinya'aaknym havikk* 'the man and the woman together' is the subject. However, she gives no detailed analysis of what the internal structure of this phrase might be. Given that she argues that *havikk* is a verb, fleshing out the analysis would be important.

The relativized noun *iipa* 'man' is within the relative clause, and it does not carry a demonstrative suffix, which appears after the last element of the whole relative clause, together with the subject marker: *-ny-ch*. When a coordinated constituent is relativized, the following sequence obtains:

(36) [tunay 'iipa thinya'aak-m havik-m '-uuyuu-ny-ch]
 [yesterday man woman-with two-DS 1-see-NOM-DEM-SUBJ]
 'ahuut-taahan-m.
 good-PL-very-TNS
 'The man and the woman I saw yesterday are very nice.'

In this sentence, once again, the relativized DPs are inside the relative clause and agreement on the main verb is plural. Thus, it seems these structures are true coordinations, not NPs with PP complements.

Mojave also has another comitative-like structure which does not trigger plural agreement on the main verb:

(37) thinya'aak-nych many m-takwer-k mat=kahwely iyem-m.
 woman-DEM-SUBJ you 2=OBJ-follow-SS Parker go-TNS
 'The woman went to Parker with you' or, literally 'The woman followed you to Parker.'

The verb *takwer* 'follow', which does not necessarily imply actual following, is used in this construction which resembles the comitative type found in English.

To summarize the data presented so far, comitatives are coordinate structures in Mojave, as such, they trigger plural agreement on the verb. The peculiarity of Mojave comitative coordination is that it involves a collective verb which carries the switch-reference marker.

2.1.5 The Analysis of Mojave Comitatives

The coordination pattern illustrated in the preceding section had, as we saw, two important properties: it involves switch-reference markers adjoined to a collective verb, and it marks object coordination with DS (cf. (30)b) and subject coordination with SS (cf. (30)a), the opposite pattern of Hopi. The two patterns are schematized in (38). Clearly, a straightforward Conjunction Reduction analysis would yield the wrong results for Mojave.[33]

(38) a. [NP with-NP]$_{subj}$ Collective V=SS V-PL.
 b. NP [NP and NP]$_{obj}$ Collective V=DS V-PL.

---

[33] I owe this observation, as well as the discussion of the following analysis to David Ganelin.

Recall Munro's (1980) observation that coordinated sentences in Mojave would be better translated as 'the X and the Y, being two, did something'. I think this observation gives us an important clue about the structure of these sentences. Note that there are two overt verbal heads in such a translation, and arguably, in the original Mojave sentences. On the one hand, the presence of these two heads explains why there are switch-reference markers: in effect, there are two clauses. The representations are schematized in (39)a, c, for subject and object conjunction respectively, and glossed as (39)b, d, respectively.

(39) a. [NP and NP]$_i$ Coll-V$_i$ =SS V-PL.
b. The NP and the NP, who were two, VP-ed.
c NP$_i$ [NP and NP]$_j$ Coll-V$_j$ =DS V-PL.
d. The NP$_{sub}$ VP-ed [the NP and the NP]$_{obj}$, who were two.

When subjects are conjoined, the subject of the main verb and the subject of the collectivizing verb are the same; when the objects are conjoined, the subject of the main verb is different from the subject of the collectivizing verb, which happens to be the conjoined object of the main verb.

On the other hand, I noted above that the collective verb surfaces with coordination. From the perspective adopted in this book, Mojave overtly instantiates the second functional head that I proposed for coordination in general. The main difference would be that conjunction is unspecified in general (cf. (12)), but in Mojave it is specified as a collective head. The structure proposed for Mojave conjunction is the following:

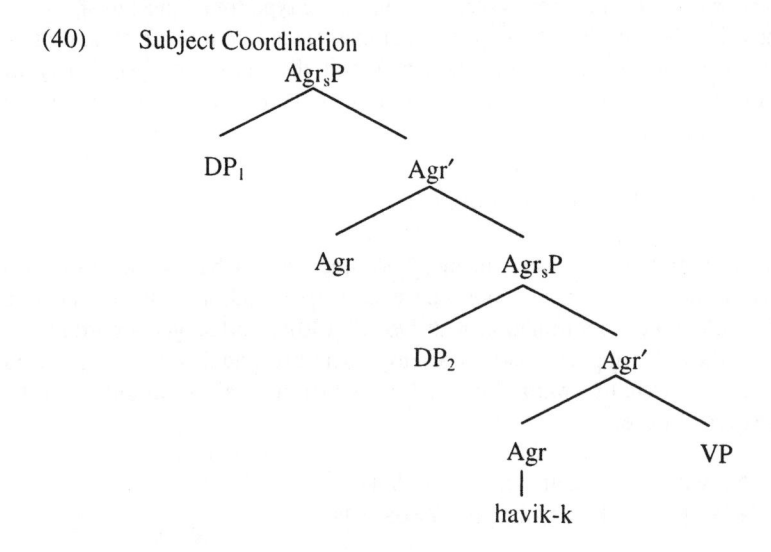

(40)   Subject Coordination

```
              Agr_sP
             /      \
          DP_1      Agr'
                   /    \
                 Agr    Agr_sP
                       /     \
                     DP_2    Agr'
                            /    \
                          Agr    VP
                           |
                         havik-k
```

In the case of objects, the structure would be the one in (41).[34] In this case, the two coordinated objects are in the specifier of Agr$_o$P.

---

[34] IP is shorthand for TP and Agr$_s$P.

(41)   Object Coordination

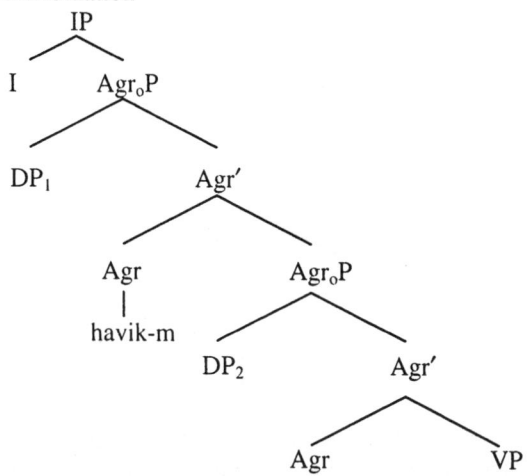

```
                IP
               /  \
              I   Agr₀P
                 /    \
               DP₁    Agr'
                     /    \
                   Agr   Agr₀P
                    |    /    \
                 havik-m DP₂   Agr'
                              /   \
                            Agr    VP
```

Note that the existence of a collective verb in coordinated structures in Mojave is problematic for analyses that treat conjunction always as group forming. If the meaning of the conjunction is group formation, what does the collective verb do in such structures? Rather, this language seems to show that coordination is overtly propositional.

To summarize this section, I have suggested that Mojave overtly instantiates the structure of coordination I have proposed. The key difference is that Mojave has the lexical entry for conjunction more specified than languages like English or Spanish.

2.2   Coordination of Other Categories

In the preceding section, I have presented an analysis of switch-refence phenomena that supports a sentential analysis of coordination. Further evidence along the same lines comes from the observation made by Van Oirsouw (1987) and Zoerner (1995) that languages that have categorically restricted uses of conjunction limit it to CP and NP coordination (for example Kru languages, as quoted in Van Oirsouw 1987). If coordination involves sentential functional projections across-categories, the fact that CP and NP form a natural class in Kru is not surprising, given the parallelism between CPs and DPs noted at least since Chomsky (1970). However, a more detailed analysis of Kru languages would be necessary to see if they provide evidence in favor or against the hypothesis presented in this book.

The general structure for coordination that I have been proposing is the following one:

(42)

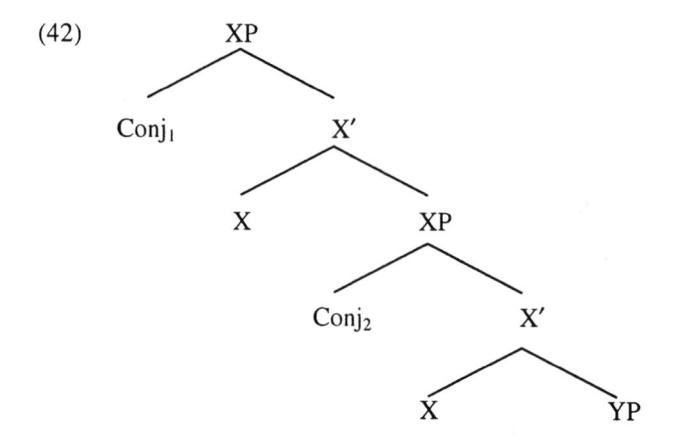

```
        XP
       /  \
    Conj₁   X'
           /  \
          X    XP
              /  \
           Conj₂   X'
                  /  \
                 X    YP
```

In this schema, the first X represents the conjunction, the second X any sentential functional projection, such as INFL, Agr, etc. Thus, a coordination of subjects would have the following structure[35]:

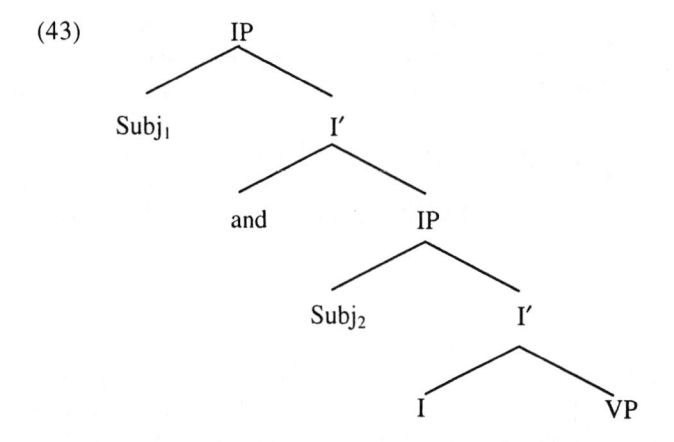

(43)

```
         IP
        /  \
     Subj₁   I'
            /  \
          and    IP
                /  \
             Subj₂   I'
                    /  \
                   I    VP
```

In the following sections, I will address coordination of other categories. In particular, I will look at coordination of adverbs, clauses, inflectional projections (aspect), heads and morphemes (I will take illustrate the analysis for PP-coordination and adjectival coordination cases in chapter 4, section 2.5).

2.2.1 Coordination of Adverbs

Let us now turn adverbial coordination. Consider a sentence like (44). The meaning of such a sentence involves two events of going to the bank, so the conjunction must join two separate events, EvP1 and EvP2 (these event projections can be mapped to

---

[35] One of the obvious consequences of the structure in (43) is that the conjoined DPs are not constituents in the traditional sense, an issue I will return to in 3.

an existing functional projection within the extended CP, perhaps to Stowell's 1995 and Zagona's 1998 ZeitP). The actual derivation depends on whether right-adjunction is available or not. Let us assume that adverbials are right-adjoined to a maximal projection, in this particular case, TP.[36] The representation appears in (45).

(44)   Mary went to the bank on Tuesday and on Thursday.

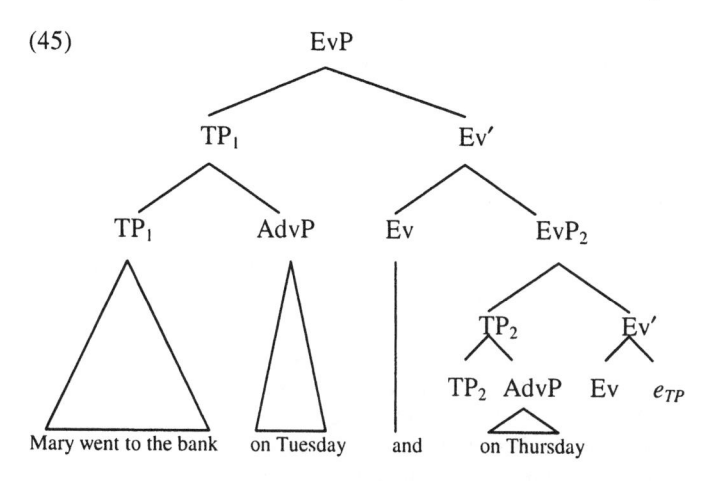

(45)

```
                           EvP
                          /   \
                       TP₁     Ev'
                      /   \    /  \
                   TP₁  AdvP  Ev   EvP₂
                                    /   \
                                  TP₂    Ev'
                                  / \    / \
                               TP₂ AdvP Ev  e_TP

         Mary went to the bank   on Tuesday   and   on Thursday
```

In this derivation, the joined categories are two Event Phrases. Each TP is in the specifier of an EvP, which anchors TP to speech time. In this particular case, each event is different only in its temporal anchoring with respect to speech time, but the content of each event (thematic relations, etc.) is identical. Suppose that Ev represents temporal anchoring to speech time, this would be reflected in the feature specification of each ev head. In the lower EvP₂, the TP is either base-generated in the spec of EvP2, or moves there from the complement position of Ev₂. TP₂ is identified as being of the same type as TP₁ either by movement of the lower Ev₂ to the higher Ev₁, or else by coindexing of the two TP projections. This insures that thematic relations and temporal relations are identical in both cases.

The structure in (45) places adverbs as adjoined to TP, not in specifier positions, hence it is not compatible with Bowers (1993) and Cinque (1999), who suggest that adverbs occupy uniquely identified specifier positions, because they cannot be stacked, as shown below:

(46)   *John will possibly likely come tomorrow.

Note that the ban against two adverbs of the same kind is not a restriction on the semantic interpretation as the following paraphrase shows:

(47)   It is possible that John will likely come tomorrow.

---

[36] The analysis could be recast without using right-adjunction by inserting an additional category.

Although this claim is true for a certain set, distributional restrictions do not seem to hold for all of them: temporal adverbials can co-occur, both in English and in Spanish:

(48) a. John came this morning at three.
b. John came at three this morning.

(49) a. Berta vino esta mañana a las tres.
Berta came this morning at the three
'Berta came at three this morning.'
b. Berta vino a las tres esta mañana.
Berta came at the three this morning
'Berta came at three this morning.'

Locative adverbs, on the other hand, do show some restrictions, both in English and in Spanish, as shown in (50) and (51).[37]

(50) a. Janet went into his bedroom in the apartment.
b. *Janet went in the apartment into his bedroom.
c. *Janet went into the apartment in his bedroom.
d. *Janet went in his bedroom into the apartment.
e. ?Janet went into the apartment into his bedroom.

(51) a. Berta entró a su cuarto en el apartamento.
Berta entered to her room in the apartment
'Berta went into her room in the apartment.'
b. *Berta entró en el apartamento a su cuarto.
Berta entered in the apartment in her room
'Berta went into the apartment in her room.'
c. *Berta entró al apartamento a su cuarto.
Berta entered to-the apartment to her room
'Berta went into the apartment to her room'
d. *Berta entró en su cuarto al apartamento.
Berta entered in her room to-the apartment
'Berta went into her room to the apartment'
e. *Berta entró en su cuarto en el apartamento.
Berta entered in her room in the apartment
'Berta went into her room in the apartment'

---

[37] I owe the English judgements to Barry Schein. An anonymous reviewer points out that in other contexts, the order is free, as seen in (i)-(ii). It is not clear whether this suggests a structural difference between examples like (50) and (i)-(ii).

(i.) Jon lives near the beach in Hawaii.
(ii.) Jon lives in Hawaii near the beach.

Sentences (51)b is good only in an absolute, clause-like interpretation of the adverb: 'Once in the apartment, Berta entered her room,' however, this interpretation requires a pause between the verb and the first PP, and between the first PP and the second one. The need for a pause suggests the existence of some additional structure. (51)e is acceptable only under a relative clause interpretation where Berta entered in the room she has in the apartment, implying that she has other rooms in other places. In these reading, (51)e is similar to (52).

(52) Berta entró en su cuarto del apartamento.
Berta entered in her room of the apartment
'Berta went into her room in the apartment (not the one in the house).'

The examples above suggest three types of adverbial modifiers with respect to iteration: those that allow multiple iteration (like temporal modifiers), those that never allow it (for example, the one in (51)c), and those which are possible if one of them restricts the other, as in (51)e. In the pre-Minimalist Theory of X-bar structure, this asymmetry could be easily captured by postulating that the ones that cannot be iterated occupy specifier positions, since there is only one specifier per projection, only one adverb should be licensed (essentially, Cinque's and Bowers' analysis). However, if multiple specifiers are introduced (as in Chomsky 1995), there must be an additional assumption that only one specifier of the same type can be licensed per head. This assumption is not unproblematic, since licensing of multiple subjects is attested in East Asian languages, as Chomsky points out. Thus, it remains to be defined when heads license more than one specifier and when they license only one.[38]

With that caveat in mind, I will assume that the adverbs that cannot be iterated occupy specifier positions and are subject to licensing by a head, for this reason, only one of them can appear; adverbs that can be freely iterated are adjoined to maximal projections. For adverbs that can be restrictively iterated, namely those cases in which one of the adverb restricts the meaning of the other, I will assume that one of them is within the scope of the other. If the higher one is in the specifier, then the lower one will be in an X′ projection.

Finally, let me return to the analysis of propositional adverbs, whose distribution was given in chapter 2. Recall the basic generalization: propositional adverbs modify predicational projections. Among them, INFL, conjunctions and adjectives. Let us assume, following Collins (1988a) and several other authors, that adverbs modify heads or perhaps X′ projections. For the case of propositional adverbs that modify DPs in subject position, illustrated below, the structure would be the one in (54).

---

[38] Chomsky (1995) argues that languages are parametrized with respect to the possibility of checking a feature twice. In particular, multiple subjects in Icelandic are explained because this language allows two specifiers of the same type per projection. This cannot be a parameter in a strict sense, since double subjects are optional in Icelandic, and even impossible in certain contexts.

(53) Viviana siempre y   Lucía a veces   comen manzanas.
Viviana always and Lucia sometimes eat   apples
'Viviana always, and Lucia sometimes, eat apples.'

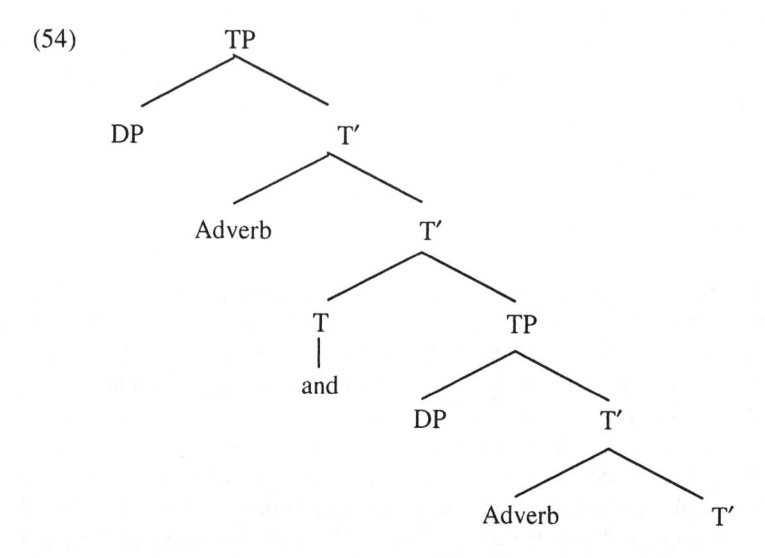

(54)
```
                TP
               /  \
             DP    T'
                  /  \
              Adverb  T'
                     /  \
                    T    TP
                    |   /  \
                   and DP   T'
                           /  \
                       Adverb  T'
```

Each of the adverbs modifies projection of the appropriate type.

2.2.2 Clausal Coordination

For the case of clausal coordination, the derivation would involve two events, as in the case of (44), except that the events do not have to be identical, even though they have to share speech time, which probably distinguishes coordinated clauses from juxtaposed clauses. Thus, an example like (55) would be derived as in (56). One way to account for the difference between the structure of conjoined adverbs (in (45) above) and the structure of conjoined clauses in (56) is to suggest that in the latter derivation, the lower event head will not raise to the specifier the higher head, unlike in the case of conjoined adverbs. This yields independent temporal readings for conjoined clauses but co-dependent temporal readings for adverbial coordination.

(55)   John arrived home and Mary will leave today.

(56)

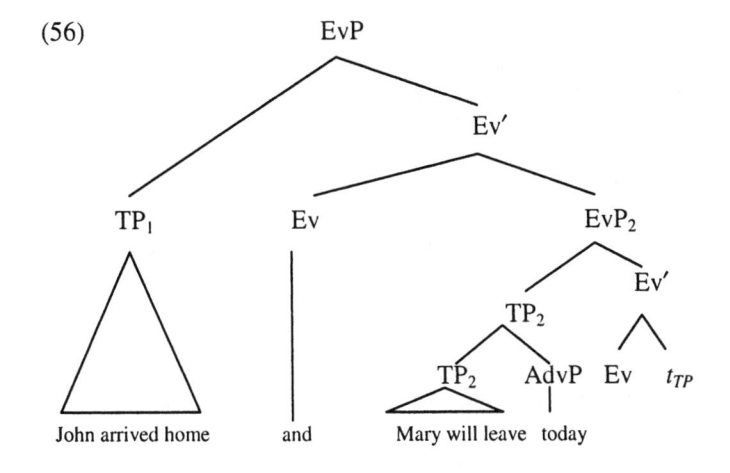

```
              EvP
             /    \
           /       Ev'
         /        /    \
       TP₁      Ev     EvP₂
       /\       |      /   \
      /  \     and   TP₂    Ev'
     /    \          / \    / \
  John   arrived   TP₂ AdvP Ev t_TP
         home      /\   |
                  /  \ today
                Mary will leave
```

2.2.3 Aspectually restricted Conjunction in Southern Quechua

In Camacho and Sánchez (1999), we analyzed the distribution of one of several conjunctions in Southern Quechua that correlates three properties: it must be interpreted collectively, it must be related to non-stative predicates and it cannot appear with objects, as summarized below.

Southern Quechua has three conjunctive morphemes (cf. Cusihuamán 1970, Calvo-Pérez 1993): *-wan, -pas* and *-nti*. However, *-nti* is the most restricted of the three: it can only coordinate subjects, not objects (cf. (57)), unlike the other two (examples from Camacho and Sánchez 1999)[39].

(57) a. *[T'anta-ta-nti, aycha-ta-nti] apa-mu-rqa-nku.
    bread-ACC-CONJ meat-ACC-CONJ take-DIR-PAST-3P.PL
    '(They) brought bread and meat (collectively).'
 b. *[Waqcha-kuna-man-nti qapaq-kuna-man-nti] qulqi-ta qu-ru-nku.
    poor-PL-DAT-CONJ rich-PL-DAT-conj money-ACC give-PAST-3P '(They) gave the money to the poor and the rich (collectively).'

Aspectually, *-nti* can only appear with non-stative predicates, not with statives (cf. (58)a vs. b). The other conjunctions are not aspectually restricted.

(58) a. Wiraqucha-kuna yana-kuna-ntin llaqta-man puri-rqa-nku.
    lord-PL servant-PL-CONJ town-towards go-PAST-3.PL
    'The lords and the servants marched towards the town.'

---

[39] As far as I can tell, *-nti* can optionally appear before both conjuncts or before one of them.

b. *Wasi-y   wasi-yki-nti   sumaq   ka-nku.
   house-1P.SG   house-2P.SG-CONJ   beautiful be-3.PL
   'My house and your house are beautiful'

Finally, the morpheme -*nti* is interpreted as a collective conjunction. Thus, the DPs must be understood either as participating in the same event, or as participating at the same time in two closely related events. It is not possible to interpret the DPs conjoined with -*nti* as participating in two completely separate events, as the translation for (59) shows:

(59) a. skay pachaq-lla-man   haya-ra-yku   ri-ntin warmikuna-ntin.
        two hundred-LIM-DAT   arrive-PAST-1-EXCL man-CONJ women-CONJ
        '(We) reached almost two hundred between men and women.'
     b. Juan Maria-ntin   wawa-ta   q'epi-nku.
        Juan Maria-CONJ baby-ACC   carry-3P.PL
        'Juan and Maria carry the baby.'
     c. *Juan Maria-ntin   wawa-ta q'epi-nku.
        Juan Maria-CONJ baby-ACC carry-3.PL
        'Juan and Maria each carry the baby.'

These data suggest that different readings of coordination correlate with different aspectual properties of predicates, and that aspectual properties correlate with certain structural positions in the tree. This is the analysis we proposed in Camacho and Sánchez (1999). Following Beghelli and Stowell (1997), we assumed that certain readings correlate with certain structural positions. In particular, Beghelli and Stowell argue that distributive quantifiers are interpreted in a Distributive Phrase that is located within the extended IP projection.

To account for why only subjects are possible with -*nti*, I will extend the results of the analysis presented in Camacho (2000b). There, it is argued that collectivity can only be a property of projections located high in the tree. The evidence suggests that there are two types of languages with respect to coordination-like comitativity: the first type correlates comitatives with a collective interpretation and with subject orientation, the second one does not (i.e. comitatives can appear in object positions, but they need not be interpreted collectively). The proposal made in Camacho (2000b) is that the fact that obligatory subject orientation and obligatory collectivity go together is not a coincidence, but rather that it follows from the way in which semantic interpretation is read off syntactic structures. In particular, I assume that the main clausal event is located in IP and that collectivity is a matter of how the main event of a sentence is construed. Thus, collectivity will only apply to subjects. If this claim is correct, we can explain why -*nti* shows the two of the three features (collectivity and subject-orientation): only subjects can be truly collective.[40]

Thus, Southern Quechua provides us with evidence that conjunction may exclusively target projections high in the structure of a sentence.

---

[40] The analysis does not explain why -*nti* also requires non-stativity.

2.2.4 Coordination of Verbal Projections

In the second chapter, I presented evidence that when verbal projections are conjoined, they must be temporally parallel. It was argued that A and B below must bear the same temporal value.

(60) Lucía [$_A$ entra] y [$_B$ sale]

Clearly, however, A and B cannot be heads, if the analysis developed so far is correct. In this analysis, all conjuncts are either specifiers or complements, hence maximal projections (see also Kayne 1994 for a similar conclusion). On the other hand, the facts about the scope of the adverb argued that A had to be a temporal projection at least in cases where a temporal adverb had scope over both conjuncts. This suggests that A is TP in this example. Let us see how it would fit within the proposal being developed.

Suppose the numeration for (60) includes at least the elements in (61). Several things make this numeration special: first, there are two unusual categories A and B. The first one is the familiar conjunction head which is underspecified for all features except for +PROP. The second one stands for the second temporal head, which I will argue, is also underspecified for tense. The only way this head will be specified is by movement of the lexically specified temporal head, which explains why both must have the same temporal features. Each TP will merge separately, yielding the structures in (62).

(61) Numeration for *Lucía sale y entra*
{ Lucía, pro, entra, sale, A, B, T, NOM }

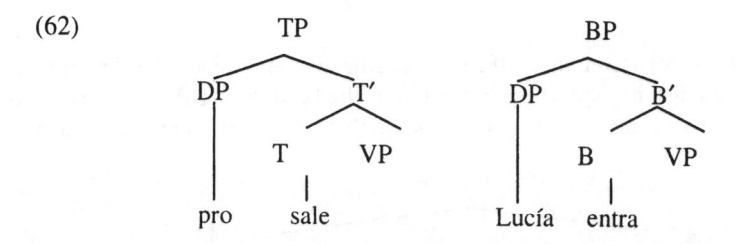

(62)

```
        TP                          BP
       /  \                        /  \
      DP   T'                     DP   B'
      |   / \                     |   / \
     pro T   VP                 Lucía B   VP
         |   |                        |   |
             sale                         entra
```

At this stage, the conjunction is still in the numeration. If it merges with the fully specified T, the result would be (63).

(63)

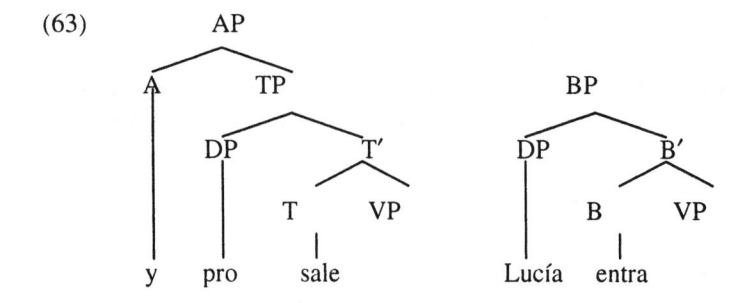

[Tree diagram: AP with A "y" and TP (DP "pro", T' → T "sale", VP); separate BP (DP "Lucía", B' → B "entra", VP)]

These two syntactic objects will have to merge to yield a single sentence. Once they do, the result will be (65). In this structure, the conjunction has projected, but it is still underspecified.

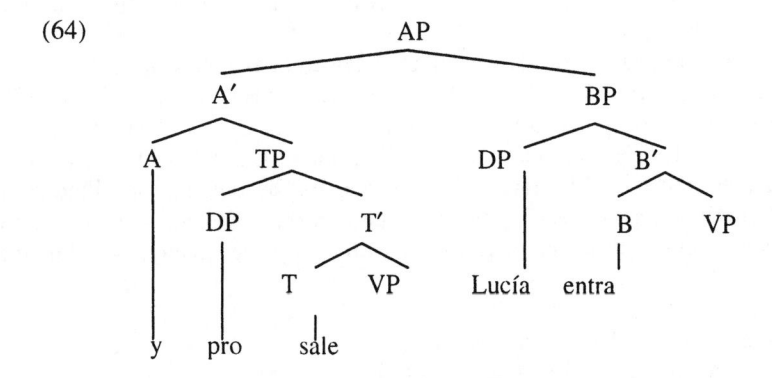

(64)

[Tree diagram: AP dominating A' and BP. A' contains A "y" and TP (DP "pro", T' → T "sale", VP). BP contains DP "Lucía" and B' (B "entra", VP).]

In (64), the second conjunct, BP, is a specifier of AP. Since the directionality parameter of Spanish has specifiers to the left of the head, then BP must move to the left, as in (66). This is also consistent with Kayne's (1994) antisymmetry proposal.

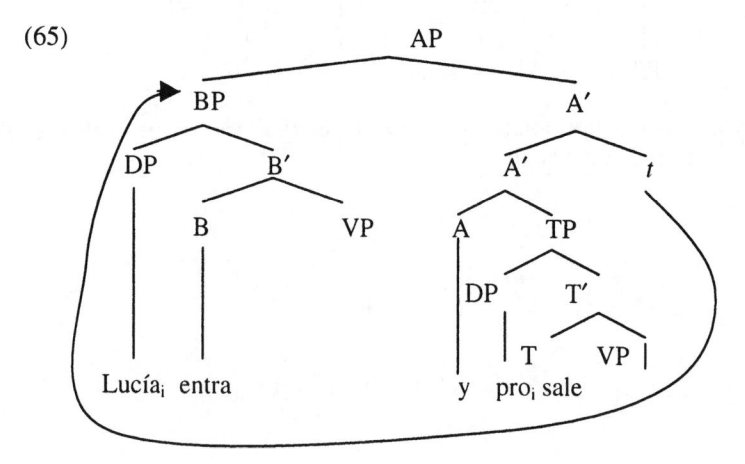

(65)

[Tree diagram: AP with BP moved to the left (DP "Lucía$_i$", B' → B "entra", VP) and A' containing A' (A, TP with DP, T' → T, VP; "y pro$_i$ sale") and trace t.]

At LF, following the logic developed up to now, T^0 raises to A^0, $T^0 + A^0$ moves to B^0, yielding (66). Through these two movements, A^0 and B^0 are specified as temporal heads with the same features as T^0.

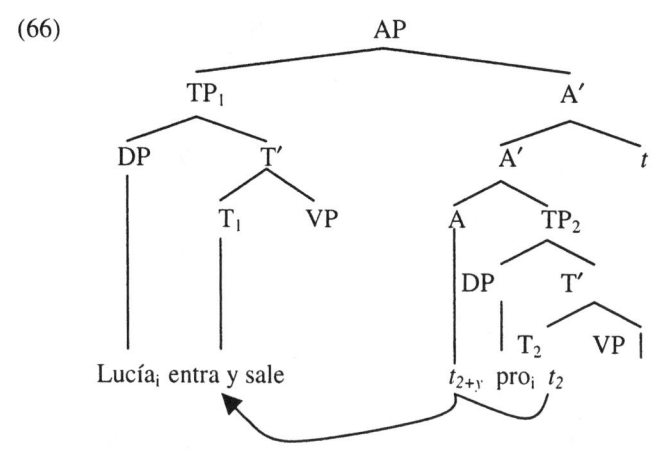

(66)

```
                        AP
                       /  \
                     TP₁    A'
                    /  \   /  \
                  DP    T' A'   t
                       / \  / \
                      T₁ VP A  TP₂
                                / \
                               DP  T'
                                   / \
                                  T₂  VP
               Lucíaᵢ entra y sale  t₂₊ᵧ proᵢ t₂
```

One question that arises is whether the landing site for *y sale* in (66) c-commands the original position (a point brought up by an anonymous reviewer). Clearly, the T_1 head does not c-command the base position from where $y + T_2$ have moved, however, it can be argued that what is relevant for licensing traces is m-command (this is necessary for *wh*-movement to the specifier of CP, for example, where the head does not c-command the trace, but the maximal wh-projection does). Alternatively, it is possible that *sale* only raises to up to the conjunction head in (66). Since TP₁ is in the specifier of that projection, spec-head agreement will insure that all features match.

If merging is done in a different order, for example, BP with A, then the lower head (B) would move to the conjunction head (A), and these two heads would move to T. The question is whether this chain, represented in (67) can provide feature specification for the trace left by B. If we assume copy + deletion, the category being copied and deleted is B, which is underspecified. Hence, the projection BP would also remain underspecified, as would AP. This derivation would therefore crash. In other words, only a derivation that starts with T at the bottom insures proper content specification for the categories A and B.

(67) T+A+B t_{A+B} t_B

On the other hand, if we assume a representational view of chains, the chain in (67) would have a temporal specification (whatever T is), and hence, each of its positions would be identified. In this case, the derivation would converge. However, the final representation would have pro c-commanding *Lucía*, a violation of

Principle C of the Binding Theory. This will be illustrated immediately below, with a slightly different derivation.

Let us consider an alternative derivation starting from the numeration in (61). Suppose that B merges with pro, yielding (68) and (69).

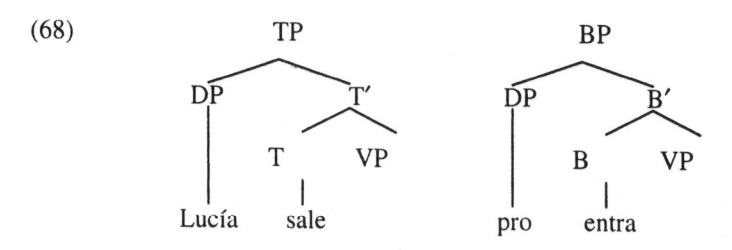

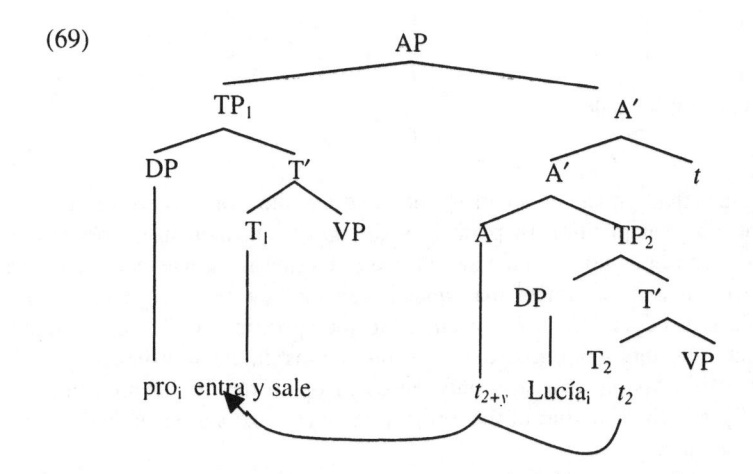

(68)

```
        TP                          BP
       /  \                        /  \
      DP   T'                     DP   B'
      |   /  \                    |   /  \
      |  T    VP                  |  B    VP
      |  |                        |  |
    Lucía sale                   pro entra
```

(69)

```
                    AP
                   /  \
                 TP₁              A'
                /  \             /  \
              DP    T'          A'   t
              |    /  \        /  \
              |   T₁   VP     A    TP₂
              |   |    |           /  \
              |   |    |          DP   T'
              |   |    |          |   /  \
              |   |    |          |  T₂   VP
           proᵢ entra y sale    t₂₊ᵧ Lucíaᵢ  t₂
```

In this derivation, pro and *Lucía* are coindexed, assuming the notion of c-command in Chomsky (1981: 166), the pronoun c-commands the R-expression, inducing a Principle C violation, as before.[41] Thus, such a derivation will not be possible.

2.2.5 Coordination, Verbal Heads and Clitics

I have argued that coordination always involves a functional projection of the sentence, such as IP, Agr₀P, etc.[42] A consequence of this proposal is that heads (and parts of words) cannot be conjoined. If they were, each conjunct would have to be

---

[41] Chomsky's definition of c-command allows it if segments of the projection that dominates α also dominate β. In order for this definition to extend to these cases, it is necessary to consider the two higher TP projections a single category. This is not implausible, given that their head has the same temporal specification by virtue of the derivation proposed.

[42] I will delay the discussion of DP-internal conjunction to chapter 3, where I deal with agreement facts.

either a specifier or a complement of the conjunction head, but in order for that to happen, they would have to be maximal categories.[43]

The ban on head coordination can be challenged in cases involving clitics and other cases of apparent morphological coordination. I will review coordination and clitics in this section and morphological coordination in the next one.

The issue of clitics and coordination has two parts. First, is it possible to conjoin two clitic-hosts with a single clitic? Second, is it possible to conjoin two clitics? Regarding the first issue, Bosque (1987) establishes the following generalization[44]:

(70) In Spanish, two coordinated verbs can share a proclitic pronoun but not an enclitic pronoun (Bosque 1987, p. 86).

This generalization can be illustrated with the following examples (from Bosque)[45]:

(71) a. Lo [leyó y resumió]   en un santiamén.
        CL read and summarized in no time at all
        'He/she read it and summarized it in no time at all.'
     b. *[Lee y resúme]lo   cuanto antes.
        read and summarize-CL as soon as possible
        'Read it and summarize it as soon as possible.'
     c. No le [importa ni interesa] lo que digan.
        not CL matters nor interests what say
        'He/she doesn't mind or care what they say.'
     d. *Debería [importar e interesar]le lo que digan.
        should matter and interest]CL what say
        'He/she should mind or care what they say.'

In Spanish, these examples contrast with the ones in (72), that involve a restructuring verb with clitic-climbing. In these cases, the conjoined verbs can share a clitic:

(72) No lo pudo [traducir ni publicar].
     not CL could translate nor publish
     'He/she couldn't translate it or publish it.'

As Bosque points out, the explanation for the ungrammaticality of (71)b, d, cannot be that hosts of enclitic pronouns cannot be conjoined, given the following contrast:

---

[43] Kayne (1994) derives the same result from his LCA: [*and* X] would result in two mutually c-commanding heads.
[44] The same generalization holds in Italian, as Kayne (1994) points out, quoting Benincá and Cinque (1990).
[45] In Spanish, proclitics are written as a separate word from the verb, whereas enclitics are written together with the verb. However, both types cliticize on the verb.

(73) a. *Para intentar [comprar o   alquilar]-lo.
         to   try   buy   or   rent-CL
         'To try to buy it or rent it.'
     b. Para intentar-lo [comprar o   alquilar].
         to   try-CL   buy   or rent
         'To try to buy it or rent it.'

In (73)a, the enclitic form is ungrammatical, for the same reasons as in (71)b, d; but in (73)b the clitic is possible even though it is enclitic, because it has climbed to the first verb. In this example, Bosque suggests coordination involves two full VPs with two clitics, with across-the-board raising of both of them.

French also disallows verbal conjunction with only one argumental clitic, as Kayne (1994) points out:

(74) *Lis- et   relis-les!
      read and reread-CL

For Bosque, the contrasts just shown follow if coordination only joins maximal phrases (a sequel of Chomsky's 1970 Lexicalist hypothesis) and enclitics are head-affixes but proclitics affix to maximal categories.[46] Thus, in (71)b, d, two heads (*lee y resume* and *importar e interesar* respectively) are conjoined and the result is ungrammatical. In general, parts of a word cannot be conjoined, as the following example shows:

(75) *re-[elaborar y   editar]
       re-elaborate and edit
      'Re-elaborate and re-edit.'

Bosque also notes that the meaning of the verbal hosts influences the possibility of having these coordinations (a point noted by Kayne 1994 as well):

(76) a. *Lo [pensó y   dijo].
          CL thought and said
          'He/she thought it and said it.'
     b. *Las [encontré y   compré].
          CL found   and bought
          'He/she found them and bought them.'

---

[46] An argument to support this partition comes from stress patterns in different dialects of Spanish: some dialects stress clitics only if they are enclitics, never if they are proclitics:

(i.)   Atráe-ló.
       'Attract it.'
(ii)   *Ló atráe.
(iii.) Lo atráe.
       'He/she attracts it'

Although the clitics are preverbal, these examples are ungrammatical because the conjoined Vs are not interpreted as part of the same event, unlike the other examples we saw previously. In fact, (76)b substantially improves if such an interpretation is forced, as below:

(77) Las encontré y compré ahí mismo.
 CL found and bought right there
 'I found them and bought them right there.'

Kayne's (1994) observations regarding clitic coordination mirror Bosque's data. He shows that clitics cannot be generally conjoined in French, as shown in (78), from Kayne:

(78) a. *Jean te et me voit souvent.
 Jean CL(2P.ACC) and CL(1P.ACC) sees often
 b. *Jean le et la vois souvent.
 Jean CL(3P.MASC.ACC) and CL(3P.FEM.ACC) sees often

Some speakers find examples like (79), similar to (78), acceptable.[47] However, those speakers who accept (79) also reject (80):

(79) ?Je lui et vous ferais un plaisir.
 I CL(3P.SG.DAT) and CL(2P.DAT) would do a favor
 'I would do you and him a favor.'
(80) *Donne-moi et lui un livre.
 Give-CL(1P.SG.DAT) and CL(3.SG.DAT) a book

Like Bosque, Kayne concludes that heads cannot be conjoined. Since clitics are heads, (80) is ungrammatical. (79) involves coordination of projections higher than the clitic, with across-the-board right-node-raising of the verb (just like in (73)b above).

The conclusion that can be drawn both from Bosque's and Kayne's data is that coordination does not target heads.

---

[47] The same holds for Spanish:

(i.) *Lo y la veo a menudo.
 CL and CL see often
 'I see him and her often.'
(ii.) *Te y me ve a menudo.
 CL and CL sees often
 'He/she sees me and you often.'

2.2.6 Morphological Coordination

The following examples show apparent cases of morphological coordination in Spanish (taken from Bosque 1987. See also Artstein 2002 and forthcoming, for an alternative view):

(81) a. Coaliciones pre- y   poselectorales
     coalitions   pre and postelectoral
     'Pre- and postelectoral coalitions'
  b. La situación política en centro- y   suramérica
     the situation political in Central and South America
     'The political situation in Central and South America'
  d. Callada- y   repetida-mente
     silent and repeated-ly
     'Silently and repeatedly'

Bosque argues that these examples involve coordination of full words, not morphological coordination. In particular, he argues that these sequences involve an empty head:

(82) [$_{Adj}$ pre-∅] y [$_{Adj}$ postelectorales]

Other possible analyses would include the following:

(83) a. [$_X$ pre-] y [$_Y$ poselectorales]
  b. [[$_{aff}$ pre-] y [$_{aff}$ post-]] electorales

Analysis (83)a argues for asymmetric conjunction between a bound morpheme (X) and a full word (Y), which violates both the principle of word integrity and the generalization that conjunction targets parallel conjuncts. Analysis (83)b, on the other hand, introduces two conjoined affixes. This analysis runs into the counterexample in (84)a, where an adverb can modify the alleged affix. Such an example would have the structure in (84)b[48]:

(84) a. Coaliciones pre e incluso   poselectorales
     coalitions   pre and even   postelectoral
     'Pre and even postelectoral coalitions'
  b. Coaliciones [[$_{aff}$ pre] e [$_?$ incluso pos]] electorales

In (84)b, the second conjunct cannot be an affix, so it must be a full word. Once again, this would violate word integrity and coordination parallelism.

Given the arguments against the alternative analyses, Bosque proposes coordination of full words with a null head in the first conjunct (cf. (82) above). The null heads in this structure must be licensed. According to him, the prefix licenses

---

[48] *E* is a notational variant of *y* when the following word begins with a vowel.

the empty head in those structures. Note that the opposite word order is ungrammatical:

(85) *Rápidamente y simple-
rapidly and simple

If something intervenes between the empty head and its licensor, the result is ungrammatical:

(86) a. La boda   más ceremoniosa- y   solemnemente celebrada
the wedding most ceremonious- and solemnly   celebrated
'The most ceremoniously and solemnly celebrated wedding'
b. *La boda   más ceremoniosamente y   solemne- celebrada
the wedding most ceremonious-   and solemnly celebrated
c. La boda   más ceremoniosa-mente y   más solemne-mente
the wedding most ceremonious-ly   and most solemn-ly
celebrada.
celebrated
'The most ceremoniously and most solemnly celebrated wedding'

Bosque argues that the ungrammaticality of (86)b is due to the licensing conditions of the empty head: the second head is not local enough (because of the intervening comparative) to license the empty head.[49] An alternative analysis would be to claim that the affixes right-node-raise and adjoin to the conjoined projection. For such an alternative, the ungrammaticality of (86)b would follow from the impossibility of adjoining the raised head -*mente* to the right conjunct, either because the higher constituent is no longer a simple adverbial coordination (it includes the comparative), or because the adjunction site is not local enough.

Why are these coordinations possible? Both types of affixes are special in that they are quasi-morphological words. *Pre/pos(t)*, can appear as an answer to a question:

(87) a. ¿La coalición fue pre o poselectoral?
The coalition was pre or postelectoral
'Was the coalition pre or postelectoral?'
b. Pos.
post
'Post(electoral)'

The affix -*mente*, on the other hand, has stress of its own, as Bosque points out, although stress is not a sufficient condition for coordination, because certain morphological compounds can also have secondary stress, but they cannot be conjoined:

---

[49] Kayne (1994) adopts a very similar analysis for parallel cases.

(88) a. Abrelatas y abrebotellas.
    opencans and openbottles
    'Can opener and bottle opener'
  b. *Abrelatas y botellas.
    opencans and bottles
    'Can and bottleopener'
  c. *Latas y abrebotellas.
    cans and openbottles
    'Cans and bottle opener'

The ungrammaticality of (88)b-c cannot be semantic, since it is possible to have an object that works both as a can opener and as bottle opener, it is even possible to refer to one, as long as no empty elements appear:

(89) Esto es abrelatas y abrebotellas en uno solo.
    this is opencans and openbottles in one only
    'This is a can opener and a bottle opener all in one.'

Examples (88)b-c conjoin an empty verbal root with two nominal endings. The opposite configuration, namely two conjoined verbal bases and a shared noun, is also ungrammatical:

(90) a. Caza-talentos y roba-talentos
    hunt-talents and steal-talents
    'Talent hunter and talent stealer.'
  b. *Caza y roba talentos
    hunt and steal talents
    'Talent hunter and stealer'

The general principle that accounts for all the ungrammatical examples is that heads cannot be conjoined. As mentioned earlier, Bosque argues that the grammatical cases involving adverbs and prefixes (cf. (81) above), as well as the grammatical examples with clitics from the preceding section (cf. (71)a, c, and (72) above) are possible because these affixes adjoin to a maximal projection, unlike other affixes, which adjoin to heads. Since coordination only applies to non-heads, only phrasal clitics, prefixes like *pre-* and adverbs with *-mente* can be conjoined in Spanish.

To summarize this section, I have argued, based on Kayne and Bosque, that heads and parts of words cannot be coordinated. The few apparent counterexamples can be explained by claiming that the conjuncts are not heads but maximal projections with a null head. In the analysis presented here, the ban on head coordination follows from the very way conjunction is conceived: each conjunct must be a specifier or complement, hence it must be maximal.

3. DERIVING CONSTITUENCY EFFECTS WITHOUT A COORDINATION PHRASE

The analysis presented in the preceding sections postulates that conjoined elements do not form a constituent. Furthermore, the conjunction does not form a constituent with the second conjunct, contrary to standard assumptions, beginning with Ross (1967) and many others since. In the structure proposed in this book, repeated in (91), there is no single constituent that groups all conjuncts and the conjunction leaving all other nodes out.

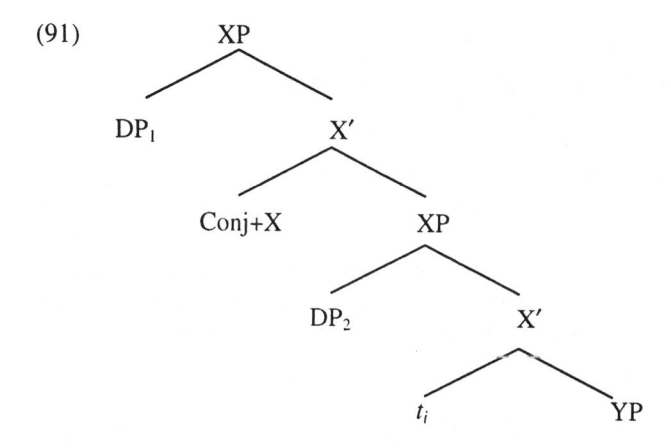

(91)

```
           XP
          /  \
        DP₁   X'
             /  \
         Conj+X  XP
                /  \
              DP₂   X'
                   /  \
                  tᵢ   YP
```

Rather, each conjunct is the specifier (or complement) of a different projection. However, the fact is that conjoined DPs have several properties of single constituents: together they can trigger plural agreement (cf. (92) in Spanish), they can act as antecedents of anaphors (cf. (93)), they can bind infinitival PROs (cf. (94)) and they can undergo DP movement (cf. (95)). In the case of agreement, both conjuncts determine agreement, and it is typically not possible for one of them to trigger agreement individually.[50]

(92) [Daniel$_i$ y Álvaro$_j$] salieron$_{i+j}$ /*salió$_i$.
   Daniel and Alvaro went out(3.PL)/*(3.SG)
   'Daniel and Alvaro went out.'

(93) Jim and Will enjoyed themselves/*himself.

(94) I told the dog$_i$ and the cat$_j$ to PRO$_{i+j}$ behave.

(95) Donald$_i$ and Daisy$_j$ seem to t$_{i+j}$ be happy.

---

[50] I have already mentioned unbalanced or asymmetric coordination as an exception to this generalization See below and also chapters 1 and 3, and Johannesen 1998.

The issue of accounting for constituency effects can be divided in two parts. First, why do conjoined elements seem to move as a constituent? Second, how can conjoined elements trigger agreement and serve as antecedents for binding and control.

Before dealing with this problem directly, it should be pointed out that the idea that conjoined elements form a constituent is not unproblematic. There is a wide set of cases in which agreement is determined by only one of the conjuncts, as already discussed in chapter 2. In at least some languages, the set of conjuncts cannot bind anaphors or control PRO when there is partial agreement, as (96) shows in Arabic, (from Aoun, Benmamoun and Sportiche 1994).

(96) *Bi ibb   Kariim w Marwaan aalun.
      love(3.SG) Kareem and Marwaan themselves
      'Kareem and Marwan love themselves.'

The theory that holds that conjuncts always form a constituent must allow for a way to explain why they do not behave as such in terms of agreement and binding in examples like (96).

A second set of difficulties for treating coordinated conjuncts as constituents relates to the so-called across-the-board movement cases (cf. Williams (1978), illustrated in (97), where the *wh*-question is simultaneously extracted from both conjoined sentences:

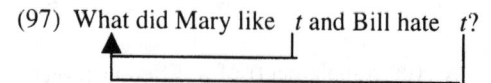

(97) What did Mary like *t* and Bill hate *t*?

In these cases, there are two initial positions for the moved element(s), and assuming that movement has taken place from both positions, they clearly do not form a constituent, unless the notion of constituenthood is extended to include items across clauses. As Williams observes, these movements are allowed so long as the moved item is structurally parallel in both conjuncts, as illustrated by the ungrammaticality of (98). Thus, across-the-board extraction constitutes a clear exception to the idea that when two phrases move to the same landing site, they must be constituents.

(98) *What did Bill buy t and bring/brought us together?

A third type of case where the relationship between constituenthood and coordination breaks down involves ellipsis, as illustrated in (99). It is generally assumed that only constituents can be coordinated, however, examples like (99)a show a case where something that is clearly not a constituent *sus padres a Miguel hoy* 'his parents to Miguel today' is a conjunct. The standard view on this exception is that several items have been deleted in that constituent, which should really have the structure in (99)b. The ellipsis analysis assumes that deletion takes place under identity with the overt item(s) in the other conjunct, however the null elements in the second conjunct can be slightly different than the overt elements in the first one. In particular, in (99)a, the missing verb must be plural because the subject is plural. Thus, strictly speaking, the null elements in the second conjunct are not identical to those in the first conjunct.

(99)   a. Juana le dio manzanas a Pedro ayer y sus padres
           Juana CL gave apples to Pedro yesterday and POSS parents
           a Miguel hoy.
           to Miguel today
           'Juana gave apples to Pedro yesterday and his/her parents did to Miguel today'
    b. Juana le_i dio_j $manzanas_k$ a Pedro ayer y sus padres e_i e_j e_k a Miguel hoy

Finally, notice that this kind of ellipsis does not occur in subordinating structures, as shown in (100). Thus, the possibility of having these unexpected constituents is directly linked to conjunction.

(100)   *Juana le dio manzanas a Pedro ayer sin que sus padres
          Juana CL gave apples to Pedro yesterday without that POSS parents
          a Miguel hoy.
          to Miguel today
          'Juana gave apples to Pedro yesterday without an his/her parents giving one to Miguel today.'

Across-the-board extraction and ellipsis illustrate two points: first, that the link between constituenthood and coordination is not as general as claimed, and second, that it is precisely the structure of coordination (as opposed to subordination, for example) that allows these kinds of exceptions.

In the following sections, I will be presenting an alternative to the standard view that coordination generally forms a constituent. This alternative explores the view that constituenthood is only an indirect requirement for movement and also for interpretation (antecedenthood for plural anaphors, control, agreement).

Given the assumptions of the analysis I have been presenting, it must be the case that when two conjuncts seem to move, they either move as separate constituents to the position where they appear in at the surface, or else, they are base-generated in the surface position, and they are coindexed with a category located in the thematic position. Each option is illustrated in (101)a and (101)b respectively. In the second option, there is a chain between each of the conjuncts and some other category I will call *conjunction pro*. This other category may have moved from the θ-position, thus being subject to constraints on movement.

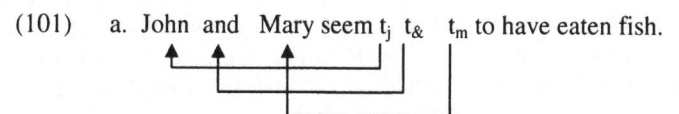

(101)   a. John and Mary seem t_j $t_\&$ t_m to have eaten fish.

b. John$_i$ and Mary$_i$ seem pro$_{i+j}$ to t$_{i+j}$ have been called t$_{i+j}$

(101)a can be construed as a subcase of Williams' (1978) across-the-board rule application. Thus, the restrictions that Williams suggests for those cases could also be generalized to all cases of coordination. Thus, ATB movement and coordination would be subsumed under a unified analysis, albeit the one that does not fall within the standard assumptions of the grammar (because it operates on discontinuous constituents). However, since Williams' ATB formulation does not explain why coordinated constituents behave in such a way, adopting (101)a would only amount to a statement on the conditions under which non-constituents can end up behaving like constituents. Instead, I will explore the second option, namely that coordinated constituents are linked to a silent phrase that moves.[51] First, I will provide evidence that suggests that conjoined constituents constitute a chain with a category that is located lower.

3.1 Evidence for Conjunction pro: Bare NPs in Spanish

The distribution of conjoined bare NPs in Spanish receives a clear explanation when viewed under the light that conjoined NPs are coindexed with a conjunction pro in a lower position. Recall the distributions regarding bare nouns and coordination presented in chapter 2, sec. 3.1. The generalization reached in that section was that bare nouns in Spanish can only appear in subject position in two cases: if they are postverbal, and if they are conjoined. These facts are illustrated below:

(102) a. *Perros pasaron ayer.
          dogs   went-by yesterday
     b. Pasaron perros ayer.
          went-by dogs yesterday
         'Dogs went by yesterday.'
     c. Perros y gatos pasaron ayer.
          dogs and cats went-by yesterday
         'Dogs and cats went by yesterday.'

It seems to be the case that (102)b is grammatical because the verb is higher than the subject. This is the underlying assumption of both Contreras's (1996) and Benedicto's (1997) analysis. In the case of Contreras, the higher position of the verb allows for government of a null category he postulates the bare DP has. In the case of Benedicto, verb-raising past the subject accounts for the existential reading, the only one available for these sentences. In both of their accounts, however, the grammaticality of (102)c is unexpected, since the verb is lower than the subject. Suppose, however, that coordination has the structure proposed in (101)b above, namely one in which the conjoined elements are coindexed with a null category

---

[51] Conceivably, ATB movement could be derived from the same idea, an option I will not explore any further.

generated in the argumental position, in this case the subject. Then, the verb would be higher than the null category, licensing it in its base position. The structure is presented in (103) for the postverbal subject case and in (104) for the conjoined case. The lower portions of the two trees are identical: the verb governs the subject in both structures.[52]

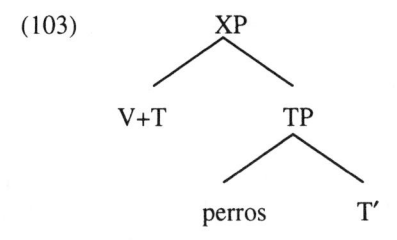

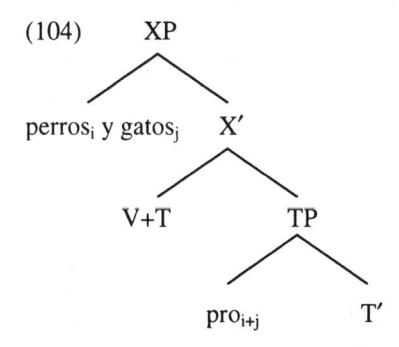

(103)
```
         XP
        /  \
      V+T   TP
           /  \
        perros T'
```

(104)
```
              XP
             /  \
     perros_i y gatos_j  X'
                        /  \
                      V+T   TP
                           /  \
                        pro_{i+j} T'
```

I do not take a stand on where the verb is located in (103) and (104). Contreras suggests bare-NPs are generated as objects and stay in situ. Since their null position is governed by the verb, this entails that the verb also stays in situ. If he is correct, then the category labelled TP above would have to be relabelled VP.[53]

Benedicto, on the other hand, locates the verb high in the tree structure, assuming Pollock's (1989) adverbial evidence; however, adverbs are not a reliable indicator in Spanish for the position of the verb, as shown in the following examples. The verb can appear to the right or to the left of adverbs like *constantly*.

---

[52] This analysis implies that the null category in (104) has the same properties of the NP subject that make it grammatical in (102)b.

[53] Contreras argues that only unaccusative verbs take bare NP subjects. Benedicto suggests the following example as counterevidence to that claim:

(i.) La carrera de medicina la estudian mujeres desde hace treinta años.
   the career of medicine CL study women from since thirty years
   'Women have studied medicine for thirty years.'

(105) a. Constantemente llegan personas a este lugar.
       constantly   arrive people   to this place
       'People constantly arrive to this place.'
   b. Llegan personas constantemente a este lugar.
       arrive people   constantly   to this place
       'People constantly arrive to this place.'
   c. Llegan constantemente personas a este lugar.
       arrive constantly   people   to this place
       'People constantly arrive to this place.'

In any event, the reasoning proposed above is consistent with a verb located high or low in the structure. What is important about this argument is that the conjoined NPs are licensed as bare-NPs because they are coindexed with a null category in a position governed by the verb. In addition to providing evidence in favor of the chain analysis of conjoined items, these facts also argue indirectly against the alternative theory sketched in (101), namely the one in which each of the conjuncts and the conjunction are extracted across-the-board. Under that analysis, the reason why conjoined bare-NPs should be possible in preverbal position but non-conjoined bare-NPs not must relate to the type of movement: coordination would force a kind of movement that ordinary NPs cannot undergo.

3.2   The Distribution of Conjoined wh-words

Consider now the following cases of *wh*-movement of conjoined phrases. The generalization to be drawn from (106) is that identical bare *wh*-phrases cannot be conjoined. By contrast, in (107), if the *wh*-word is restricted by an NP, then they can be conjoined.[54]

(106) a. *¿Quién y   quién dices que vinieron ayer?
          who and who   say that came   yesterday
          'Who and who did you say came yesterday?'
   b. Quienes dices que vinieron   ayer?
       who(PL) say that came(PL) yesterday
       'Who do you say came yesterday?'
   c. *¿Qué y   qué compraste ayer?
          what and what bought   yesterday
          'What did you buy yesterday?'
   d. ¿Qué compraste ayer?
       what bought   yesterday
       'What did you buy yesterday?'

---

[54] See below for non-identical *wh*-words.

(107) a. ¿Qué árbol y   qué poste cortaron?
       what tree and what pole cut
       'Which tree and what pole did they cut?
    b. ¿Qué hombre y   qué   mujer entraron en la tienda?
       what man   and what   woman entered in the store
       'Which man and which woman entered the store?'

Cuál 'which' is an exception to this distribution: it can be conjoined, especially in the plural, as seen in (108). However, *cuál* presupposes a noun already present in the discourse, so in this sense it behaves like (107). Its structure is the one in (108).

(108) a. ¿Cuál-es y   cuál-es ya   llegaron?
       which-PL and which-PL already arrived
       Which and which (of them) already arrived?'
    b. [cuales *e*] y [cuales *e*] ya llegaron

It has been suggested by an anonymous reviewer that (106)a, may be odd for pragmatic reasons, just as *Robin read the book and the book*. However, there are ways to make the latter example better, for example, by adding stress on *book*, but no such strategy will save (106)a. Additionally, the conjoined items in (106)a, are operators that range over variables, hence it is not obvious why there should be anything pragmatically odd. Furthermore, given that there is no plural word for *qué*, the argument that (106)c is odd because there is an alternative with a plural is not convincing. In that light, consider the following case, found in Zoerner (1995):

(109) What and what (else) did Robin buy?

I believe (and native speakers have confirmed the intuition) that it is the presence of *else* that makes the sentence grammatical. This observation suggests that English patterns like Spanish in disallowing bare *wh*-coordination but allowing a conjunction of *wh*-words if they are specified. This partition recalls Pesetsky's (1987) notion of D-linked *wh*-words. In particular, *wh*-phrases that can be conjoined are D-linked. Pesetsky's analysis proposes that D-linked *wh*-phrases do not move at LF, but are unselectively bound. Suppose that the contrast between *qué* 'what' and *qué árbol* 'what tree' is that the former must move at LF, but the latter need not. This suggests a possible explanation for the observed contrasts. In both cases, coordination has the effect of freezing the *wh*-word to remain lower than CP. This means that non-D-linked *wh*-words will not be able to move to CP, failing to check the +WH feature in C. D-linked *wh*-words, on the other hand, are unselectively bound, hence need not move.

(110)a. *¿Quién y quién dices que vinieron ayer?

b.

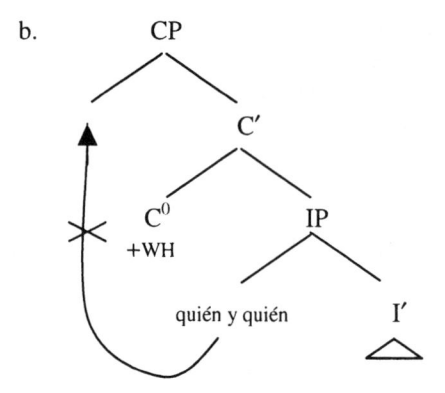

[tree diagram: CP dominating C'; C' dominates C⁰[+WH] and IP; IP dominates "quién y quién" and I'; arrow from C⁰ to "quién y quién" crossed out]

(111) a. *¿Qué árbol y qué poste cortaron?
b.

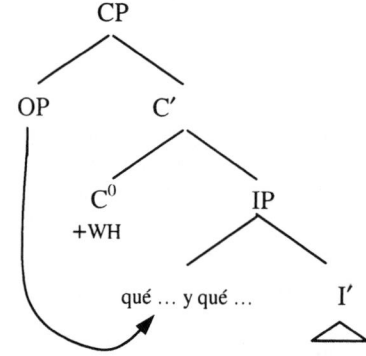

[tree diagram: CP dominating OP and C'; C' dominates C⁰[+WH] and IP; IP dominates "qué ... y qué ..." and I'; arrow from "qué ... y qué ..." to OP]

The analysis that takes D-linked *wh*-words to be bound in situ can be confirmed by scope interactions, as shown in the following examples. In a *wh*-question with a distributive quantifier, there can be a pair-list reading (cf. (112)b) or a reading in which the quantifier has wide scope over the *wh*-word (cf. (112)c). However, with a D-linked *wh*-word, only the pair-list reading is available, suggesting that the D-linked *wh*-word is lower than its non-D-linked counterpart.

(112)   a. ¿Quién se encarga   de cada niño y   cada niña?
           who   CL takes charge of each boy and each girl
           'Who is in charge of each boy and each?'
        b. Pair-list reading: Ms. Smith is in charge of Lydia, Mr. Jones is in charge of Melanie, Ms. Lopez is in charge of Miguel.
        c. Wide-scope for *cada* reading: As for Miguel, Mr. Jones and Ms. Lopez are in charge, as for Lydia, Ms. Jones and Ms. Rossi are in charge, etc.

(113)   a. ?¿Quién se encarga   de cada niño y   niña?
           who CL takes charge of each boy and girl
           'Who is in charge of each boy and girl?'
        b. Pair-list reading: Ms. Smith is in charge of Lydia, Mr. Jones is in
           charge of Melanie, Ms. Lopez is in charge of Miguel.
        c. *Wide-scope for *cada* reading.

As an anonymous reviewer points out, bare *wh*-words that are not identical can be conjoined (see (114)). The crucial point about this example is whether its structure involves coordination of two object *wh*-words or coordination of two clauses with deletion of material in one of them. If the latter analysis is correct, then the generalization that bare *wh*-words cannot be conjoined would still hold.

(114)   Who and what did you see?

In order to test whether (114) involves separate events, I will turn to verbs that require a collective object, such as *gather*.[55] This verb requires an object that is interpreted collectively. Thus, it is impossible to have a singular object, or one interpreted distributively, as shown in (115). Based on these facts, one can assume that *gather* imposes a single event interpretation.

(115)   a. Jen gathered many paitings.
        b. *Jen gathered the/a painting.
        c. *Jen gathered a painting and a drawing respectively.

For some speakers, *gather* is better with inanimate objects, but also marginally possible with human objects, as in (116).

(116)   ?Jen gathered (together) all the students.

Consider now the examples in (117). The distribution of *wh*-questions is parallel to that of regular objects: inanimate objects with *gather* are better than animate objects. However, the conjunction *who* and *what* becomes much more degraded, as seen in (117)c. One possible explanation for the ungrammaticality of this sentence is based on the fact that *gather* requires a collective object, as I have already mentioned, but the conjunction of *who* and *what* forces a distributive interpretation. This explanation can be confirmed by the contrast in (118), suggested by Jane Grimshaw. The second sentence, which treats the object as a single collection, is ungrammatical, whereas the first one, which allows a distributive interpretation of objects (and hence multiple events of gathering) is better.

(117)   a. What did John gather together in his studio?
        b. ?Who did you gather together for the meeting?
        c. *Who and what did you gather?

---

[55] Thanks to Jane Grimshaw for subtle judgements on the following sentences.

(118) a. Which paintings and which students did John gather together in his studio before his death?
b. *Which paintings and students did John gather together in his studio before his death?

The paradigms with *gather* suggest the following conclusions: a conjunction of bare *wh*-words is only possible when they are treated as separate events, suggesting that the structure involves two clauses with deleted material. Second, the contrast between non-D-linked *wh*-words and D-linked *wh*-words ((118)c vs. a) is also present in this case: only D-linked *wh*-words can be conjoined, or, to be more precise, only D-linked *wh*-words can have a multiple event interpretation.

In general, these data also argue in favor of the suggestion that conjoined categories do not move, but must be related to another category placed lower in the tree. When the conjoined category must move (for example, to check a +WH feature), then the sequence becomes ungrammatical.

In the following section, I will flesh out how the proposed chain analysis involving a conjunction pro would work out. The idea rests on a theory of how syntactic categories are formed. In particular, I suggest that categories are a collection of features, which can be spread out over different positions in a structure, along the lines of what autosegmental theory proposed for phonological features.

3.3 Local Insertion of Features and Movement

One of Chomsky's (1995) proposals is to replace the notion of movement of categories with feature-movement plus pied-piping of the category. This move opens the way to an alternative view of movement where lexical categories are no longer inserted with all their features fully specified. Instead, lexical items are bundles of features tied together by a categorial label. These bundles can contain partially unspecified values, and, conversely, features can be inserted in a different syntactic position than the matrix. Each matrix is identified by the categorial feature, which acts as a label. Let us call this matrix a *categorial matrix*.[56] Thus, the lexical entry *John* would have the representation in (119), with possibly other features in its matrix that are not relevant for our purposes.[57]

---

[56] In this view, the categorial feature plays a special role: it identifies the matrix. It is like the root-node/timing-tier in autosegmental phonology. There is an issue of whether it plays any other role. In particular, Chomsky argues that this feature is interpretable, but as Fabio Pianesi has pointed out to me, the information the categorial label carries might be retrievable from the semantic structure of the sentence.

[57] Underspecified features are preceded by an underscore line: _ϕ represents underspecified ϕ-features.

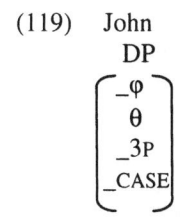

(119) John
$$\text{DP} \begin{bmatrix} -\varphi \\ \theta \\ \_3\text{P} \\ \_\text{CASE} \end{bmatrix}$$

In this representation, the feature 3P 'third person' is independently represented from the feature φ. In the typical case, feature insertion will result in a representation where all the features appear together under the same matrix, as in (119) above, but another possibility is to have different features inserted in different structural positions in the tree. To illustrate this case, consider the following examples from Latin American Spanish (cf. Bonet 1995). (120) illustrates a paradigm where each sentence has a singular direct object and a plural indirect object. When the indirect object is clitic left-dislocated, the clitic that appears is plural, as in (120)b. When both the direct and the indirect object are clitic left-dislocated, a rule is triggered by which the clitic *le* becomes *se*, as shown in (120)c. (cf. Perlmutter 1971 among others). Unlike *le*, *se* does not show number alternation. Interestingly, however, the direct object clitic becomes plural, and the intuition is that it does so precisely because the indirect object plural marking cannot surface on the indirect object clitic. The fact that this number migration is triggered by the presence of *se* is shown in (120)d, where the direct object clitic is, once again, singular, as expected (cf. Bonet 1995 for many other examples of feature migration).

(120) a. Donamos el cuadro$_i$ a los nieto-s$_j$
 donated the picture.SG to the grandchild-PL
 'We donated the picture to the grandchildren.'
 b. A los nieto-s$_j$ le-s$_j$ donamos el cuadro$_i$
 to the grandchild-PL CL-PL donated the picture(SG)
 'The grandchild-PL, we donated the picture to them.'
 c. A los nieto-s$_j$, el cuadro$_i$ se$_j$ lo-s$_i$ donamos
 to the grandchildren-PL, the picture CL CL-PL donated
 'The children, the picture, we donated it to them.'
 d. El cuadro$_i$ lo$_i$ donamos a los nieto-s$_j$
 the picture, CL(SG) donated to the grandchild-PL
 'The picture, we donated it to the grandchildren.'

Under the current assumptions, these facts can be accounted for if the lexical entry for *se* can be optionally marked with the feature plural, but this feature has no slot within *se*'s categorial matrix for the feature to be realized. Hence, it can be inserted in the syntactic position for the categorial matrix of *lo*. In the diagram below, *se*'s underspecified slot for number is filled in with the PL feature from *lo*.[58]

---

[58] One fact this analysis does not account for is when this type of feature migration can occur. Bonet's (1995) intuition is that it is restricted to clitic systems. See also Grimshaw 1999 for an Optimality Theory analysis of these facts.

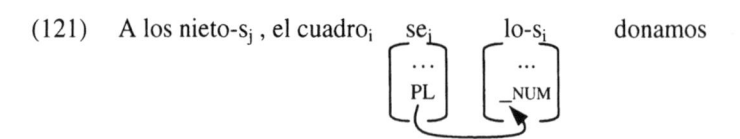

(121)   A los nieto-s$_j$, el cuadro$_i$ se$_i$ lo-s$_i$ donamos
$$\begin{bmatrix} \cdots \\ \text{PL} \end{bmatrix} \begin{bmatrix} \cdots \\ \text{NUM} \end{bmatrix}$$

Assuming that features can be inserted independently of matrices, one can view movement as an operation by which a matrix fills its unspecified matrix slots. Take a sentence like (122), with the derivation in (123). In (123)a, the categorial matrix of the lexical item has merged with V^{MAX}. The matrix of the nominal includes the categorial label [DP], a θ-role [AGENT], unspecified CASE, unspecified φ-features, and possibly other features. The θ-role must be specified, if, as I am assuming, it is assigned/checked in the spec of VP. The independently available CASE and φ nominal features are inserted in the specifier of IP. In order for the categorical matrix to specify its CASE and φ-feature slots, it must move to the specifier of IP, as illustrated in (123)b. After raising, the matrix is fully specified, and the relevant features are checked against the inflectional head. In this view, there is no pied-piping of categories as a result of feature movement, rather, categories move because they must have their unspecified features filled. Thus, like in incorporation analyses, features are not present in the lexical category to begin with, however, unlike in incorporation analyses, the lexical category has a matrix which determines which features must be specified.[59]

(122)   Jane seems to have arrived.

---

[59] This proposal may offer an alternative response to the old debate between representational or derivational constraints. It is possible that representational constraints affect certain features (those that are inserted where checked) but derivational constraints will affect other features (those that move).

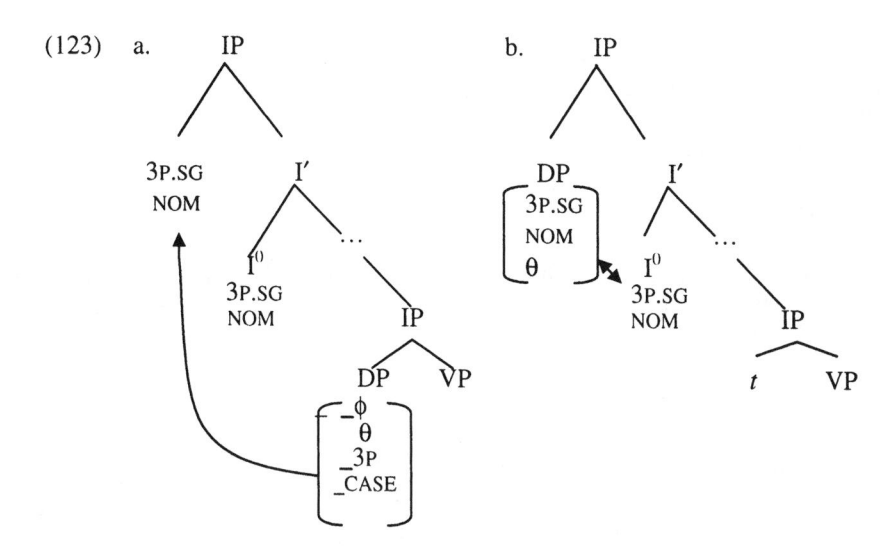

(123) a. [IP tree: 3P.SG NOM ... I' with I⁰ [3P.SG NOM] and IP containing DP [−φ, θ, −3P, −CASE] and VP]

b. [IP tree: DP [3P.SG NOM θ] and I' with I⁰ [3P.SG NOM] and IP containing t and VP]

The case of A-bar movement is somewhat different. Take example (124)a in Spanish, with the partial representation in (124)b before movements of any kind (features are inserted at checking projections):

(124) a. ¿Quienes dices que trajeron el regalo?
   who(PL) say that brought(PL) the gift
   Who do you say brought the gift?

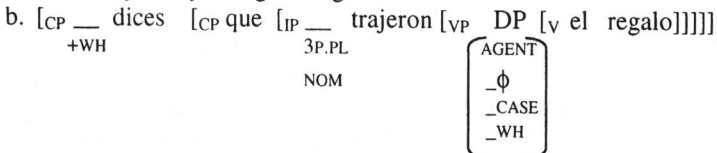

b. [CP __ dices [CP que [IP __ trajeron [VP DP [V el regalo]]]]]
   +WH   3P.PL   ⎡AGENT⎤
                                NOM   ⎢ −φ ⎥
                                                   ⎢−CASE⎥
                                                   ⎣ −WH ⎦

The lower position gets the DP feature, the theta role, and unspecified CASE and φ-features. Spec of IP gets the CASE and φ-features (we know there is a φ-feature because the *wh*-word shows overt plural agreement). Finally, the higher CP position gets a *wh*-feature. After movement, the fully specified DP matrix will finish in the spec of CP position. The overt phonological word will be pronounced there as well.

The usual locality constraints will prevent the features of a subject from ending up specifying the DP matrix of an object. This proposal differs from Baker's (1988) incorporation theory only in positing the categorial matrix, which provides a trigger for movement and constrains the possible targets to those positions where the unspecified features can be specified. Thus, a DP matrix in the spec of VP will only be able to potentially raise to the functional projections where accusative or nominative are checked, since only those positions will have the relevant φ-features to specify the values of the matrix.

One can wonder why features would be inserted independently of the matrix just to have the matrix raise to fill its slots. A possible answer is economy: if features are inserted at the point in the structure where they are checked, this restricts feature movement. This view suggests that economy should be computed not only on categories, but also on features.

The mechanism just described involves a distributed chain of syntactic features tied together by a categorial matrix. In the default case, feature insertion at the checking projection is the optimal state; however, languages can vary as to which features must be inserted where. For example, a given language may force insertion of agreement features lower in the chain, leaving case stranded in the higher position. Before turning to coordination, I will address the issue of head movement under this system.

3.3.1 Aux-to-Comp inversion

I have suggested that features must be inserted locally at their checking projection. In the previous section, I gave examples of what this would entail for XP movement. In this section, I will turn to how this idea can shed light on certain cases of head movement, using facts come from Aux-to-Comp inversion in English. Pesetsky (1989) has suggested that Aux-inversion does not involve movement of the auxiliary to Comp, but rather lack of subject raising.[60] He argues that English has a type of counterfactual construction that involves inversion, as in the following examples:

(125) a. Should it rain, we would get wet.
       b. Had Mary bought bread, we could have made sandwiches.

The properties of this construction are the following: first, it involves auxiliaries or modals which can independently occur in *if* counterfactuals, and second, those auxiliaries or modals can also appear in the past tense. Thus, *can, could, were to* (in the meaning of obligatoriness) cannot appear, but *should, had, were to, were* can. Pesetsky argues that this partition is the same as Pollock's (1989) observation that only non-θ-assigning verbs can raise in English, as illustrated below.

(126) a. Does John like ice cream?
       b. *Likes John ice cream?

Note, however, that *do*, which is a non-θ-assigner (cf. (126)a) can appear in *if* counterfactuals and in the past tense, but cannot appear in inversion counterfactuals:

(127) a. If he did come, we would go.
       b. *Did he come, we would go.

Pesetsky's conclusion is that *do* does not really move to C. Rather, it is inserted at PF. One interesting feature about counterfactual auxiliaries is that they do not show agreement features. Within the current framework, this means that the φ-

---

[60] These facts, as well as the reference of Pesetsky's article were pointed out to me by Kyle Johnson.

features of the verb are merged in IP, where they are checked against the subject. The higher auxiliary, on the other hand, does not show φ-features because they are not inserted with it. It also lacks independent temporal values, therefore tense features would not be inserted with it either. An alternative interpretation of Pesetsky's idea that *do* is inserted in C at PF is that its categorial matrix, void of any content, is inserted there, but features are inserted in situ. Let me now return to the specific issue of movement and coordination.

3.4 Coordination, Movement and Local Insertion

The notion of distributed categories provides us with a way to formalize the idea that coordination entails a chain between the conjuncts and a silent category. Recall the notion, briefly sketched in diagram (101)b above, repeated below.

(128)   John$_i$ and Mary$_i$ seem   pro$_{i+j}$ to   t$_{i+j}$ have been called   t$_{i+j}$

The extension of local feature insertion to coordination entails that part of the features of the chain are inserted in the lowest position, and they move to the two conjuncts.

In the case of conjoined subjects, the agreement features of the conjoined DPs will always be generated in the specifier of the agreeing IP. Take, for example, the sentence in (129)a, with the numeration in (129)b that has the matrix specification for each of the relevant categories. In that numeration, DP$_x$ is the silent category that will match the feature specifications of each of the conjuncts (the category labelled pro in (128)). This category is plural, and I will assume that plurality can be taken as a sum of singularities, hence the presence of two distinct, binary features SG. Additionally, this category will receive the thematic role in VP, as we will see directly below. The conjunction has copied the feature specification of the category I. The structure of the clause, once categories have merged, would be the one in (130).

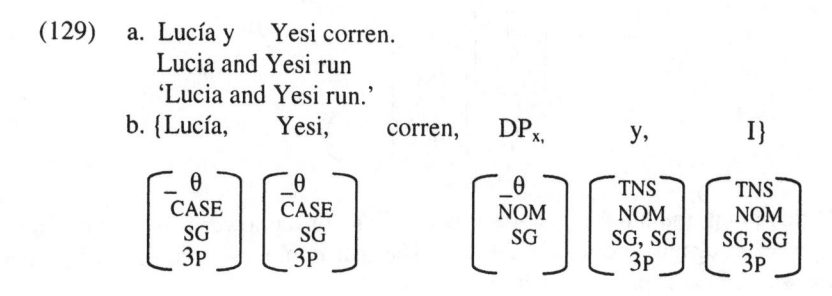

(129)   a. Lucía y   Yesi corren.
        Lucia and Yesi run
        'Lucia and Yesi run.'
     b. {Lucía,   Yesi,   corren,   DP$_x$,   y,   I}

$$\begin{bmatrix} \theta \\ \text{CASE} \\ \text{SG} \\ \text{3P} \end{bmatrix} \begin{bmatrix} \theta \\ \text{CASE} \\ \text{SG} \\ \text{3P} \end{bmatrix} \begin{bmatrix} \theta \\ \text{NOM} \\ \text{SG} \end{bmatrix} \begin{bmatrix} \text{TNS} \\ \text{NOM} \\ \text{SG, SG} \\ \text{3P} \end{bmatrix} \begin{bmatrix} \text{TNS} \\ \text{NOM} \\ \text{SG, SG} \\ \text{3P} \end{bmatrix}$$

(130)

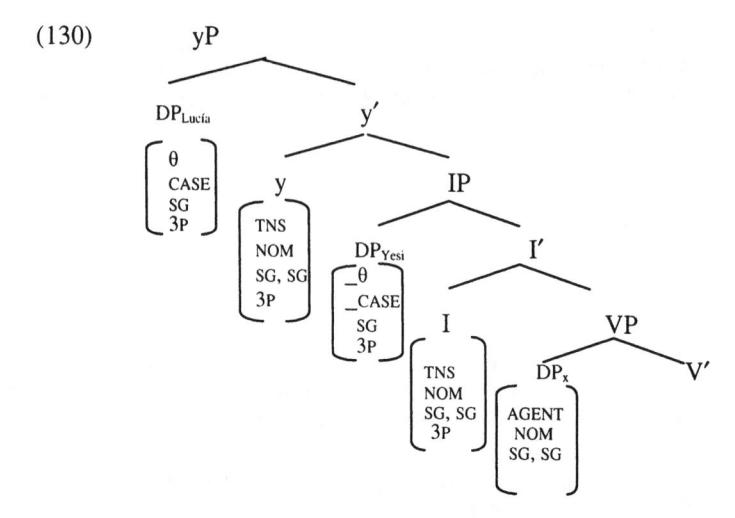

```
           yP
          /  \
   DP_Lucía   y'
   ⎡ θ    ⎤  / \
   ⎢ CASE ⎥ y   IP
   ⎢ SG   ⎥ ⎡TNS⎤  / \
   ⎣ 3P   ⎦ ⎢NOM⎥ DP_Yesi  I'
            ⎢SG,SG⎥ ⎡ θ  ⎤  / \
            ⎣3P ⎦ ⎢_CASE⎥ I   VP
                  ⎢ SG  ⎥ ⎡TNS ⎤ / \
                  ⎣ 3P  ⎦ ⎢NOM ⎥DP_x  V'
                          ⎢SG,SG⎥ ⎡AGENT⎤
                          ⎣ 3P ⎦ ⎢NOM ⎥
                                 ⎣SG,SG⎦
```

The lower DP_x matrix receives its theta-role in spec, VP. It then moves to the spec of IP (cf. (131)), where it fuses with the matrix DP_{Yesi}. This fusing operation can be viewed as a partial copying, since the categories are not identical. It will only be possible when there are no incompatible features between the categories that undergo fusion. The resulting matrix (labelled $DP_{Yesi/x}$) will have its theta role and case slots filled/specified. Its number specification will include two singulars (see below), and will check the D features in I, in particular, Case.

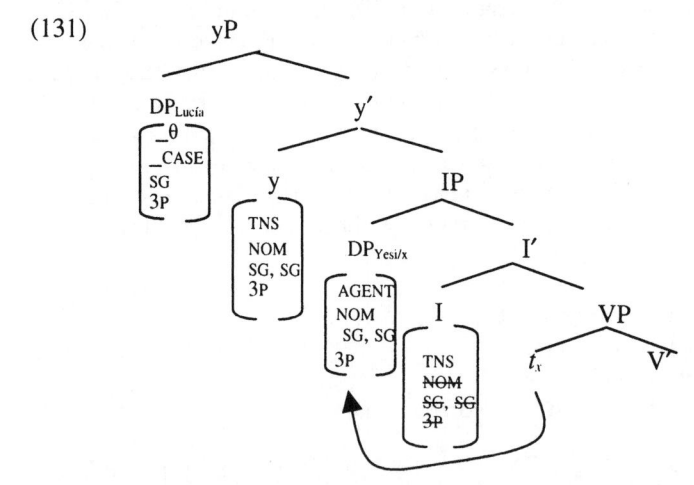

(131)

```
           yP
          /  \
   DP_Lucía   y'
   ⎡ θ    ⎤  / \
   ⎢_CASE ⎥ y   IP
   ⎢ SG   ⎥ ⎡TNS⎤  / \
   ⎣ 3P   ⎦ ⎢NOM⎥ DP_Yesi/x  I'
            ⎢SG,SG⎥ ⎡AGENT⎤  / \
            ⎣3P ⎦ ⎢NOM ⎥ I   VP
                  ⎢SG,SG⎥ ⎡TNS ⎤ / \
                  ⎣ 3P ⎦ ⎢N̶O̶M̶⎥ t_x   V'
                         ⎢S̶G̶,S̶G̶⎥
                         ⎣ 3̶P̶ ⎦
```

At this point, the number feature specifications of the lower I are deleted, after being checked against the matrix $DP_{Yesi/x}$. The matrix moves up to spec of yP and merges with $DP_{Lucía}$, with the result in (132).

(132)

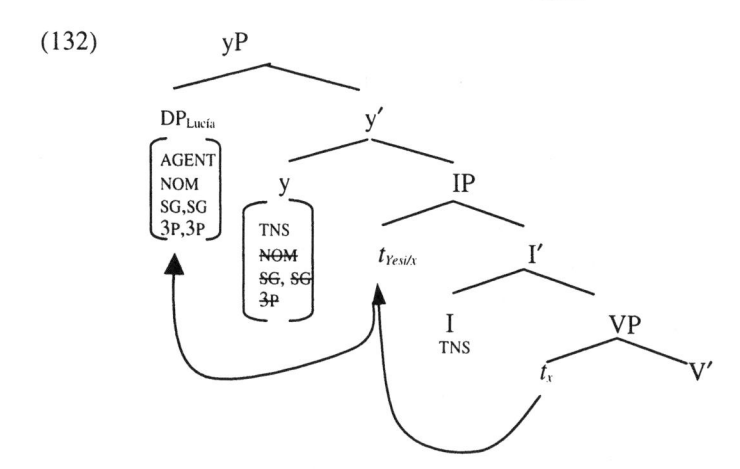

```
              yP
             /  \
      DP_Lucía   y'
      ⎡AGENT⎤   / \
      ⎢NOM  ⎥  y   IP
      ⎢SG,SG⎥ ⎡TNS⎤
      ⎣3P,3P⎦ ⎢N̶O̶M̶⎥  t_{Yesi/x}  I'
              ⎢S̶G̶,S̶G̶⎥           / \
              ⎣3̶P̶  ⎦           I   VP
                               TNS   \
                                t_x   V'
```

The formal features in y are deleted, and only TNS remains. The interpretable features in DP remain.

The analysis has several unusual theoretical assumptions to which I now turn. First, it introduces a new syntactic operation, *fusion*, which takes two categories that are partially identified and turns them into a single one whose features share from both of the initial categories. One can view this operation as a subtype of Merge, in which neither of the merging categories project, but rather the resulting one shares features of both. Second, the analysis makes some assumptions on how features can be represented. Thus, a matrix specification can have more than one feature, in particular, a matrix can have two instances of 3P, or two instances of SG. The latter will yield a semantic plural, the former will typically yield a 3p. However, it is conceivable that a language would allow two 1P. feature-specifications to be interpreted as a DUAL. Consider the following example quoted in Corbett (2000, p.197) from Slovene (cf. Lenček 1972, p. 60):

(133) Tonček   in   Marina   sta   prizadevn-a
       Tonček(SG.MASC) and   Marina(SG.FEM) be(DU)   assiduous-DU.MASC
       'Tonček and Marina are assiduous.'

In this example, a coordination of singulars agrees with a dual verb. Within the proposed system, this would be achieved by checking two individual singular features against each of the I^0 categories.

Let me now turn to a case in which the person features of the conjuncts do not match. This case is illustrated in (134), where a first person pronoun and a third person DP are conjoined; the agreement specification on the verb is 1P. PL. The derivation for this example would be the same as the one already seen, except that the lower I would be specified as 1P, SG, SG. When the lower DP_x matrix merges with the DP_Marta in the spec of the lower IP, the person feature will not be deleted on the I^0, because of a person mismatch. The DP matrix will move further up to the spec of yP, and there the resulting matrix will be specified as 1P/3P. This specification will be able to delete the 1P feature on y^0. However, in order for the lower I⁰ 1P specification to be deleted, this head will have to raise to y⁰, where it will find a feature to match its person feature, as in (136).

(134) Yo y Marta canta-mos.
I and Marta sing-1P.PL
'Marta and I sing'

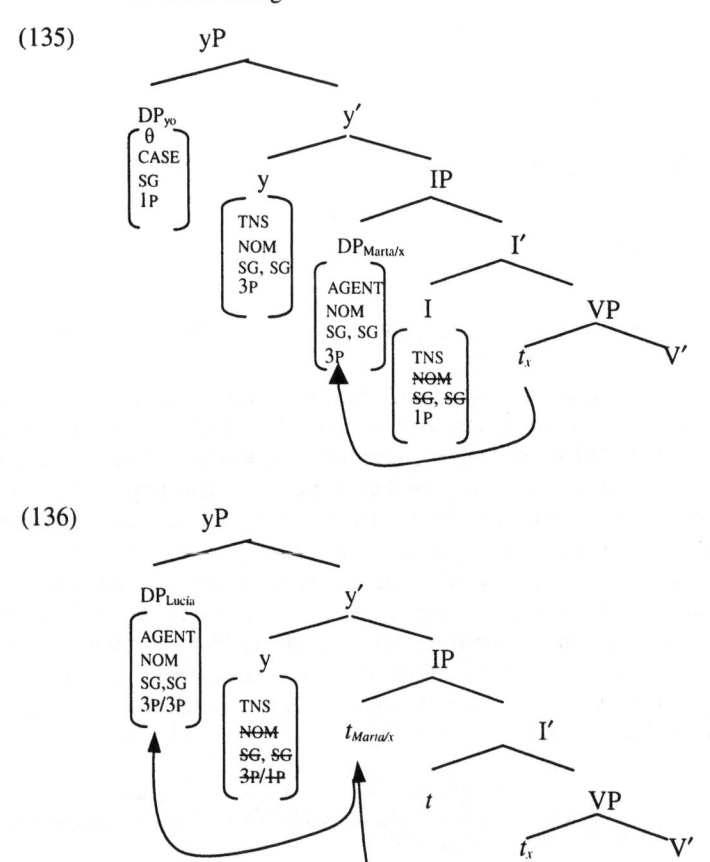

(135) [tree diagram]

(136) [tree diagram]

Two points should be noted. First, the resulting nominal matrix has the following characteristics: it shares the features of both nominal matrices, resulting in a category that is plural (SG + SG) and has the person specifications 1P/3P. Second, nothing in this analysis prevents the symmetric outcome: a conjunction of 1st and 3rd person nominals matching a 3rd person, plural verb. In this system, the fact that such combination seems to be universally dispreferred will follow from an independent person scale (1>2>3). I believe this is the correct way of viewing it, since the choice of 1st person agreement on the verb in such cases does not seem to follow from syntactic restrictions. In particular, for example, it does not see to be subject to word order asymmetries, unlike number (partial checking).

The approach I am presenting here shares some characteristics with Dalrymple and Kaplan's (2000) approach to feature resolution. One essential difference stems from the fact that these authors assume an LFG framework. One of the similarities relates to how the features of a conjoined constituent are represented. For example, in an example like (137), from their article (p. 778), 'José y yo' is an hybrid object which includes each conjunct (with individual feature specifications like PERSON 3, NUM SG) and a specification for settings of the whole conjunct (like PERSON 1, NUM PL). This can be seen as the non-derivational version of the analysis I have just presented, with one minor difference: for Dalrymple and Kaplan, plural is a primitive feature, whereas for me it is a sum of singulars.

(137) José y yo habla-mos   /*hablá-is   /*habla-n
       Jose and I speak-1P.PL/speak-2P.PL/speak-3P.PL
       'Jose and I speak.'

Note that feature resolution is not always the outcome of conjoining constituents with different feature settings. In the Bantu languages, it is possible to coordinate two nouns that belong to the same class, as Dalrymple and Kaplan (2000, p. 771) point out, however, it is impossible to coordinate nouns that belong to classes 5/6 and 7/8 respectively, as shown in the Xhosa examples in (138), quoted from those authors.[61]

(138) a. umfana   nomfazi   bayagoduka.
           young.man(1/2) and.young.woman(1/2) go.home(1/2)
           'The young man and the young woman are going home.'
       b. *Igqira   neanuse   ayagoduka
           doctor(5/6) and.diviner(7/8) go.home(5/6)
       c. *Igqira   neanuse   ziyagoduka
           doctor(5/6) and.diviner(7/8) go.home(7/8)

Case checking will have slightly different properties. As I already observed, conjunction sometimes blocks case assignment. This can be seen in the following paradigm from Zoerner (1995):

(139) a. *Me left.
       b. Robin and me left.
       c. Me and Robin left.
       d. *Kim saw I.
       e. Kim saw Robin and I.

---

[61] 5/6 indicates that the singular of the noun belongs to class 5 and the plural to class 6, as is standard practice when quoting Bantu nominals.

The data in (139) can be interpreted as suggesting that only the first conjunct checks CASE (cf. Johannessen 1998 for a similar analysis). In the current framework, this means that a case feature is only inserted in the higher IP position, not in the lower one. Lack of an overt case feature results in default CASE.

This framework incorporates Corbett's (1983) resolution rules into the grammar, without any need to include feature percolation. For theories of coordination that postulate a coordinated constituent, it is necessary to explain how features of two DPs within a conjunction phrase are passed up to the higher node. In the present theory, φ-feature differences between DPs are computed indirectly, by spec-head agreement between each of the DPs and the inflectional head.

3.5   Binding and Control binding and control

As I pointed out, conjoined DPs can be antecedents of anaphors and infinitival subjects. In the analysis of coordination where conjuncts form a plural-like constituent, the possibility of binding and control is easily predicted, since plurals independently act as antecedents and controllers. In the current framework, this follows from the fact that there is an additional DP matrix (the so-called conjunction pro) introduced in the spec of VP, which can act as the antecedent for the anaphor. This analysis also accounts for the fact that individual conjuncts cannot bind an anaphor:

(140)   a. Mercedes$_i$ y   Daniel$_j$ se$_{i+j}$ vieron.
        Mercedes and Daniel CL   saw
        'Mercedes and Daniel saw each other/themselves.'
     b. *Mercedes$_i$ y   Daniel$_j$ se$_i$ vio.
        Mercedes and Daniel CL   saw
        'Mercedes and Daniel saw herself'
     c. *Eleni and Sofia saw herself.

In theories that propose a Conjunction Phrase, this follows from the fact that the individual conjuncts do not c-command outside ConjP, so they cannot be antecedents for anaphors. In the current theory, it follows from the fact that the DP inserted in the spec of VP carries the φ-features of both conjuncts. Such theories also predict that binding should be possible inside this phrase. Munn (1993) argues that elements within coordination cannot be antecedents, as shown in the following examples from his work:

(141)   a. *John saw a video of the men$_i$ and each other$_i$.
     b. The candidates$_i$ saw a video of them$_i$ and each other$_i$.
     c. *Fred saw a video of them$_i$ and each other$_i$.
     d. *Either John or a picture of himself will suffice.

Munn suggests that *them* cannot be considered the antecedent of the anaphor in (141)b because of examples like (141)c, where the pronoun cannot be the antecedent of the anaphor.[62]

Munn accounts for the contrast between (141)a, b, by distinguishing between binders and antecedents. The condition on antecedents is that they must be thematic. In Munn's theory, the condition on antecedents is that they must be thematic. In his theory, conjuncts are non-thematic (they are predicates); rather the whole conjunction phrase (his BP) is thematic, so individual conjuncts cannot be antecedents. Thus, (141)a is ungrammatical because the anaphor lacks an antecedent (although the pronoun is its binder); whereas (141)b is grammatical because the subject is the antecedent of the anaphor. Similar examples exist in Finnish and Russian (cf. Munn 1993).[63]

Let us assume that the distinction between binders and antecedents is appropriate. In Munn's analysis, this is due to the fact that conjuncts are predicates, not arguments, hence they cannot be antecedents. In my proposal, conjoined elements are specifiers of propositional functional projections, so there must be a different source for the distinction between antecedent and binder. The general aim is to bar conjuncts from being antecedents (but not binders) of a referentially dependent expression within the coordination. The following definition accomplishes that goal:[64]

(142) A DP cannot be the antecedent of a referentially-dependent expression if it is in the specifier of the same projection as the dependent element.

4. CHAPTER SUMMARY

This chapter has provided the empirical justification for the propositional content of conjunction. I have argued that the data concerning sentential adverbs, as well as evidence from switch-reference languages and languages with aspectually restricted conjunctions like Quechua form a natural class in that they all involve predicational projections. I have proposed that the structure for coordination is one in which each conjunct appears in the same structural position (following *licensing symmetry*, cf. chapter 2). This is done by splitting a functional projection in two parts, one headed by the regular functional head, the other one by the conjunction, an underspecified head whose content gets contextually determined by the regular functional head. Given this proposal, we find a natural way to explain why no heads are conjoined.

---

[62] According to Munn, (141)b is interpreted in the following way: "on the assumption that the candidates never make speeches together, [(141)b] can refer to a single video in which each of the candidates appear (separately) making speeches. If each candidate saw this video, then [(141)b] is a possible description of what they did."

[63] Note that (141)b should be out because the pronoun is coindexed with an R-expression in its binding domain.

[64] As an anonymous reviewer points out, this view is compatible with Williams' view in which binding relations are computed on theta-structure, not on constituent structure.

Finally, I have presented an alternative analysis of agreement and movement, based on two notions: first, the notion of local insertion of features, second, postulating a conjunction pro. For A-movement, I have argued that the relevant features (φ, case) do not move, but are inserted locally in the checking domain position and later the categorial matrix with the unspecified values for the features moves to the checking domain, where it is fully specified. For A-bar movement, the same holds true. However, in this case, movement from IP may be restricted in the case of conjoined *wh*-words, since they do not form a constituent.

For agreement, binding and control, I have suggested deriving antecedent binding facts from the interaction between conjunction pro, which carries the set of features of both conjuncts and anaphors. In the next chapter, I will turn to agreement asymmetries.

CHAPTER #4

COORDINATION AND AGREEMENT

In chapter 3 I argued that coordination involves a two identical projections that host the conjuncts in their respective specifiers. This analysis predicts that certain phenomena should affect only one of those segments. In this chapter I will argue that partial agreement is an operation restricted to one of the specifiers. Partial agreement displays two important characteristics. There is a typological correlation regarding word order and a division that depends on interpretive possibilities. After presenting the data, I will turn to the analysis of the different patterns in the current framework.

1. THE DISTRIBUTION OF PARTIAL AGREEMENT

1.1 Word Order and Partial Agreement

In many languages, partial agreement is sensitive to word order. For example, in Arabic, Spanish and Brazilian Portuguese, if a given conjoined sequence has the language's canonical word order (in all three cases, SVO), agreement cannot be partial, but must be computed taking into account all conjuncts (*full agreement*); in the alternative VS word order, agreement can be full or partial. A valid generalization is that if a language has alternative word orders and shows partial agreement, it will show it in the non-canonical word order.

The following examples from Morrocan Arabic (MA) show word-order dependent partial agreement:[65]

(1) a. Mša umar w ali. (MA)
    left(3P.MAS.SG) Omar and Ali
    'Omar and Ali left.'
  b. * umar w ali mša. (MA)
    Omar and Ali left(3P.MAS.SG)
    'Omar and Ali left.'
  c. umar w ali mšaw.
    (MA) Omar and Ali left(PL.)
    'Omar and Ali left.'

---

[65] Unless otherwise stated, Arabic examples come from Aoun, Benmamoun and Sportiche 1994.

A few apparent counterexamples to the generalization concerning word order and partial agreement have been presented in the literature. Johannessen (1996), for example, quotes the following examples from German:

(2) a. Aber links war die Binnenalster und
but left was(SG) the(NOM.SG) inner-Alster(NOM.SG) and
die weissen Lichtreklamen.
the(NOM.SG) white(PL) light-ad(NOM.PL)
'But to the left were the inner Alster (lake) and the white light-ads.'
b. Alt und jung will nun die Zeichen
old(NOM.SG) and young(NOM-SG) want- to(3P.SG) now the signs
sehen.
see(SG)
'Old and young now want to see the signs.'

(2) shows alternative word orders: VS in (2)a and SV in (2)b. The latter example, however, does not seem to be a true case of partial agreement, rather it seems to be a case of semantic agreement, as the one displayed by English.[66] This example requires the subject to be interpreted collectively, something like 'all the people, the entire population, wants to see the sign'. If the verb is put in plural, the meaning changes to something like 'the young people and the old people, both groups of population want to see the signs'. These partially agreeing subjects are restricted to a few nouns, only those that can be interpreted as a collectivity and also seem to require that the denotation of the nouns together exhaust the possible references of the predicate. So, for example, substituting 'old and young' for 'mothers and fathers' in (2)b is not felicitous because not everyone in the population can be classified into mother and fathers.[67] There is also another difference between both sentences: the first one becomes ungrammatical if embedded, the second one is still grammatical:

(3) a. *Ich glaube dass links die Binnenalster und
I believe that left the(NOM.SG) inner-Alster(NOM.SG) and
die weissen Lichtreklamen war.
the(NOM.SG) white(PL) light-ad(NOM.PL) was(SG)
'I think that the inner Alster (lake) and the white light-ads were to the left.'

---

[66] The following discussion regarding the German data owes much to Roland Hinterhölzl.
[67] Johannessen argues that German does not have semantic agreement in the way English does. However, all her examples show is that the distribution of semantic agreement in German is different from that of English.

b. Ich glaube dass alt und jung will nun
   I think that old(NOM.SG) and young(NOM.SG) want-to(3P.SG) now
   die Zeichen sehen.
   the signs see(SG)
   'I think that old and young now want to see the signs.'

1.2 PF and LF Agreement Patterns

Conjoined structures with partial agreement can be divided in two types: those that behave as if agreement had no interpretive consequences (i.e. the coreference possibilities are still those of the whole coordinated structure), which I will call *PF agreement* structures, and those where agreement patterns do have interpretive consequences, which I will call *LF agreement* structures.[68] Czech is an example of a PF agreement language, as shown in (4), from Johannessen (1996); Irish is another example (cf. (5), from McCloskey 1986): in both cases, a plural anaphor can refer back to the conjoined DPs despite singular agreement on the verb. Lebanese Arabic illustrates the second type. As (6), from Aoun, Benmamoun and Sportiche (1994) shows, a verb requiring a plural subject cannot be licensed by a DP coordination if agreement is partial:

(4) Má se rád Jan i Petr.
    has(SG) REFL(SG/PL) glad(SG) Jan and Petr
    'Jan and Petr love themselves.'

(5) Bhíos pro-féin agus Tomás ag caint le chéile
    be(PAST.1P.SG) pro-EMPH and Thomas talk(PROG) with each other
    'Thomas and I were talking to one another.'

(6) *Bi ibb Kariim w Marwaan aalun.
    love(3P.SG) Kareem and Marwaan themselves
    'Kareem and Marwan love themselves.'

1.3 PF Agreement

I the following sections, I will review the distribution of PF agreement in several languages. As I already mentioned, PF agreement can be characterized by not saying that the interpretive possibilities of conjoined phrases are the same as those of conjoined phrases with full agreement. In other word, the fact that there is partial agreement seems to be a PF phenomenon.

---

[68] As we will see, however, a language can have both types of agreement, each in different constructions.

1.3.1 Irish

In addition to the example in (5)a, Irish also has other cases of PF-partial agreement.[69] McCloskey (1986) and McCloskey and Hale (1984) show that partial agreement is possible in the configuration V/P/N [pro and NP], where the pro is licensed by the agreement features of the governing category (examples from McCloskey 1986):

(7) a. Go raibh an-aithne acu pro-féin agus Daidí Jim ar
 COMP be(PAST) great-acquaintance at pro-EMPH and Daddy Jim on
 a chéile.
 each other
 'that they and Daddy Jim knew each other well' (lit.) 'that there was great acquaintance on each other at them and Daddy Jim.'
 b. A ghabháltas pro-féin agus a mháthar.
 3P.SG.MAS holding pro-EMPH and 3P.SG.MAS mother(GEN)
 'His own and his mother's holding.'

(7)a shows a coordinated term of a preposition, and (7)b a coordinated possessive. McCloskey points out that the only fully acceptable case across dialects of Irish is the first example, the second and the third progressively degrade both in acceptability and range of dialects where it is accepted. McCloskey and Hale's original analysis makes use of the notion of government. They suggest that an agreement element governs the pro thus identifying it. Although Irish shows the added feature of conjoining a pro, which most languages disallow, this is clearly an instance of partial agreement, with the added interest that it is the only possible pattern in this language.

In addition to the examples above, in the following ones we can see that Irish allows a plural anaphor, or a collective predicate (examples from McCloskey and Hale 1984):

(8) a. Dá mbéitheá féin agus Rachel ag gabhail i gcleamhnas.
 if be(COND.2.SG) REFL and Rachel go(PROG) in engagement
 'If you and Rachel were getting engaged.'
 b. Go mbeinn-se agus tusa mór len a chélie.
 COMP be(COND.1.SG)-CONTR and you great with each other
 'That you and I would be very friendly with each other.'

Irish shows no contrast with respect to the possibility of having plural anaphors between stage-level and individual-level predicates.[70] This fact will become relevant when we compare the PF agreement pattern with the LF agreement paradigm.

---

[69] The suggestion that Irish agreement might be purely a PF phenomenon is an idea originally due to Jim McCloskey transmitted to me by Joseph Aoun.

[70] Stage-level predicates are those that indicate temporary properties of the subject, such as *available*, individual-level predicates indicate permanent properties.

1.3.2 Spanish Adjectival Agreement

Adjectives in Spanish obligatorily agree in number and gender with the noun they modify, as illustrated in (9)a-b. (9)c is ungrammatical because the adjective is masculine and the head noun is feminine. In (9)d, on the other hand, the adjective is singular but the head noun plural.

(9) a. La mesa   redond-a
       the table(FEM)   round-FEM
       'The round table'
   b. Las mesa-s   redond-a-s
       the table(FEM)-PL round-FEM-PL
       'The round tables'
   c. *La mesa   redond-o.
       the table(FEM)   round-MASC
   d. *Las mesa-s   redond-a.
       the table(FEM)-PL round-FEM.SG

In general, when two DPs are conjoined, it is always possible to have full agreement on the adjective. If both nouns are masculine, the adjective is masculine, plural (cf. (10)a). If only one of the nouns is masculine, the adjective shows masculine, plural agreement (cf. (10)b), at least this is the normative solution, although there is variation, as I will show below. If both nouns are feminine, the adjective is feminine, plural (cf. (10)c).

(10) a. El secretari-o   y el coordinador   peruan-o-s
       the secretary-MASC and the coordinator(MASC) peruvian-MASC-PL
       'The Peruvian secretary and the Peruvian coordinator'
    b. El   secretari-o   y la coordinador-a   peruan-o-s
       the secretary-MASC and the coordinator-FEM peruvian-MASC-PL
       'The Peruvian secretary and the Peruvian coordinator'
    c. La secretari-a   y la coordinador-a peruan-a-s
       the secretary-FEM and the coordinator-FEM peruvian-FEM-PL
       'The Peruvian secretary and the Peruvian coordinator'

In all of the examples above, the adjective has scope over both nouns. It is also possible to have partial agreement with the last conjunct, and typically the adjective has scope over that conjunct as well. However, in some cases, it is possible to have partial agreement with the second conjunct and still have scope over both conjuncts.[71]

The two possible agreement patterns when the conjoined DPs have different gender are full, default masculine agreement, as in (10)b and (11)a or gender agreement with the closest conjunct (cf. (11)c-d, in particular, and (12)). In some

---

[71] All of these examples are based on the ones collected by Fernández Ramírez (1995) from written sources. I have made minor modifications in some of them. Grammaticality judgements are my own.

cases, number agreement can also be with the closest conjunct (cf. (11)d), (12)b). In all of these cases, the adjective can have scope over both conjuncts. This fact is particularly noticeable in (11)d, because number agreement is singular:[72]

(11) a. Ejerce   influencia en el crecimiento   y   la
       exercises influence in the growth(MAS.SG) and the
       reproducción   genétic-o-s.
       reproduction(FEM.SG) genetic-MAS-PL
       'He/she/it exercises influence in the genetic growth and reproduction.'
   b. Ejerce   influencia en la reproducción   y el
       exercises influence in the reproduction(FEM.SG) and the
       crecimiento   genétic-o-s.
       growth(MAS.SG) genetic-MAS-PL
       'He/she/it exercises influence in the genetic growth and reproduction.'
   c. Ejerce   influencia en el crecimiento   y la
       exercises influence in the growth(MAS.SG) and the
       reproducción   genétic-a-s.
       reproduction(FEM.SG) genetic-FEM-PL
       'He/she/it exercises influence in the genetic growth and reproduction.'
   d. Ejerce   influencia en la reproducción   y el
       exercises influence in the reproduction(FEM.SG) and the
       crecimiento   genétic-o.
       growth(MAS.SG) genetic-MAS(SG)
       'He/she/it exercises influence in the genctic growth and reproduction.'

(12) a. ?El pensamiento   y (la) acción   polític-a-s.
      the thinking(MAS.SG) and (the) action(FEM.SG) political-FEM-PL
      'Political thinking and action'
   b. El pensamiento   y (la) acción   política.
      the thinking(MAS.SG) and (the) action(FEM.SG) political(FEM.SG)
      'Political thinking and action'

Non-local partial agreement is not possible, as illustrated below:

(13) a. *Ejerce   influencia en la reproducción   y el
       exercises influence in the reproduction(FEM.SG) and the
       crecimiento   genétic-a-s.
       growth(MAS.SG) genetic-FEM-PL
   b. *Ejerce   influencia en la reproducción   y el
       exercises influence in the reproduction(FEM.SG) and the
       crecimiento   genétic-a.
       growth(MAS.SG) genetic-FEM.SG

---

[72] Wide scope is much more difficult to obtain with partial agreement in feminine and singular, as in (11)b.

c. *Ejerce influencia en el crecimiento y la
exercises influence in the growth(MAS.SG) and the
reproducción genétic-o.
reproduction(FEM.SG) genetic-MAS.SG

Prenominal elements (determiners and certain adjectives) can only agree with the closest DP, as shown in (14). These examples show that both the determiner and the prenominal adjective must agree with the first nominal *gracia* 'grace'[73]:

(14) a. La supuest-a gracia y encanto
the(FEM.SG) alleged-FEM(SG) grace(FEM.SG) and charm(MAS.SG)
italian-o.
Italian-MAS(SG)
'The alleged Italian grace and charm'
b. *Las supuest-a-s gracia y encanto
the(FEM.SG) alleged-FEM-PL grace(FEM.SG) and charm(MAS.SG)
italian-o/italian-o-s.
Italian-MAS.SG/-MAS-PL
c. *Los supest-o-s gracia y encanto
the(MAS.PL) alleged-FEM(SG) grace(FEM.SG) and charm(MAS.SG)
italian-o/italian-o-s.
Italian-MAS(SG)/MAS-PL

To summarize, it is possible to have partial agreement in number and gender between the adjective and the closest conjunct, maintaining wide scope of the adjective over both conjuncts. Partial agreement is obligatory with prenominal elements.

In the case of PP conjunction, full agreement is the default solution, as before: plural number and masculine if there is a masculine noun, otherwise feminine:

(15) a. Pretendiendo oponer a su serenidad y a su
Pretending oppose to his serenity(FEM.SG) and to his
indiferencia suprem-a-s.
indifference(FEM.SG) supreme-FEM-PL
'Pretending to oppose to his supreme serenity and indifference.'

---

[73] (14)c contrasts with (11)a, b, although the postnominal part of each example is very similar. Note, however, that what causes the ungrammaticality in the latter example is the lack of agreement between *supuestos* and *gracia*.

b. Lo más importante es que cada una disponga del
CL most important is that each one(FEM) have available of-the
espacio y de la tierra necesari-o-s para su perfecta
space and of the land(FEM-SG) necessary-MAS-PL for his perfect
prosperidad.
prosperity
'The most important thing is that each of us disposes of the necessary space and land for his perfect prosperity.'

In the case of PP coordination, partial agreement in gender and number with the second conjunct (with wide scope interpretation of the adjective) is much worse, however, partial agreement in gender and full agreement in number is only slightly marginal, as shown in (17)b:

(16) a. *Que cada una disponga del espacio y de la tierra
 that each one have available of-the space and of the land(FEM.SG)
 necesari-a.
 necessary-FEM(SG)
 b. ?Que cada una disponga del espacio y de la tierra
 that each one have available of-the space and of the land(FEM.SG)
 necesari-a-s.
 necessary-FEM-PL
 'That each one have the necessary space and land.'

(15) and (16)b raise a paradox (as the editors of Fernández Ramírez 1995 point out). Agreement between adjectives and nouns is taken to be local. This is why a postnominal adjective cannot agree only with the first conjunct (cf. the ungrammaticality of (13)b). In particular, agreement is usually assumed to be DP-internal. However, full agreement in (15) and partial agreement in gender in (16)b is clearly not DP-internal. In both sets of examples, the two DPs are inside PPs. In the first case, the fact that there is full agreement suggests that the adjective must have a position higher than both DPs, but there is no constituent that includes only both DPs. The structure for (15)a is schematically shown in (17)a. In (16)b, on the other hand, the adjective agrees partially in gender (indicated by a dotted line in (17)b), fully in number, and also has wide scope.[74]

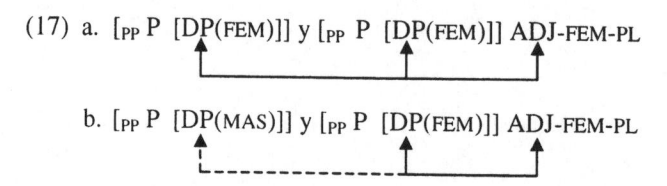

(17) a. [$_{PP}$ P [DP(FEM)]] y [$_{PP}$ P [DP(FEM)]] ADJ-FEM-PL

b. [$_{PP}$ P [DP(MAS)]] y [$_{PP}$ P [DP(FEM)]] ADJ-FEM-PL

There are two important points about these facts. First, they can be classified as PF agreement, since partial or full agreement does not necessarily correlate with

---

[74] These contrasts can be reproduced with the masculine as well.

differences in interpretation. Second, they suggest one of two possible analyses: either there is an agreement projection above DP and even above PP, or else, there is some version of right-node-raising, perhaps along the lines of Kayne's (1994) analysis of right-node-raising. I will return to the analysis of these cases below.

1.3.3 Clitic Agreement with Accusatives in Dialects of Spanish

Spanish shows wide variation with respect to the morphological properties of the clitic system.[75] It has been proposed that clitics in Spanish are agreement markers (cf. Silva-Corvalán 1981, Franco 1993 and references in the latter), so in this sense, the variation that I am going to describe, which can be classified in two distinct dialects, *dialect A* and *dialect B*, is an instance of partial agreement.[76] In both dialects, partial agreement displays features of gapping. In dialect B, the full agreement pattern has an additional characteristic: a coordination of two DPs with a single preposition is interpreted collectively, whereas a conjunction of two PPs is interpreted distributively. In all cases, however, singular agreement supports plural dependencies. Both dialects are accusative clitic-doubling, and both only allow doubling of animates (as described by Jaeggli 1982). However, neither are River Plate Spanish; dialect A is drawn from a Chilean speaker, dialect B from Peruvian speakers. Data from datives in dialect B also correspond to dialects that do not double accusatives.

For partial agreement, both dialects pattern in the same way: it is only available when the conjuncts are PPs (vs. a conjunction of prepositional terms), and the second conjunct is separated by a heavy pause, indicated by a comma in the examples. The contrast is illustrated in (18):

(18) a. *Lo   vi   a   Juan y   Pedro.
         CL(SG) saw to   Juan and Pedro
         'I saw Juan and Pedro.'
     b. Lo   vi   a   Juan, y   a Pedro.
         CL(SG) saw to   Juan and to Pedro
         'I saw Juan and Pedro.'

Sentences such as (18)b also allow the adverbs like *también* 'too', *ayer* 'yesterday', *hoy* 'today' (cf. (19)a, b), which usually appear in gapping constructions. These adverbs cannot appear when the clitic is plural[77]:

(19) a. Lo   vi   a   Juan, y   a Pedro también.
        CL(SG) saw to   Juan and to Pedro also
        'I saw Juan and Pedro also.'

---

[75] Thanks to Alfredo Arnaiz, Liliana Paredes and Liliana Sánchez for judgements, and to Germán Westphal for judgements and discussion of the data from this section and the next one.
[76] In other analyses, Spanish clitics are not considered agreement markers.
[77] (19)c is acceptable with a different structure, what Milner 1987 calls *interpretive chains*.

b. Lo vi a Juan ayer, y a Pedro hoy.
   CL(SG) saw to Juan yesterday and to Pedro today
   'I saw Juan yesterday and Pedro today.'
c. #Lo-s vi a Juan (hoy) y a Pedro ayer.
   CL-PL saw to Juan (today) and to Pedro yesterday
   'I saw Juan today and Pedro yesterday.'

Dialects A and B are different in the full agreement paradigm. Dialect A disallows coordination of two PPs (cf. (20)b). Dialect B, on the other hand, allows both possibilities (cf. (21)).[78]

(20) a. Lo-s vi a Juan y Pedro.   (Dialect A)
        CL-PL saw to Juan and Pedro
        'I saw Juan and Pedro.'
     b. *Lo-s vi a Juan y a Pedro.
        CL-PL saw to Juan and to Pedro
        'I saw Juan and Pedro.'

(21) a. ?Lo-s vi a Juan y Marta.   (Dialect B)
        CL-PL saw to Juan and Marta
        'I saw Juan and Marta.'
     b. Lo-s vi a Juan y a Marta.
        CL-PL saw to Juan and to Marta
        'I saw Juan and Marta.'

The contrast in (20) would follow if a coordination of two PPs (as in (20)b) always involves coordination of higher nodes with gapping (along the lines of Aoun, Benmamoun and Sportiche's (1994) analysis of the Arabic data, see below). This would explain why it is not possible to have full agreement in those cases: there is no nominal, plural-like coordinated node to agree with.

In dialect B, coordination of two PPs forces a distributive reading and a conjunction of two DPs terms of a preposition tends to correlate with a collective reading. This is illustrated by the contrast in (22). Distributive readings (forced by *respectivamente* 'respectively') are very marginal when only one preposition appears, as in (22)c. Note that when the preposition is totally absent, as in (22)b, the distributive reading is possible.[79]

(22) a. Visitaron a Juan y Marta.
        visited to Juan and Marta
        'They visited Juan and Marta.'

---

[78] *A* is strictly not a preposition, but an animacy marker/case marker.
[79] The preposition *a* in (22)a appears because the object is animate.

b. Visitaron San Francisco y   San Diego respectivamente.
   visited   San Francisco and San Diego respectively
   'They visited San Francisco and San Diego respectively.'
c. ??Visitaron a Juan y   Marta respectivamente.
   visited   to Juan and Marta respectively
   'They visited Juan and Marta respectively.'
d. Visitaron a Juan y   a   Marta respectivamente.
   visited   to Juan and   to Marta respectively
   'They visited Juan and Marta respectively.'

In Clitic Left Dislocation (CLLD) structures we find the same contrast between dialects. Both dialects disallow partial agreement:

(23) a. *A Juan y   Pedro, lo   vi.
        to Juan and Pedro CL(SG) saw
     b. *A Juan y   a Pedro, lo   vi.
        to Juan and to Pedro, CL(SG) saw

However, once again, the full agreement paradigm shows a difference. As before, dialect A allows a coordination of two DPs but not of two PPs (cf. (24)a vs. b). Dialect B, on the other hand, completely disallows coordination of two DPs (cf. (25)a).

(24) a. A Juan y   Pedro, lo-s   vi.   (Dialect A)
        to Juan and   Pedro, CL-PL saw
        'Pedro and Juan, I saw them.'
     b. *A Juan y a Pedro, lo-s vi.
        to Juan and to Pedro, CL-PL saw
        'Juan and Pedro, I saw them.'

(25) a. ??A Juan y   Marta, lo-s   vi.   (Dialect B)
        to Juan and Marta CL-PL   saw
        'Juan and Marta I saw them.'
     b. A Juan y   a   Marta, lo-s vi.
        to Juan and   to Marta CL-PL saw
        'Juan and Marta I saw them.'

To summarize, partial agreement is possible in dialects A and B only if both of the conjoined direct objects are preceded by the marker *a*, and if there is a pause. The possibility of having an adverb suggests these are gapping structures. In clitic left dislocated structures, on the other hand, partial agreement is not possible at all. Full agreement, shows a diverging pattern: dialect A only accepts a single marker *a* (both in non-dislocated and dislocated structures), whereas in dialect B the single marker structure is slightly deviant. The differences between both dialects are summarized in the following table:

Table 1. Agreement paradigms for the accusative, dialects A and B

	Dialect A		Dialect B	
Partial agreement	Sg. → pause, también	gapping	Sg. → pause, también	gapping
Full agreement	a [DP y DP]	gapping	a [DP y DP]	collective
	[a DP] y [a DP]	*	[a DP] y [a DP]	distributive
CLLD	a [DP y DP]	√	a [DP y DP]	*
	[a DP] y [a DP]	*	[a DP] y [a DP]	√

Although datives in dialects A and B have a different distribution, it should be observed from the start that grammatical examples with partial agreement in both dialects do not require a pause between both conjuncts, as they do in the case of accusatives. In dialect A, singular marking on the clitic is only possible with two PPs, as with accusatives:

(26) a. *Le di un libro a Juan y Marta. (Dialect A)
    CL(SG) gave a book to Juan and Marta
    'I gave a book to Juan and Marta.'
  b. Le di un libro a Juan y a Marta.
    CL(SG) gave a book to Juan and to Marta
    'I gave a book to Juan and Marta.'

However, when the dative is not peripheral, it is not possible to have singular agreement, unless the constituent after the dative is clearly dislocated:

(27) a. *Le dije a Juan y a Pedro la verdad.
    CL(SG) told to Juan and to Pedro the truth
    'I told Juan and Pedro the truth.'
  b. Le dije a Juan y a Pedro, la verdad.
    CL(SG) told to Juan and to Pedro, the truth
    'I told Juan and Pedro the truth.'

The full agreement paradigm is also the same as for accusatives: only a single preposition *a* is possible:

(28) a. Le-s di un libro a Juan y Marta. (Dialect A)
    CL-PL gave a book to Juan and Marta
    'I gave a book to Juan and Marta.'
  b. *Le-s di un libro a Juan y a Marta.
    CL-PL gave a book to Juan and to Marta
    'I gave a book to Juan and to Marta.'

Clitic Left Dislocated constituents also show the same distributional pattern, only full agreement is possible:

(29) a. *A Juan y Marta, le   di   un libro.
        to Juan and Marta, CL(SG) gave a book
        'Juan and Marta, I gave them a book.'
    b. A Juan y   Marta, le-s   di   un libro.
        to Juan and Marta, CL(PL) gave a book
        'Juan and Marta, I gave them a book.'
    c. *A Juan y a Marta, le   di   un libro.
        to Juan and to Marta, CL(SG) gave a book
        'Juan and Marta, I gave them a book.'
    d. *A Juan y a Marta, le-s di   un libro.
        to Juan and to Marta, CL-PL gave a book
        'Juan and Marta, I gave them a book.'

The distribution is summarized in table 2:

Table 2. Dative Clitics in Dialect A

	[P DP] y [P DP]	P [DP y DP]
Full agreement	*	√
Partial agreement	√ (but * if moved)	*

Partial agreement in dialect B datives is only possible if the DPs are not dislocated, as shown in (30). Only (30)a-b, the non-dislocated versions of the sentences are grammatical, regardless of whether the conjunction joins DPs (cf. (30)a vs. c) or PPs (cf. (30)b vs. d).

(30) a. Le   di   un libro a Juan y   Marta.
        CL(SG) gave a book to Juan and Marta
        'I gave a book to Juan and Marta.'
    b. Le   di   un libro a Juan y a Marta.
        CL(SG) gave a book to Juan and to Marta
        'I gave a book to Juan and Marta.'
    c. *A Juan y Marta le   di   un libro.
        to Juan and Marta CL(SG) gave a   book
    d. *A Juan y a Marta le   di   un libro.
        to Juan and to Marta CL(SG) gave a book
    e. A Juan y   a Marta le-s di   un libro.
        to Juan and to Marta CL-PL gave a   book

As in all other cases, when the clitic is singular, it is still possible to have a restrictive relative clause whose subject refers back to both conjoints:

(31) Le   di   un libro al   hombre y   a la mujer que vinieron.
     CL(SG) gave a book to-the man   and to the woman that came(PL)
     'I gave a book to the man and the woman that came.'

To summarize the distribution, both partial and full agreement patterns are possible in dialect B in non-dislocated word orders. In dislocated structures, however, only full agreement is possible.

1.3.4 Czech

Johannessen (1996) quotes Czech as a PF agreement language. A distributive quantifier (formed by a preposition with the meaning 'at the rate of' and the distributed object) is possible with partial agreement, and so is a plural reflexive anaphor (examples from Johannessen 1996):

(32) a. Po   jednom jablku   sneỳdl   Jan a Petr.
       at-the-rate-of one(LOC) apple(LOC) ate(3P.SG) John and Peter
       'John and Peter ate an apple each.'
    b. Má   se   rád   Jan i Petr.
       has(3P.SG) REFL(SG/PL) glad(SG) John and Peter
       'John and Peter love themselves.'

In the first sentence, the distributive quantifier *po* 'each' distributes over both subjects, despite the fact that the verb is singular. The second sentence, on the other hand, involves a reflexive anaphor that is interpreted with respect to each of the conjuncts, despite the singular number on the verb.

1.4 LF agreement

In the following sections I will review a range of cases where partial agreement has interpretive consequences: agreement determines the type of antecedent that can appear. Since agreement can involve person, number and gender, it is possible that a language will show semantically relevant agreement with respect to only one of those categories. Typically, number agreement will be semantically relevant, but gender and person will not. We will see examples of this type from Arabic, Brazilian Portuguese and Spanish.

1.4.1 Arabic

According to Aoun, Benmamoun and Sportiche (1994) (henceforth ABS) Arabic is a LF agreement language: partial agreement in Arabic does not license plural elements. Munn (1999), however, has questioned this claim, arguing that ABS's examples only show cases of syntactically required plural agreement, not semantically required plurality. In this section, I will review the relevant data.

According to ABS, partial agreement always occurs in the VS word order in the dialects of Arabic that have it.[80] When the word order is VS, the verb can fully agree

---

[80] In addition to the data from ABS, this section relies on judgments provided to me by Lina Choueiri.

with the first DP in Lebanese Arabic (LA) and Morrocan Arabic (MA) (cf. (33)a, b); whereas in Standard Arabic (SA), it agrees in gender with the first DP (cf. also Mohamad (1989)). When the order is SV, the verb cannot agree partially with the closest S, as seen in ((33)c, d).

(33) a. Mša   umar w   ali.   (MA)
        left(3P.MAS.SG) Omar and   Ali
        'Omar and Ali left'
    b. Raa   Kariim w Marwaan.   (LA)
        left(3P.MAS.SG) Kareem and Marwaan
        'Kareem and Marwaan left'
    c. * umar w   ali mša.   (MA)
        Omar and Ali left(3P.MAS.SG)
    d. *Kariim w Marwaan raa .   (LA)
        Kareem and Marwaan left(3P.MAS.SG)

With partial agreement, anaphors cannot take both conjuncts as antecedents:

(34) a. Kariim w Marwaan bi ibbo   aalun.   (LA)
        Kareem and Marwaan love(3P.PL) themselves
        'Kareem and Marwaan love themselves'
    b. Bi ibbo   Kariim w Marwaan   aalun.
        love(3P.PL) Kareem and Marwaan themselves
        'Kareem and Marwan love themselves'
    c. *Bi ibb   Kariim w Marwaan   aalun.
        love(3P.SG)   Kareem and Marwaan themselves
        'Kareem and Marwan love themselves'

The same pattern holds for other constructions which require a plural antecedent: collective predicates and quantifiers like *both* or *together*. All three of these items are possible with the fully agreeing conjoined phrases, but not with the partially agreeing counterparts (see ABS). I will illustrate the cases of b- uu 'together' and the verb 'meet':

(35) a. umar w Sa id mšaw   b- uu   l-l-mədrasa.   (MA)
        Omar and Said went(PL) with-both to-the-school
        'Omar and Said went to school together.'
    b. *Mša   umar w Sa id b- uu   l-l-mədrasa.
        went(3P.MAS.SG) Omar and Said with-both to-the-school
    c. * umar mša   w   ali mša b- uu .
        Omar went(3P.MAS.SG) and Ali left with-both

(36) a. *Lta a   Kariim w   Marwaan.   (LA)
        met(3P.MAS.SG) Kareem and Marwaan
    b. Lta o   Kariim w   Marwaan.
        met(PL) Kareem and   Marwaan

'Kareem and Marwaan met.'

Additionally, if there is a distributive quantifier like *killwaa ad* 'each' in LA, which can only quantify over plural elements, it can only appear with the fully agreeing version, not the partial agreement one:

(37) a. Kariim w Marwaan akalo təffee a kill waa ad.
Kareem and Marwaan ate(PL) apple each one
'Kareem and Marwaan each ate an apple.'
b. * akal Kariim w Marwaan təffee a kill waa ad.
ate(3-MAS.SG) Kareem and Marwaan apple each one
'Kareem and Marwaan each ate an apple.'
c. * akal Kariim w Marwaan təffee a kill waa ad.
ate(3P.S) Kareem and Marwaan apple each one
'Kareem and Marwaan each ate an apple'

ABS argue that partial agreement (agreement with the first conjunct) involves clausal coordination, so the structure of a sentence like (38)a would be (38)b or (38)c, where there are two full clauses. The second VP deletes, leaving only the first one, and the common VP adjunct is right-node-raised and adjoined to the conjunction site:

(38) a. Neem Kariim w Marwaan f -l-biit. (LA)
slept(3P.MAS.SG) Kareem and Marwaan in-the-room
'Kareem and Marwaan slept in the room.'
b. [Kareem VP] and [Marwaan VP] [in the room]
c. [VP Kareem] and [VP Marwaan] [in the room]

This accounts for why there is partial agreement with the first conjunct: the verb is part of the first sentential conjunct, hence it agrees with the first subject.[81] It also explains why no elements requiring plural antecedents are possible: at no point is there a plural-like antecedent, since there are two clauses.

For the case of full agreement, two DPs are conjoined and they are the subject of a single clause. This explains why full agreement allows collective verbs, plural quantifiers and anaphors: the subject is a constituent formed by the DP coordination.

Munn (1999) questions whether these paradigms show semantically plural agreement or only syntactically plural agreement. Thus, a syntactically singular but semantically plural noun like *jamaa* 'group' is ungrammatical with *sawa* 'together', in contrast to a syntactically (and semantically) plural noun like *rijal* 'men', as shown in below (sentences and judgements from Munn 1999):

---

[81] In fact, this is only one of the solutions ABS suggest, another one is some version of Williams's (1978) across-the-board movement, which will extract the verb simultaneously from both clauses, although this by itself does not account for agreement, as ABS point out.

(39) a. el-jamaa   raa et.
       the-group left(FEM.SG)
       'The group left.'
    b. *el-jamaa raa et   sawa.
       the-group left(FEM.SG) together
    c. el-rijal   raa u   sawa.
       the-men left(MAS.PL) together
       'The men left together'

According to Munn, elements like *sawa* 'together' and *lta a* 'met' cannot be used to support ABS's clausal analysis, because they show a syntactic plurality requirement, not a semantic one, given that they are not compatible with semantic plurals like *el-jamaa* 'the group'. Rather, these elements only show a "*formal* licensing requirement that requires a *syntactic* plural (Munn 1999, 646)". The reason why (36) is ungrammatical is that the verb requires a syntactic plural, and the subject is syntactically singular (but perhaps semantically plural). In their reply to Munn, Aoun et al. (cf. Aoun, Benmamoun and Sportiche 1999) point out the following problem in Munn's logic. Suppose that the coordination of DPs in (39)a is semantically plural. Given that the verb in the latter example is singular, what is number of this conjunction of DPs? If it is syntactically plural, then (38)a should be grammatical, under Munn's assumption that *lta a* only requires syntactic plurality. If the conjoined DPs are syntactically singular, then it should trigger singular agreement, contrary to fact.

There are additional complications in LA: in this language it is possible to have two subjects in a construction which involves the progressive auxiliary *keen*. The agreement pattern when the auxiliary appears is as follows: if the subject precedes the auxiliary, there is agreement with the conjoined phrase (cf. (40)), if the subject follows the auxiliary but precedes the verb, there can be full agreement (cf. (41) a) or partial agreement between the auxiliary and the first conjunct (cf. (41)b), as in cases of VS order without the auxiliary (cf. (33)b)).

(40) Kariim w Marwaan keeno am yil abo.   (LA)
     Kareem and Marwaan were ASP playing(PL)
     'Kareem and Marwaan were playing.'

(41) a. Keeno Kariim w   Marwaan am   yil abo.
        were Kareem and Marwaan ASP playing(PL)
        'Kareem and Marwaan were playing.'
     b. Keen   Kariim w   Marwaan am yil abo.
        was(3P.MAS.SG) Kareem and Marwaan ASP playing(PL)
        'Kareem and Marwaan were playing.'

The problem is that the main verb must be plural in these examples. Since (41)b has partial agreement on the auxiliary, this means, following ABS's logic, that there are two clauses. However, if there are two clauses, what is the main verb agreeing with?[82] This paradigm is problematic for ABS's analysis (as pointed out to me by Barry Schein).

Additionally, in these cases, it is still possible to have an anaphor (judgements provided by Lina Choueiri):

(42) Keen　　　　Kariim　w　Marwaan　am　yil abo　ma ba ˌun.
was(3P.MAS.SG) Kareem　and Marwaan ASP　playing(PL) with each other
'Kareem and Marwaan were playing with each other.'

Aoun and Benmamoun's (1999) explanation for this apparent problem is that the auxiliary does not show agreement with the first conjunct, but default agreement. This can be seen in cases where the first conjunct is feminine (43)a and also in the fact that a plural DP is also possible (43)c (examples from Aoun and Benmamoun 1999):

(43) a. *Keenet　　　　Nadia w　Zayna　am yil abo.
　　　　was(3P.FEM.SG) Nadia and　Zayna ASP　playing(PL)
　　b. Keen　　　　Nadia w　Zayna　am yil abo.
　　　　was(3P.MAS.SG) Nadia and Zayna ASP playing(PL)
　　　　'Nadia and Zayna were playing.'
　　c. Keen　　　　le-wleed　　am yil abo.
　　　　was(3P.MAS.SG)　the children ASP playing(PL)
　　　　'The children were playing.'
　　d. Keen　　　　Kariim w　Marwan　am　tidrib-un
　　　　was(3P.MAS.SG) Karim and Marwan ASP　beat(FEM.SG)-CL(PL)
　　　　lm　allme.
　　　　the teacher
　　　　'Karim and Marwan, the teacher used to beat them.'

According to Aoun and Benmamoun, the higher auxiliary verb does not agree with the postverbal subjects. Rather, these examples are bi-clausal, the auxiliary has an expletive subject. As (43)d shows, the auxiliary is higher than a clitic left-dislocated element (*Karim w Marwan*). This supports the view that the higher auxiliary is in a higher clause.

A second, related paradigm has to do with stage-level vs. individual-level predicates.[83] Stage-level predicates contrast with individual-level predicates with respect to the availability of plural anaphors:

(44) a. *Keen　Kariim w　Marwan　ixwe la-ba ˌun.
　　　　was(SG) Kareem and Marwan brothers to each other
　　b. *Keen　Kariim w　Marwan　ilmaan　tnaytinun.
　　　　was(SG) Kareem and Marwaan　German(PL)　both

---

[82] This fact is common to other languages which show the SV/VS contrast, for example Brazilian Portuguese and Spanish, see below.

[83] This contrast was suggested to me by Barry Schein. Judgements are from Lina Choueiri.

c. ?Keen Kariim w Marwaan mabsuṭiin laba ḍun.
 was(SG) Kareem and Marwaan happy(PL) for each other
 'Kareem and Marwan were happy for each other.'

The logic of ABS' analysis suggests that (44)a, b are bi-clausal whereas (44)c is a true DP coordination.

1.4.2 Brazilian Portuguese

Brazilian Portuguese is also a language with a limited range of partial agreement, according to Munn (1993), who quotes the following data: a conjoined subject with a copular verb *estar* triggers full agreement in number on the verb and on the adjective, as well as default (masculine) agreement on the adjective (if at least one of the conjuncts is masculine), as shown below.

(45) a. A janela   e o portão   estavam abert-o-s.
 the window(FEM) and the door(MAS) were(PL) open-PL-MAS
 'The door and the window were open.'
 b. *A janela   e o portão   estava abert-o.
 the window(FEM) and the door(MAS) was(SG) open-MAS(SG)
 'The door and the window were open.'
 c. *A janela   e o portão   estava abert-a.
 the window(FEM) and the door(MAS) was(SG) open-FEM(SG)
 'The window and the door were open.'

In the order VS, agreement both in number and gender may be with the closest conjunct, just as in Arabic (cf. (46)).

(46) a. Estava abert-a   a janela   e o portão.
 was(SG) open-FEM the window(FEM) and the door(MAS)
 'The door and the window were open.'
 b. ??Estavam abert-o-s   a janela   e o portão.
 were(PL) open-MAS-PL the window(FEM) and the door(MAS)
 'The door and the window were open.'
 c. *Estava abert-o   a janela   e o portão.
 was   open-MAS(SG) the window(FEM) and the door(MAS)
 'The window and the door were open.'

With the copular verb *ser*, agreement must be full even in the order V-S-Adj[84]:

---

[84] Munn (1999) gives a grammatical example of *ser* and partial agreement, but this involves a clefted structure: *fui eu e as meninas que compramos as flores* 'it was I and the girls that bought the flowers.' Agreement patterns in clefts are not necessarily the same as in non-clefts.

110   CHAPTER #4

(47) a. São   os   meninos e   as   meninas educad-o-s.
         are(PL) the boys   and the girls   polite-MAS-PL
         'The boys and the girls are polite.'
     b. *São   os   meninos e   as   meninas educad-a-s.
         are(PL) the boys   and the girls   polite-FEM-PL
         'The boys and the girls are polite.'
     c. *E   o   menino e   a   menina educad-o-s.
         is(SG) the boy   and the girl   politeMAS-PL
         'The boy and the girl are polite.'
     d. *E   o   menino e   a   menina educad-a-s.
         is(SG) the boy   and the girl   polite-FEM-PL
         'The boy and the girl are polite.'

Finally, the following examples with *estar* in the order V-S-Adj complete the paradigm[85]:

(48) a. Estava a janela   e o   portão   aberto.
         was(SG) the window(FEM) and the door(MAS) open(SG-MAS)
         'The window and the door were open.'
     b. *Estava a janela   e o   portão   aberta.
         was(SG) the window(FEM) and the door(MAS) open(SG-FEM)
         'The window and the door were open.'
     c. ?Estava o portão   e a janela   aberta.
         was(SG) the door(MAS) and the window(FEM) open(SG-FEM)
         'The window and the door were open.'
     d. ?Estava a janela   e o portão   abertos.
         was(SG) the window(FEM) and the door(MAS) open(PL-MAS)
         'The window and the door were open.'

The data above show that Brazilian Portuguese has a parallel paradigm to the one seen for Arabic where the auxiliary shows partial agreement but the adjective shows full agreement. Like Arabic, the cases of plural agreement are stage-level, (cf. (44)a, b) vs. (44) c) in Arabic, (47)c vs. (48)d in Brazilian Portuguese). This suggests that a similar analysis is possible in those cases as well.

Munn (1999) argues that Brazilian Portuguese also shows that partial agreement does not go hand in hand with semantic singularity. In particular, following Schmitt (1997), he argues that absolutive participials allow partial agreement and allow group readings:

(49) a. Arrumad-a-s   as sala-s   e o quarto,...
         tidied-up-FEM-PL the living.room(FEM)-PL and the bedroom(SG)
         'Once the living-room and the bedroom were tidy,...'
     b. *Arrumad-o-s   as sala-s   e o quarto,...
         tidied.up-MAS-PL the living.room(FEM-PL) and the bedroom(MAS.SG)

---

[85] Thanks to Marcello Santos for the judgements.

c. Combinad-a   a prata   e o ouro,
combined-FEM(SG) the silver(FEM) and the gold(MAS)
a Maria tinha o suficiente para fazer um anel.
the Maria had the enough   to make a ring
'With the gold and the silver combined, Maria had enough to make a ring.'

In both Brazilian and Spanish, absolute clauses are allowed only with transitive and unaccusative verbs. However, another very important feature of absolutive participials is that they must be perfective. In particular, only those adjectives and participials that can appear with *estar* can appear in absolute participials (cf. Bosque 1990, Suñer 1990, Hernanz 1991). If this is correct, absolute clauses would be a subcase of the stage/individual-level paradigm we have already seen for Arabic and Brazilian Portuguese. And if the lead from Arabic is correct, then it is possible to reanalyze these cases as involving biclausal structures.

1.4.3 Spanish Subject-Verb Agreement

Spanish has, to a minor extent, the patterns of both Arabic and Brazilian Portuguese. Although sentences with partial agreement are marginal, there is a clear contrast between the SV word order, for which agreement must be full, and VS word order, for which partial agreement is marginally possible.

(50) a. Juan y Marta llegaron.
        Juan and Marta arrived(PL)
        'Juan and Marta arrived.'
     b. *Juan y Marta llegó.
        Juan and Marta arrived(SG)
     c. Llegaron   Juan y Marta.
        arrived(PL) Juan and Marta
        'Juan and Marta arrived.'
     d. ?Llegó   Juan y Marta.
        arrived(SG) Juan and Marta

(51) a. Juan y Marta estaban sentados.
        Juan and Marta were   sitting(PL)
        'Juan and Marta were sitting.'
     b. *Juan y Marta estaba sentad-o/sentad-o-s.
        Juan and Marta was   sitting-MAS(SG)/MAS-PL
     c. ?Estaban Juan y Marta sentado-s.
        were(PL) Juan and Marta sitting-PL
        'Juan and Marta were sitting.'
     d. ??Estaba Juan y Marta sentado-s.
        was(SG) Juan and Marta sitting-PL

e. *Estaba Juan y   Marta sentad-o/sentad-a.
   was(SG) Juan and Marta sitting-MAS(SG)/FEM(SG)
f. *Estaba   sentad-o   Juan y   Marta.
   was(SG) sitting-MAS(SG) Juan and Marta

The best cases of partial agreement involve unaccusative verbs, as in example (50)d. The aspectual copula *estar* is marginal if the adjective is final, as seen in (51)d. However, this example is still better than the ones where the adjective has partial agreement (cf. (51)e, f).[86] As in Brazilian Portuguese, there is a contrast between the aspectual copula *estar* and the regular copula *ser*: the counterpart of (51)d with *ser* is ungrammatical:

(52) *Era   Juan y   Marta felic-es.
     was(SG) Juan and Marta happy-PL

Transitive verbs do not show partial agreement:

(53) a. Juan y   Marta trajeron   un libro.
        Juan and Marta brought(PL) a book
        'Juan and Marta brought a book.'
     b. *Juan y Marta trajo   un libro.
        Juan and Marta brought(SG) a   book
        'Juan and Marta brought a book.'
     c. *Trajo   un libro Juan y   Marta.
        brought(SG) a book Juan and Marta
        'Juan and Marta brought a book.'
     d. *Trajo   Juan y   Marta un libro.
        brought(SG) Juan and Marta a   book
        'Juan and Marta brought a book.'

Finally, the participial paradigm in Spanish is different from the one in Brazilian Portuguese presented at the end of the preceding section.[87] Although partial agreement with the closest conjunct is possible (cf. (54)c), the contrast between the grammaticality of that sentence and the ungrammaticality of (55)a suggests that these cases involve LF agreement, since singular agreement does not license a plurality like the one required by *combinada* 'combined'.

(54) a. Arreglad-a-s   la sala   y el   cuarto,...
        tidied-up-FEM-PL the living.room(FEM.SG) and the bedroom(MAS.SG)
        'Once the living-room and the bedroom were tidy,...'

---

[86] If the first conjunct were second person, agreement would have to be full.
[87] Munn (1999) claims Spanish has the same distribution as Brazilian Portuguese Native speaker judgements (including my own), suggest this is not the case.

b. Arreglad-o-s la sala y el cuarto,...
   tidied-up-MAS-PL the living.room(FEM.SG) and the bedroom(MAS.SG)
   'Once the living-room and the bedroom were tidy,...'
c. Arreglad-a la sala y el cuarto,...
   tidied-up-FEM(SG) the living-room-(FEM.SG) and the bedroom(MAS.SG)
   'Once the living-room and the bedroom were tidy,...'

(55) a. ?*Combinada la plata y el oro, María tuvo
   combined(FEM.SG) the silver(FEM) and the gold(MAS) Maria had
   suficiente para hacer un anillo.
   enough to make a ring
   b. Combinadas la plata y el oro, María tuvo
   combined(FEM.PL) the silver(FEM) and the gold(MAS) Maria had
   suficiente para hacer un anillo.
   enough to make a ring
   'With the gold and the silver combined, Maria had enough to make a ring.'
   c. Combinados la plata y el oro, María tuvo
   combined(MAS.PL) the silver(FEM) and the gold(MAS) Maria had
   suficiente para hacer un anillo.
   enough to make a ring
   'With the gold and the silver combined, Maria had enough to make a ring.'

1.4.4 Summary

Spanish, Brazilian Portuguese and Arabic have patterns of partial agreement in sentences where there are two agreeing heads (auxiliary and main verb, or copular verb and adjective). In all three languages, partial agreement with the first agreeing head is possible if the subject follows it, in all three languages the other agreeing head must display full agreement, and all three languages favor partial agreement with stage-level predicates. Unlike Arabic and Spanish, Brazilian Portuguese allows plural dependencies. In the following section, I will turn to the analysis of these differences.

2. ANALYSIS

To my knowledge, there are four explicit proposals to account for the partial agreement paradigm (cf. Bahloul and Harbert (1992), Benmamoun (1992), Johannessen (1993, 1996, 1998), Aoun, Benmamoun and Sportiche (1994), Aoun and Benmamoun (1999) and Munn (1996, 1999)).

2.1 Bahloul and Harbert (1992), Benmamoun (1992), Munn (1999)

These two analyses rely on the crucial distinction between spec-head agreement and government, using a conjunction projection with a conjunct in the specifier and one in the complement position. Thus, partial agreement takes place under government, full agreement under spec-head. There are two arguments against this analysis, as Aoun and Benmamoun (1999) point out: given that the verb raises past the subject, there is a spec-head configuration during the derivation where full agreement could take place, so it is not clear why it does not. This objection is only tenable under the strong assumption that agreement must take place if the right spec-head configuration exists.

The second objection to the analysis is that it does not explain why plural anaphors are not possible. Assuming that the antecedent of anaphors are DPs, and if the conjunction projection is a DP for the relevant purposes, the fact that the verb agrees with one of the conjuncts should not determine whether the conjoined DP can act as a plural antecedent. In other words, Arabic should be like Irish in those cases. In order to overcome this objection, the analysis would have to argue that it is the φ-feature morphology of the verb that determines antecedenthood, not the actual DPs. However, this predicts that all languages with partial agreement should disallow plural dependencies, contrary to fact.

2.2 Johannessen (1993, 1996, 1998)

As we saw in chapter 2, Johannessen also proposes conjunction phrase (CoP) with the first conjunct in its specifier and the second one in its complement. Partial agreement falls within what Johannessen calls unbalanced coordination, where only one of the conjuncts determines the feature specification of the whole coordination.[88] When agreement is partial, the specifier of CoP agrees with the head Co. By this agreement relation, the whole CoP inherits the features of the first conjunct. CoP, in turn, is in the spec of IP, triggering partial agreement. The fact that CoP will have features of one of the conjuncts explains why plural anaphors are not possible.

For the case of partial agreement of the Arabic type, Johannessen argues that the CoP is merged at the CP level, and has sentences as conjuncts (following ABS). Presumably, this reflects the fact that VS has the verb higher than IP, as ABS argue. In both Johannessen and ABS's analyses, there must be a further operation that deletes material in the second conjunct under identity.

Johannessen's analysis has difficulties accounting for the word order asymmetry. Given the analysis of partial agreement described above, it should not matter whether the order is VS or SV, in both cases partial agreement should be available.

In the case of what I have called PF agreement languages (those that license plural dependencies), like Czech or German, Johannessen (1996) states: "when a

---

[88] Partial agreement is just a lexical property of languages, not a consequence of structural properties, as it is in ABS.

coordinate subject does have a plural interpretation, we can deduce that CoP has attached to the subject NPs of the input structures, yielding actual NP coordination (p. 671)." It is not clear, however, how features from both conjuncts percolate up to the higher CoP, since one of the conjuncts is in complement position.

2.3 Aoun, Benmamoun and Sportiche (1994), Aoun and Benmamoun (1999)

As I have already shown, ABS propose two different structures: partial agreement involves a coordination of two sentences with gapping. Full agreement, on the other hand, involves a coordination of DPs within a single sentence.

In the VS word order, the verb has moved higher than IP. There are two arguments for this additional movement. First, it is possible to show for Moroccan Arabic that the verb must be higher than IP in VS sentences without coordination, since the subject must precede sentential negation in verbless sentences (cf. (56)a, b). The fact that negation is sentential can be shown because it licenses NPIs (cf. (56)c-e). Since the verb precedes the subject, which in turn precedes sentential negation, and negation is higher than IP, the verb must be higher than IP.

(56) a. Omar ma-ŝi f-d-dar. (MA)
   Omar NEG at-the-home
   'Omar is not at home.'
 b. *Ma-ŝi Omar f-d-dar.
   NEG Omar at-the-home
 c. Omar ma m a   tta wa   d.
   Omar NEG with any one
   'Omar is not with anyone.'
 d. *Ma Omar m a   tta wa d.
   NEG Omar with any one
 e. ma-ŝi kull wa d qra   tta ktab.
   NEG every one   read any book

Second, there is a contrast in acceptability between true gapping cases without a remnant, marginal in Arabic (cf. (57)a), and partial agreement cases, which are fine without a remnant (cf. (33) above, repeated below as (58)). (57)b shows a grammatical example of gapping with a remnant.

(57) a. ??Omar z a   w Karim. (MA)
   Omar came(3P.MAS.SG) and Karim
 b. Omar z a l-barə w Karim l-yum. (MA)
   Omar came(3P.MAS.SG) yesterday and Karim today

(58) a. Mša   umar w ali. (MA)
   left(3P.MAS.SG) Omar and Ali
   'Omar and Ali left.'

b. Raa   Kariim w   Marwaan.   (LA)
   left(3P.MAS.SG) Kareem and Marwaan
   'Kareem and Marwaan left.'

ABS suggest that the fact that the verb is higher than the gapping site accounts for the difference, although it is not clear why this should be the case. In general, the mystery remains as to why the verb must move to FP in order to license gapping without a remnant, and why [SV and S] is not possible with this type of structure.

In order to account for PF agreement languages (one of which is Standard Arabic), Aoun and Benmamoun (1999) build on one of the properties of Standard Arabic VS word order: when the subject follows the verb (VS), the verb only has person and gender (not number) features. In (59)a, number surfaces as default, singular, despite the fact that the subject is plural. When the subject precedes the verb, the verb has person, number and gender:

(59) a. waqafa   l- awlaadu.
       stood(3P.MAS.SG) the-children
       'The children stood.'
    b. al- awlaadu waqafuu.
       the-children stood(3P.MAS.PL)
       'The children stood.'

Based on Benmamoun (2000a, b), Aoun and Benmamoun (1999) suggest that in VS word order in Standard Arabic, the number feature on the verb appears on the subject. This is possible because the verb and the subject merge postsyntactically. In some sense, number is spelled-out periphrastically, as tense may be in other languages (cf. section 2.5.1 for details on postsyntactic merger). This option is not available in Lebanese or Moroccan. If the merger analysis is correct, cases of partial agreement in Standard Arabic are really examples of full agreement in disguise, and this explains why plural dependencies are possible.

Extending this analysis to other languages is viable as long as they show the morphosyntactic effects Standard Arabic shows. Irish is also a good candidate for postsyntactic merger, as Aoun and Benmamoun (1999) suggest.

2.4 An Alternative Proposal for LF agreement

The task in this section is to incorporate some of the insights from the analyses presented in previous sections into the framework I have been proposing so far. The basic dichotomy established throughout this chapter is that partial agreement phenomena can be classified in two types: cases where agreement has semantic consequences (LF agreement) and those cases where it does not (PF agreement). The second dichotomy is the correlation between partial agreement and non-canonical word order, which also holds in some languages. I will look at LF and PF agreement cases in turn, and I will suggest the possibility that there are actually two types of PF agreement languages.

2.4.1 Subject-verb LF Agreement

Languages with LF agreement have the basic property that the verb agreement pattern determines the coreference possibilities, as seen in previous sections. These languages come in two varieties: those that are sensitive to word order (Lebanese, Spanish, Brazilian Portuguese, etc.) and those, much less frequent, that are not (German). First I will propose an analysis for word-order-sensitive languages.

Partial agreement languages sensitive to word order only show partial agreement in the non-canonical word order (namely VS for SVO languages, SV for VSO languages). Arabic, for example, is an SVO language which only shows partial agreement in the VS configuration. Assuming that an SVO language has the specifier preceding the head, and assuming also that agreement is only in spec-head configuration, this means that the verb and the agreeing conjunct (the first one in the case of Arabic) are not overtly in the relevant agreement configuration. It follows, then, that either agreement is covert, or there is a null pronominal expletive in the specifier of the projection where V is.

ABS argue precisely against an analysis of agreement in Arabic in which an expletive pro triggers agreement when the subject is postverbal:

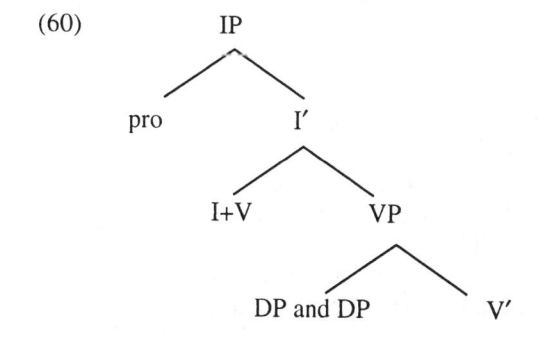

(60)
```
         IP
        /  \
      pro   I'
           /  \
         I+V   VP
              /  \
         DP and DP  V'
```

The arguments against this analysis are the following: in LA, the agreement morpheme must be affixed to the complementizer *inna*. If the subject is pronominal, the complementizer can either fully agree with it (cf. (61)a) or show default 3rd person singular agreement (cf. (61)b):

(61) a. Fakkar   inne (ana) ru t.
  thought(3P.MAS) that(1P.SG) (I) left(1P.SG)
  'He thought that I left.'
 b. Fakkar   inno   (ana) ru t.
  thought(3P.MAS) that(3P.MAS.SG) (I) left(1P.SG)
  'He thought that I left.'

When the subject is fully lexical, however, the morpheme attached to the complementizer cannot agree with it (cf. (62)a,b), but must take default 3rd person agreement, as in (62)c, d:

(62) a. *Fakkar   innun   l-baneet raa o.
        thought(3P.SG) that(3P.PL) the-girls left(3P.PL)
    b. *Fakkar   inna   Zeena raa it.
        thought(3P.MAS) that(3P.FEM) Zeena left(3P.FEM)
    c. Fakkar   inno   l-baneet   raa o.
        thought(3P.MAS) that(3P.MAS.SG) left(3P.PL) the-girls
        'He thought that the girls left.'
    d. Fakkar   inno   Zeena raa it.
        thought(3P.MAS) that(3P.MAS.SG) Zeena left(1.FEM)
        'He thought that Zeena left.'

When the lexical DP subject is postverbal, full agreement is not possible either. Complementizer agreement thus groups pronominals vs. other categories. If an expletive pro were available in the conjoined, partial agreement examples above, it should pattern with pronominals and trigger full agreement in the VS word order. However, full agreement is not possible (cf. (63)a, b), only default agreement is (cf. (63)c, d):

(63) a. *Fakkar   innun   raa o   l-baneet.
        thought(3P.SG) that(3P.PL) left(3P.PL) the-girls
        'He thought that the girls left.'
    b. *Fakkar   inna   raa it   Zeena.
        thought(3P.MAS) that(3P.FEM) left(3P.FEM) Zeena
        'He thought that Zeena left.'
    c. Fakkar   inno   raa o   l-baneet.
        thought(3P.MAS) that(3P.MAS.SG) left(3P.PL) the-girls
        'He thought that the girls left.'
    d. Fakkar   inno   raa it   Zeena.
        thought(3P.MAS) that(3-MAS.SG) left(1P.FEM) Zeena
        'He thought that Zeena left.'

This evidence argues against the expletive agreement proposal only if one assumes that null expletives and pronominals should pattern the same. In that case, one would expect expletive agreement to follow the distribution in (61). Although referential pro and overt referential pronominals do behave in the same way, this need not carry over to overt and null expletives. For example, English *it* can only trigger 3rd person agreement, whereas non-expletive pronouns also come in 1st/2nd. Although this does not settle ABS's objection directly, it lends some credibility to an alternative.

Be that as it may, here we will explore the second option: partial agreement in word order-sensitive languages is always covert. Recall that ABS argue that the VS+S structures are instances of gapping. Although a more detailed analysis of gapping structures will be presented in chapter 5, I will anticipate aspects of the proposal here. Following insights from Zoerner (1995), the proposed structure for gapping would be the one below.

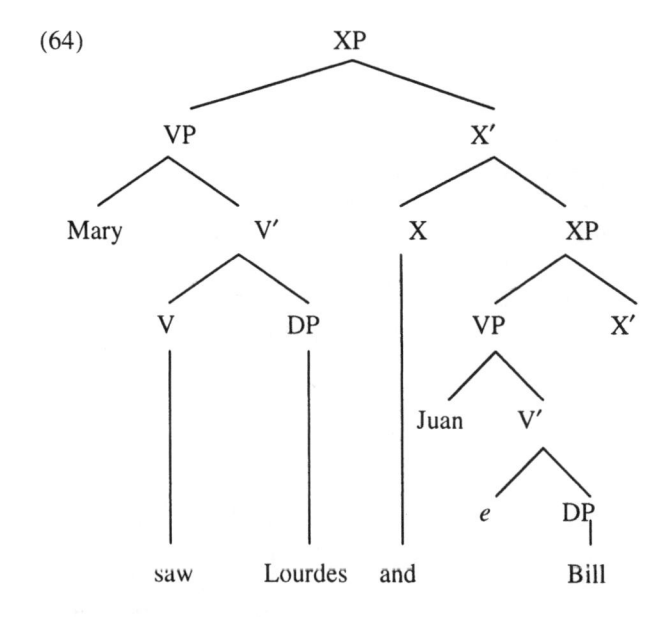

(64)

```
                        XP
                       /  \
                     VP    X'
                    /  \  /  \
                 Mary  V' X   XP
                      / \    /  \
                     V  DP  VP   X'
                            / \
                         Juan  V'
                              / \
                             e   DP
                             
                   saw  Lourdes and  Bill
```

In this structure, X is a predicational phrase headed by the conjunction, which has each conjunct in a specifier (see chapter 5 for details). Assuming this structure, the VS word order coordination in Arabic (cf. (38)a, repeated as (65)) can be analyzed as in (65)b. Unlike for ABS, I claim that the VP modifier *fə-l-biit* 'in the room' is inside the second conjunct, not right-node-raised. Arguments in favor of this analysis are given in chapter 5, sec. 2.1.

(65) Word Order Sensitive-Partial Agreement at spell-out
    a. Neem   Kariim w Marwaan fə-l-biit.   (LA)
       slept(3P.MAS.SG) Kareem and Marwaan in-the-room
       'Kareem and Marwaan slept in the room.'

b.

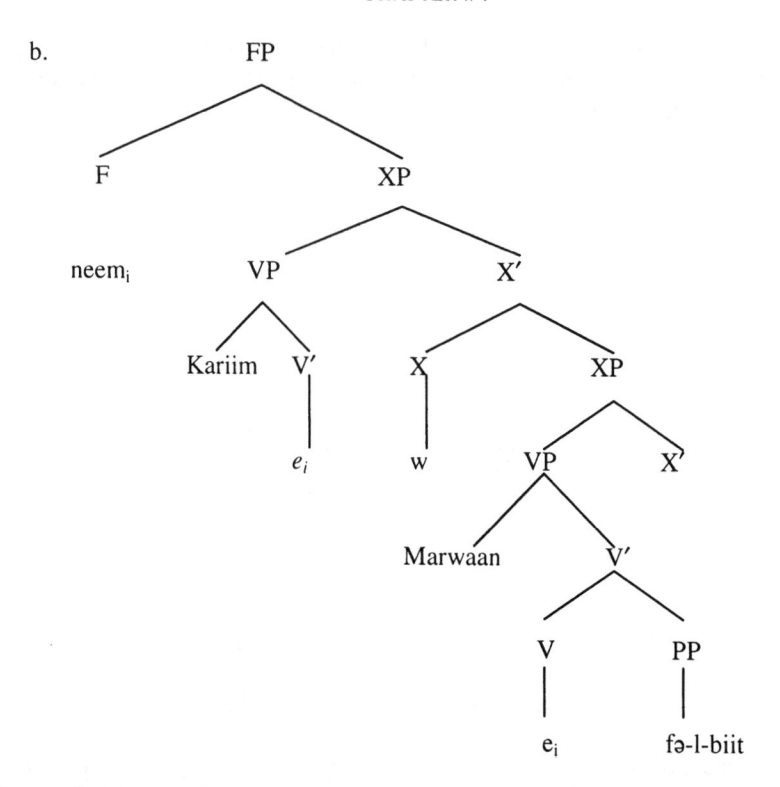

```
              FP
             /  \
            F    XP
          neemᵢ  /  \
               VP   X'
              /  \  / \
          Kariim V' X  XP
                 |  |  / \
                eᵢ  w VP  X'
                     /  \
                Marwaan V'
                        / \
                       V   PP
                       |   |
                      eᵢ  fə-l-biit
```

After spell-out, the higher subject will move to the spec-FP, checking agreement with the verb in F^0, as shown in (66).[89] Note that only the closest conjunct can move to spec-FP because movement of the lower conjunct would entail a minimality violation.

---

[89] This analysis violates Ross' Coordinate Structure Constraint, since one of the conjuncts moves out of the conjoined structure.

(66) VS-arabic2 Word Order Sensitive-Partial Agreement after spell-out.

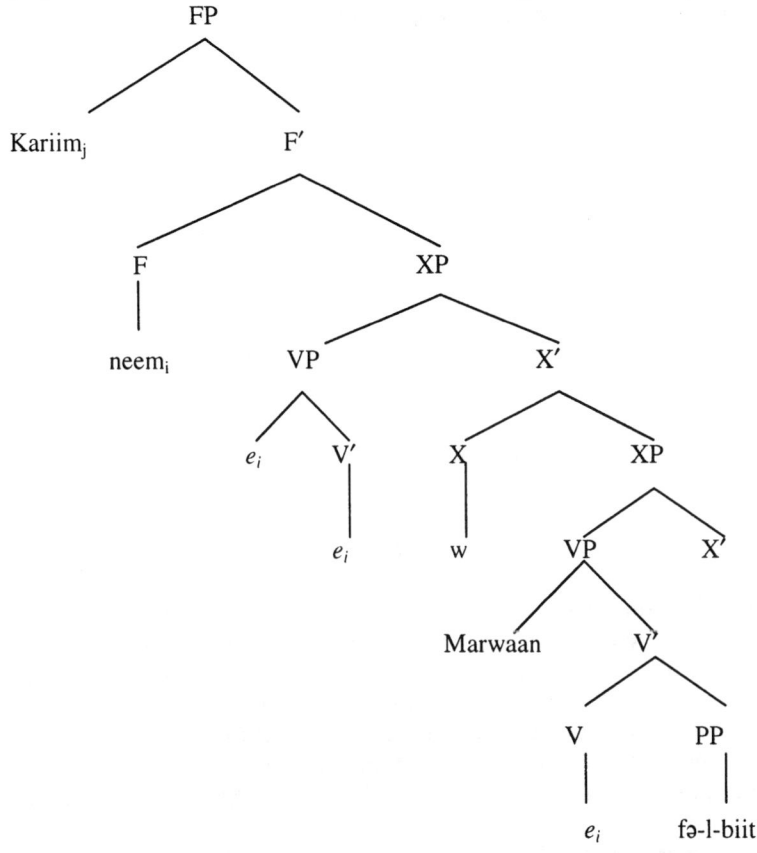

```
                    FP
                   /  \
          Kariim_j      F'
                      /    \
                     F      XP
                     |     /  \
                  neem_i  VP    X'
                         / \   /  \
                       e_i  V' X    XP
                            |  |   /  \
                           e_i w  VP    X'
                                 /  \
                            Marwaan  V'
                                    /  \
                                   V    PP
                                   |    |
                                  e_i  fə-l-biit
```

As in ABS' analysis, the reason why there cannot be plural anaphors is that there is no plural antecedent: the two DP subjects are not in the right configuration. Unlike in ABS's analysis, the system I am proposing allows generation of the φ-features of the verb in F, which explains why partial agreement is restricted to VS configurations in an SVO language.[90]

Languages showing partial agreement between the second conjunct and the verb are also accounted for: the verbal φ-features are inserted in the head of the second conjunction projection (IP, for example), yielding spec-head agreement with that conjunct. This seems to be the case in the Latin example quoted by Corbett (1983) (originally from Gildersleeve 1948):

---

[90] Generating the verb in F introduces an asymmetry: a θ-role can be assigned in the VP without the verb, but the DP matrix must always be present.

(67) a. Et ego et Cicero meus flagitabit.
 and I and Cicero my will-demand(3P.SG)
 'Both I and my Cicero will demand (it).'

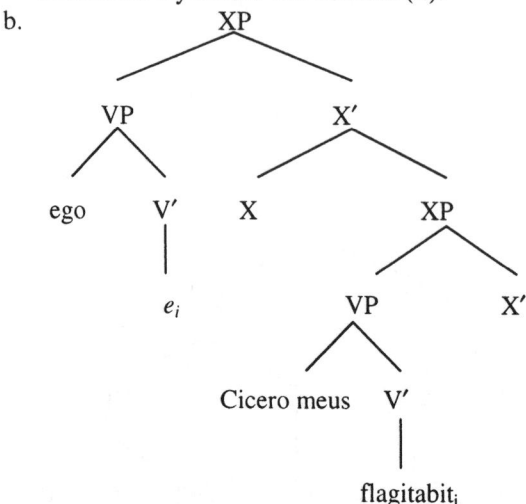

b.
```
              XP
           /      \
         VP        X'
        /  \      /  \
      ego   V'   X    XP
            |       /    \
            e_i    VP     X'
                  /  \
            Cicero meus  V'
                         |
                    flagitabit_i
```

For these cases, the higher V would have to be licensed through an indirect spec-head mechanism. The lower verb agrees with its specifier (*Cicero meus*). Given that V^0 is the head of VP, the features of the head will be present in the maximal projection. Since the VP is in the specifier of XP, it will agree with the head of XP, and in turn the features of XP will percolate through the extended XP projection. This will insure that the higher X^0 will inherit the features of the lower X^0 projection, and hence trigger agreement with the VP in the specifier of the higher XP.[91]

Sporadic quotes of languages where partial agreement is not with the closest conjunct exist in the literature. Without a more detailed analysis of those languages, it is not possible to know whether they could be integrated in this proposal. For example, Corbett (1983) quotes an example in Slovene (from Toporisic 1972), where the distant conjunct triggers partial agreement:

(68) Groza in strah je prevzela vso vas.
 horror(FEM.SG) and fear(MAS.SG) has seized(FEM.SG) whole village
 'Horror and and fear have seized the whole village.'

In this example, the verbal past participle *prevzela* 'seized' is feminine and it agrees with the first noun *groza* 'horror'. Additionally, the verb is singular, also showing partial agreement.

Serbo-Croat also shows distant agreement (cf. Corbett 1983 for the original source of the example):

---

[91] Note that if Latin is SOV, the configuration in (67)a would simply be the symmetric counterpart of languages like Spanish or Arabic, already seen.

(69) Ona   stalna   duboko urezana svijetla   i   sjene   koje
     Those constant deeply cut   ligths(NEUT.PL) and shades(FEM.PL) which
     je   naslikao umjetnikov kist   bila su   jac̀ya
     has painted the   artist's brush were(NEUT.PL) stronger(NEUT.PL)
     od   realne svijetlosti.
     than real   light
     'Those constant, deeply cut lights and shades which the artist's brush painted were stronger than real light.'

In this example, the first conjunct is neuter plural and the verb agrees with it although the second conjunct is closer. The analysis of these examples is challenging, because they seem to violate locality constraints that are at the center of most analyses of partial agreement.

I noted that several partial agreement paradigms were affected by the stage/individual-level properties of the predicate. Lebanese Arabic, for example, showed cases with a singular auxiliary and a plural main verb where the availability of plural anaphors bound to the plural main verb was restricted to stage-level predicates (cf. (44), repeated below):

(70) a. *Keen   Kariim w   Marwan   ixwe   la-ba ḍun.
        was(SG) Kareem and Marwan brothers to each other
     b. *Keen Kariim w Marwan   ilmaan tnaytinun.
        was(SG) Kareem and Marwaan German(PL) both
     c. ?keen   Kariim w   Marwan   mabsuṭiin la-ba ḍun.
        was(SG) Kareem and Marwaan happy(PL) for each other
        'Kareem and Marwan were happy for each other.'

The same contrast could be observed in Brazilian Portuguese and Spanish with respect to *ser, estar* (cf. (47)c, d vs. (48)d, repeated below):

(71) a. *E   o menino e   a   menina educad-o-s.
        is(SG) the boy   and the girl   polite-PL-MAS
        'The boy and the girl are polite.'
     b. *E   o menino e a   menina educad-a-s.
        is(SG) the boy   and the girl   polite-PL-FEM
        'The boy and the girl are polite.'
     c. ?Estava a janela   e   o   portão   abert-o-s.
        was(SG) the window(FEM) and the door(MAS) open-PL-MAS
        'The window and the door were open.'

For the case of the Arabic auxiliary construction, Aoun and Benmamoun (1999) argued that there was an extra expletive that agreed with the auxiliary whereas the main verb agrees with the full subject. This account can be generalized. It can be argued that *estar* involves a biclausal structure, with the second clause headed by an aspectual projection. *Ser*, on the other hand, involves a single clause. If the analysis is correct, the stage-level in Arabic and in Spanish and Brazilian Portuguese share a biclausal structure and an expletive.[92]

2.5 PF Agreement Analysis

Cases of PF agreement include subject-verb agreement in Irish, Standard Arabic, German and Czech, postnominal adjectival agreement in Spanish and clitic agreement in Spanish. To account for these cases, I will adopt a version of Aoun and Benmamoun's (1999) and Benmamoun's (2000b) postsyntactic merger proposal.

2.5.1 Aoun and Benmamoun's (1999) Postsyntactic Merger for Standard Arabic

Aoun and Benmamoun (1999) and Benmamoun (2000b) analyze partial agreement with coordination in Standard Arabic as involving a postsyntactic merger between the verb and the first conjunct. This merger is an instance of rebracketing under adjacency: when the verb and the noun merge, the φ-features on the noun and the ones on the verb are licensed, and they are spelled-out as a single element on the verb. (72)a shows the configuration before merger, with number features on both categories, (72)b shows the end result.

(72) a. [V affix$_{num}$] [NP affix$_{num}$]
b. [[V affix$_{num}$] NP]

The analysis just presented accounts for a fact about Standard Arabic: number features must appear on the verb if a null element (a trace or a pro) is in the subject position. Since the merger is sensitive to the phonological nature of the elements, it follows that null elements will not be able to merge postsyntactically:

(73) a. ayyu l- awlaadi naz a uu.
which the-children succeeded(3P.MAS.PL)
'Which children passed?'
b. * ayyu l- awlaadi naz a a.
which the-children succeeded(3P.MAS.SG)

(74) a. kun-na ya- kul-na.
be-PAST(3P.FEM.PL) 3P-eat-FEM.PL
'They were eating.'
b. *kaan-at ya- kul-na.
be-PAST(3P.FEM.SG) 3P-eat-FEM.PL

---

[92] The same correlation between expletives and stage/individual-predicates can be observed in English, as is well-known:
(i.) There is a doctor available.
(ii.) *There is a doctor altruistic.

It is possible to extend this analysis to the coordination framework I am proposing: at the level of syntax, before the derivation branches off to the interpretive component, the structural configuration allows for plural antecedenthood. Postsyntactically, the first conjunct will raise to the specifier of the projection headed by the verb, yielding the PF partial agreement paradigm.

2.5.2 *Irish*

Irish is also a good candidate for the postysntactic merger analysis. This language has a morphological alternation between so-called analytic and synthetic verbal forms. Analytic forms only show tense and mood, no agreement morphology whatsoever; synthetic forms, on the other hand, show tense, mood, person and number marking (cf. McCloskey and Hale (1984). If the subject of a clause is phonologically specified, the analytic form must appear (cf. (75)a vs. (75)b). If the subject is null, the verb must be in the synthetic form, as in (75)c (examples from McCloskey and Hale 1984):

(75) a. Chuirfeadh Eoghan isteach ar an phost sin.
 put(COND) Owen in on that job
 'Owen would apply for that job.'
 b. *Chuirfinn mé isteach ar an phost sin.
 put(COND.1.SG) I in on that job
 c. Dá gcuirfeá insteach ar an phost sin gheobhfá é.
 if put(COND.2.SG) in on that job get(COND.2.SG) it
 'If you applied for that job, you would get it.'

Unlike in Standard Arabic, traces in Irish appear only with the analytic form, but pro appears with the synthetic form (cf. McCloskey and Hale 1984), as shown in (76)a and (76)b respectively.

(76) a. Chan mise a chirfeadh t isteach ar an phost sin.
 COP+NEG me COMP put(COND) in on that job
 'It is not me that would apply for that job.'
 b. Dá gcuirfeá isteach ar an phost sin gheobhfá é.
 if put(COND.2.SG) in on that job get(COND.2.SG) it
 'If you applied for that job, you would get it.'

Following Aoun and Benmamoun's (1999) analysis, analytic forms in Irish would be a case of postsyntactic merger: the relevant φ-features are present on the DP and on the verb. After merger, only one set of features will surface on the DP.

A potential problem for this account comes from a class of verbs McCloskey (1996) calls *salient unaccusatives*. These verbs have the general syntactic configuration [V P NP]. They have a single argument that is headed by a preposition (not a case marker, as convincingly argued by McCloskey), and there is ample syntactic evidence that the PP is not in the canonical position of the subject. However, these forms also appear with the analytic form. Following the postsyntactic merger analysis, the sole argument would have to merge with the verb, but there is an intervening preposition.

McCloskey (1996) argues that Irish transitive and intransitive clauses systematically differ from salient unaccusatives in that the former have an agreement projection which hosts the strong nominal feature (namely, the feature that drives the Extended Projection Principle), whereas the latter lack this projection altogether. Since salient unaccusatives lack the agreement projection, there is no expletive, and a PP argument is possible. In some sense, salient unaccusatives are licensed without a nominal subject. In both structures, the verb is in a higher temporal projection.

Suppose we extend the postsyntactic merger to salient unaccusatives and claim that the analytic form signals the absence of an agreement projection (in the case of salient unaccusatives). Then, the prediction is that transitive and intransitive clauses should not have analytic forms, since those types of clauses always have an agreement projection. However, as I mentioned earlier, they do appear with analytic forms of the verb. On the other hand, there is evidence that the subject raises out of the VP internal position regardless of the analytic/synthetic distinction. For example, in infinitival sentences, the subject is to the left of the verb; in the progressive construction, which involves two verbs, the subject is to the left of the progressive, etc. Since raising of the subject out of VP is independent of the analytic/synthetic alternation, either the agreement projection is not directly linked to the analytic/synthetic distinction (assuming the reason for raising is to satisfy the EPP feature in the agreement projection) or else the agreement projection is not responsible for subject raising.

Of these two possibilities, the second one is less attractive, since the assumption that the (lack of the) agreement projection is responsible for subject raising accounts for many of the distributional properties of salient unaccusatives and even transitive and intransitive verbs. Rather, let us pursue the first option: the agreement projection is not always linked to the analytic/synthetic alternation. It is possible that the analytic form is a manifestation of two phenomena: either postsyntactic merger (in the case of transitive and intransitive verbs) or lack of a syntactic projection of agreement (in the case of salient unaccusatives). This solution preserves the basic intuition that the lack of morphological marking for agreement features on these forms reflects lack of syntactic features, either because they are structurally absent (in the case of unaccusatives), or because they are pre-empted by those in the nominal (in the case of regular transitives and intransitives). The two possibilities reflect pre-spell-out merger (unaccusatives) or post-spell-out merger (transitives and intransitives). In the case of the salient unaccusatives, lack of agreement is syntactic, it reflects syntactic properties and it has syntactic effects. In the case of transitive and intransitive verbs, lack of agreement does not have syntactic effects.

The analysis just sketched can be extended to coordination. Recall that Irish has conjoined null pronominals (cf. examples below). McCloskey points out that conjoined pronominals (whether null or lexical) must always appear with some particles.[93] They appear in the first conjunct and they appear with the synthetic form (examples from McCloskey and Hale 1984):

(77) a. Dá mbeinn-se   agus tusa ann.
        if be(COND-1.SG) -CONTR and you there
        'If I and you were there.'
    b. An mbéitheá   féin agus bean an ti   sásta?
        Q be(COND.2.SG) REFL and the-woman-of-the-house satisfied
        'Would you and the woman of the house be satisfied?'

Clearly, postsyntactic merger has not taken place, since the verb form is synthetic. Suppose, however that postsyntactic merger in Irish may surface either on the NP or on the verb, if the NP is null. Analytic forms (with features on the NP) would merge whenever possible, synthetic forms otherwise (when the pronominal is null).

Notice that synthetic and analytic forms are not in free distribution: if there is a synthetic form, it is not possible to use the analytic one plus a pronoun, for example, suggesting a preference for spelling out the φ-features on the verb wherever possible. The question is, why should there be analytic forms at all with full NPs, if spelling-out on the verb is preferred? The reason why this preference operates in the case of NP subjects may have to do with a principled distinction between NP features and pronominal features: the latter may be spelled-out independently as pronouns, as affixes or as clitics (cf. Everett 1996 for a treatment of pronouns, clitics and φ-feature affixes as allomorphs), whereas the NP features do not usually surface as independent morphemes.

To summarize, I have analyzed Irish as a case that involves two types of agreement-feature spell-out. The first type, postsyntactic merger, is similar to the one proposed by Aoun and Benmaoun (1999) for Arabic, with no syntactic effects; the second one reflects a lack of agreement projection, which translates also in lack of morphological marking on the verb, but with syntactic consequences (i.e. lack of subject raising). In either case, however, we expect conjoined elements to be able to serve as antecedents for plurals.

2.5.3 Agreement with Prenominal DP elements in Spanish

In previous sections I explored the adjectival agreement paradigm in Spanish that can be summarized as follows[94]: determiners and prenominal adjectives cannot have full agreement (cf. (78)-(79) and (80) respectively).[95]

---

[93] One possible explanation for this fact is that the empathic, contrastive and reflexive suffixes are all related to inflectional projections, whether verbal or nominal, as switch-reference markers in Hopi and Mojave (see chapter 2, sections 2.12 and 2.1.4 respectively).

[94] Brazilian Portuguese shows a similar pattern, according to Munn (1999).

[95] Munn (1999) argues that the contrast between full agreement prenominal elements and partial agreement postnominal elements reflects a difference between spec-head agreement and government agreement. His examples involve demonstratives vs. determiners in languages like English. However,

(78) a. La influencia y mérito
the(FEM.SG) influece(FEM.SG) and merit(MAS.SG)
'The influence and merit'
b. *Las/los influencia y mérito
the(FEM.PL/MAS.PL) influence(FEM.SG) and merit(MAS.SG).

(79) a. La supuesta imagen y reflejo
the(FEM.SG) supuesta(FEM.SG) image(FEM.SG) and reflection(MAS.SG)
'The alleged image and reflection'
b. *Las/los supuesta imagen y
the(FEM.PL)/(MAS.PL) alleged(FEM.SG) image(FEM.SG) and
reflejo
reflection(MAS.SG)
c. *Las/los supuestas/os imagen y
the(FEM.PL)/(MAS.PL) alleged(FEM.PL)/(MAS.PL) image(FEM.SG) and
reflejo
reflection(MAS.SG)

(80) a. *La/las supuestas negociación y firma tuvieron lugar en
the(SG)/(PL) alleged(PL) negotiation and signature took place in
Cali.
Cali

One question that arises is which element in the DP determines agreement. In particular, it could be argued that the determiner is responsible for agreement and an independent restriction on the determiner forces the singular on the prenominal adjective. In order to define whether it is the determiner or the noun that force agreement on the adjective, we can examine the press-headline register, where articles tend to be dropped; even here it is not possible to have a plural adjective with conjoined Ns:

(81) a. Supuesto terrorista secuestra a industrial.
alleged(SG) terrorist(SG) kidnap to industrialist
'Alleged terrorists kidnap industrialist.'
b. Supuesto [terrorista y narcotraficante] secuestra a industrial.
alleged(SG) terrorist(SG) and drugdealer(SG) kidnaps(SG) to industrial
c. [Supuesto terrorista] y [narcotraficante] secuestran a industrial.
alleged(SG) terrorist(SG) and drugdealer(SG) kidnap(PL) to industrial
'Alleged terrorist and drugdealer kidnap industrialist.'

---

in languages where determiners have overt number and gender, it is clear that there is no contrast between demonstratives (in spec, DP) and determiners (in D).

d. *Supuestos [terrorista y narcotraficante] secuestra a
   alleged(PL) terrorist(SG) and drugdealer(SG) kidnaps(SG) to
   industrial.
   industrial
e. *Supuestos [terrorista y narcotraficante] secuestran a
   alleged(PL) terrorist(SG) and drug-dealer(SG) kidnap(PL) to
   industrial
   industrial.
   'Alleged terrorist and drug-dealer kidnap industrialist.'

As (81)a shows, a non-conjoined, bare singular DP is possible in a headline context. A conjoined NP, on the other hand, can have two possible interpretations, depending on the agreement on the verb: if verbal agreement is singular, the reference of the conjoined NPs is a single item, and the adjective has scope over both conjuncts. Hence, (81)b refers to a single person who allegedly is a drug-dealer and a terrorist. If agreement is plural, the reference is to two independent entities, and the adjective only has scope over the first conjunct. Thus, in (81)c, an alleged terrorist and a drug-dealer kidnapped an industrialist. In either case, the adjective cannot be plural, as shown in (81)d, e. The ungrammaticality of (81)e probably relates to the fact that the adjective cannot have scope over both conjuncts. In other words, the adjective must remain lower than the conjunction. The ungrammaticality of (81)d, on the other hand, must be related to the referential properties of the whole DP. A plural adjective is inconsistent with singular agreement on the verb, because singular agreement determines singular reference of the DP. From these facts we can conclude that prenominal adjectives cannot agree with conjoined NPs because they are structurally lower than conjunction.

Notice the following asymmetry: whereas singular partial agreement may allow plural dependencies in PF agreement languages, plural agreement does not seem to allow for singular dependencies. If this is generally true crosslinguistically, it suggests that plural agreement is the marked option. One way to capture this observation is to assume that plural agreement is a sum of singulars, as in the system I am adopting.

Longobardi (1994) argues that in Romance, nominal arguments must be introduced by determiners: an argument must have a determiner (null or lexical). From this assumption he can derive the distribution in (82). If there is a single determiner and two conjoined Ns, agreement must be singular (cf. (82)a), but if there are two conjoined DPs, agreement must be plural (cf. (82)b). In the first case, there is a single argument (there is only one determiner), hence agreement is singular, in the second case, there are two arguments (two determiner phrases), hence agreement must be plural.

(82) a. El ayudante y colaborador mío puso/*pusieron los cuadros.
       the helper and collaborator mine put(SG)/put(PL) the paintings
    b. El ayudante y el colaborador mío *puso/pusieron los cuadros.
       the helper and the collaborator mine put(SG)/put(PL) the paintings

Notice, however, that (82)a) and Longobardi's original example in Italian (Longobardi 1994, p. 620) both involve modified nouns. The corresponding example in Spanish without the possessive is much worse, an issue I will return to below:

(83) *?El ayudante y colaborador puso/*pusieron los cuadros.
      the helper and collaborator put(SG)/(PL) the paitings

This correlation between determiner phrases, arguments and verbal number systematically holds for purely referential nouns. For abstract nominals, however, the correlation breaks down:

(84) a. La supuesta agudeza y claridad del análisis suprimieron las
       the alleged sharpness and clarity of-the analysis suppressed(PL) the
       dudas.
       doubts
       'The analysis' alleged sharpness and clarity suppressed doubts.'
    b. La supuesta agudeza y claridad del análisis suprimió las
       the alleged sharpness and clarity of-the analysis suppressed(SG) the
       dudas.
       doubts
       'The analysis' alleged sharpness and clarity suppressed doubts.'

Following Longobardi's logic, plural agreement on the verb should signal two arguments, as in (84)a, but here there is a single determiner. The natural assumption is that this example has a null determiner in the second conjunct. However, note that the adjective has scope over both conjuncts. We reach a bracketing paradox of sorts (under the assumption that scope requires c-command): the conjoined categories are DPs (illustrated in (85), where coordination is indicated with square brackets), but an adjective inside the first DP has scope outside that DP (indicated with { }).

(85) [$_{DP}$ La supuesta {agudeza] y [$_{DP}$ claridad del análisis}]

Let us assume that plural verbal agreement does entail plurality of arguments, as Longobardi suggests. This means that there are two determiners. One possible option to represent scope is to propose an empty adjective. Thus, the abstract structure would be (86). This structure resembles Kayne's (1994) analysis of right-node-raising. For Kayne, RNR structures are derived not by adjunction of the shared constituent to the right, but rather by deletion under identity of the first instance of that repeated element. In this case, the only difference is that deletion involves the second instance of the determiner and the adjective.

(86) [$_{DP}$ D A N] and [$_{DP}$ Ø$_D$ Ø$_A$ N]

Notice that deletion is directional: it can only apply to the second conjunct, as illustrated in (87).[96] This is consistent with the idea that conjuncts are c-command asymmetric: if the first conjunct asymmetrically c-commands the second one, we expect deletion to be in the second one only.

(87) a. *Ø$_i$ agudeza y la$_i$ supuesta claridad
       sharpness and the alleged clarity
    b. #La$_i$ Ø$_j$ agudeza y Ø$_i$ supuesta$_j$ claridad
       la sharpness and alleged clarity

To summarize, cases of apparent NP conjunction inside DP really involve full DP conjunctions with null structure licensed under identity.

Why can referential DPs not be licensed in this way? Recall that (82)a, repeated below, is ungrammatical if the verb is plural. Why can it not have the structure in (88)b?

(88) a. *El ayudante y colaborador mío pusieron los cuadros.
       the helper and collaborator mine put(PL) the paintings
    b. [$_{DP}$ el ayundante] y [$_{DP}$ Ø colaborador] ...

One possibility is that referential DPs require strictly disjoint referents. Since the null D is coindexed with the lexical one, they will have the same referent. If referential DPs must be strictly disjoint, such a structure would be uninterpretable. The following contrast suggests this analysis may be correct:

(89) a. *The woman and the woman came.
    b. The women came.
    c. *La mujer y la mujer vinieron.
       the woman and the woman came(PL)
    d. Esta mujer y esta mujer vinieron.
       this woman and this woman came(PL)
       'This woman and this woman came.'

Both the Spanish and the English versions of a coordination of two identical nouns are ungrammatical (cf. (89)a, c), by contrast to a plural (cf. (89)b). If the references of each NP are distinguished, for example by using a demonstrative, as in (89)d, then coordination becomes grammatical.

The analysis suggests that abstract nouns do not fix a referent in the same way as referential nouns. Although a coordination of two identical DPs with abstract nouns is equally ungrammatical (cf. (90)), the fact that two conjoined abstract DPs do not necessarily force plural verbal agreement (cf. (84)b above) suggests referentiality is fixed in a different way for abstract and for referential nouns.

---

[96] (87)b is grammatical, but not with a reading where the adjective has scope over the first noun.

(90) *La idea y la idea son buenas.
the idea and the idea are good

Finally, I observed that conjoined NPs with the same referent are only good if the NPs are modified (cf. (83) above, repeated below).

(91) *?El ayudante y colaborador puso/*pusieron los cuadros.
the helper and collaborator put(SG)/(PL) the paitings

As a generalization, this suggests that NPs alone (i.e. without adjectives or modifiers) cannot be conjoined. Depending on the correct analysis of adjectives, this generalization can be stronger. If adjectives appear in their own projections, the relevant generalization would be that NPs cannot be conjoined at all, only adjectival projections can. If adjectives are adjoined categories, then the generalization becomes much more difficult to capture. Let us assume, following Sánchez (1995), that extensional adjectives appear in a Predicational Phrase (PredP). In Sánchez's analysis, this accounts for why null nominals can only be licensed by three types of categories: extensional adjectives (cf. (92)a), relative clauses (cf. (92)b) and certain complements headed by *de* (cf. (92)c), but not by bare determiners (cf. (92)d) or intensional adjectives (cf. (92)e).

(92) a. La casa grande y la Ø chiquita.
the house big and the small
'The big house and the small one.'
b. La casa grande y la Ø chiquita que está a la derecha.
the house big and the small that is to the right
'The big house and the one to the right.'
c. La casa de madera y la Ø de piedra.
the house of wood and the of stone
'The wooden house and the stone one.'
d. *La casa grande y la Ø
The houes big and the
e. *La verdadera terrorista y la presunta Ø
the true terrorist and the alleged

Sánchez argues that the grammatical examples all share a common functional projection, PredP.[97] Suppose Sánchez and Kayne are correct, and adjectives involve such a functional category. In that case, one can advance the following generalization: the lowest category that can be conjoined inside DP is PredP (not NP). This generalization, if correct, can be explained by the analysis that I am proposing:coordination only affects functional categories with predicational content.

In the following section, we will turn our attention to agreement between conjoined DPs and PPs and adjectives.

---

[97] See Kayne (1994) for a similar analysis.

2.5.4 Postnominal Modifiers

Agreement with Postnominal Adjectives. As shown in previous sections, postnominal adjectives can have partial number and gender agreement with conjoined NPs (ex. (93)a) and DPs (ex. (93)b), even though they may have scope over both nouns. It is even possible to have partial gender agreement and full number agreement (ex. (93)c, d). Full number and gender agreement is also possible (ex. (93)e):

(93) a. El pensamiento y filosofía frances-a
   the thinking(MAS) and philosophy(FEM) French-FEM(SG)
   'French thinking and philosophy'
b. El pensamiento y la filosofía frances-a.
   the thinking(MAS) and the philosophy(FEM) French-FEM(SG)
c. El pensamiento y filosofía frances-a-s
   the thinking(MAS) and philosophy(FEM) French-FEM-PL
d. El pensamiento y la filosofía frances-a-s
   the thinking(MAS) and the philosophy(FEM) French-MAS-PL
e. El pensamiento y (la) filosofía frances-es
   the thinking(MAS) and (the) philosophy(FEM) French(MAS)-PL

The number on the adjective correlates with the number on the verb, if the DPs are subjects. PP coordination shows a more restricted pattern: number must be full if the adjective takes wide scope, but gender can be partial or default:

(94) a. Dispone del espacio y de la tierra necesari-o-s.
   has available of-the space and of the land(FEM.SG) necessary-MAS-PL
   'He/she has the necessary space and land available.'
b. Cada una dispone del espacio y de la tierra
   each one has available of-the space and of the land(FEM.SG)
   necesari-a-s.
   necessary-FEM-PL
   'Each one has the necessary space and land available.'

The possible patterns are summarized below, the adjective has scope over the bracketed material:

(95) a. D [NP$_{sg.mas}$ and NP$_{sg.fem}$] Adj$_{sg.fem}$
   b. [$_{DP}$NP$_{sg.mas}$] and [$_{DP}$ NP$_{sg.fem}$] Adj$_{sg.fem}$
   c. [$_{PP}$ DP$_{sg.mas}$] and [$_{PP}$ DP$_{sg.fem}$] Adj$_{pl.fem}$

Extending the deletion-under-identity analysis proposed for prenominal elements in the preceding section poses some difficulties. Suppose, for example that the structures for the patterns in (95) were the ones in (96) respectively:

(96) a. [$_{DP}$ D NP$_{sg.mas}$ Ø$_{Adj}$] and [$_{DP}$ Ø$_D$ NP$_{sg.fem}$] Adj$_{sg.fem}$]
b. [$_{DP}$ NP$_{sg.mas}$ Ø$_{Adj}$] and [$_{DP}$ NP$_{sg.fem}$] Adj$_{sg.fem}$]
c. [$_{PP}$ [DP$_{sg.mas}$ Ø$_{Adj}$] and [$_{PP}$ DP$_{sg.fem}$ Adj$_{sg.fem}$]]

One of the potential problems has to do with the agreement features of the null adjective and the lexical one. Suppose that the deleted adjective has the same agreement features as the other one (singular, feminine in the first two cases and plural feminine in the third one), a natural assumption, since deletion takes place under identity. The result is that the agreement features of the null adjective will not match those of the NP, a situation otherwise not attested in general in Spanish. On the other hand, if the deleted adjective has the same agreement features as the first NP (masculine, singular), then deletion is no longer under strict identity. However, deletion in the context of coordination does not always require strict identity of agreement features, as the following example shows:

(97) Marta salió$_i$ y   nostros también Ø$_i$
Marta went-out(3P.SG) and we   too

The deleted verb in this example is 1st person plural, although the overt verb is 3rd singular. Under the feature insertion analysis presented in chapter 3, sec. 3.3, if features are inserted independently of lexical items, then the null element will have no agreement features inserted with it, and hence the same category can be deleted at the same structural position.

A more serious problem has to do with the fact that the null adjective is in the first conjunct. Since the evidence already presented suggests that the first conjunct c-commands the second one, the null element would not be c-commanded by the lexical one.

The data from adjectival agreement suggests that two independent facts are related: on the one hand, the adjective can have full agreement, i.e. agreement with both conjuncts. On the other, the adjective can have scope over both nouns and show partial agreement with the second conjunct. These two observations suggest the following generalization:

(98) Postnominal adjectives can agree in higher positions when DPs or PPs are conjoined.

This generalization contradicts most analyses of the DP, which take adjectival agreement to be bounded within the DP. The paradigm presented suggests that there is an agreement projection higher than DP and higher than PP, which can also be a scopal projection.

I will suggest that these facts can be accommodated in the feature-insertion analysis proposed in previous sections. Following this idea, partial agreement reflects a local spec-head relation between the elements that agree. Thus, (93)b would have the following structure:

(99)

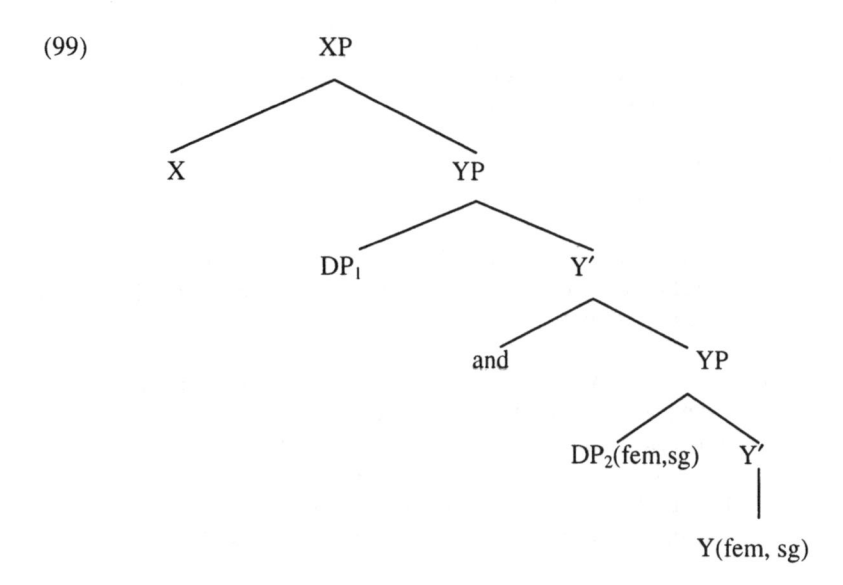

```
              XP
             /  \
            X    YP
                /  \
              DP₁   Y'
                   /  \
                 and   YP
                      /  \
              DP₂(fem,sg) Y'
                          |
                      Y(fem, sg)
```

Partial agreement takes place between the features of the lower Y and the features of DP₂ in the specifier of that lower Y. In the full agreement case (cf. (93)d), the φ-features are inserted in X and agreement is covert. In the case of partial agreement in gender but full agreement in number (cf. (93)c), the gender feature is inserted in the lower head Y, but the number feature is in X.[98] Since XP is the projection where full agreement can be triggered, I will assume this is an agreement projection AgrP. The fact that the adjective can have scope over both conjuncts suggests that it raises covertly to X⁰.

Notice that the configuration in (93)a and the structure in (99) are very similar to that of subject-verb agreement already seen: partial agreement between the second conjunct and the agreeing head. It would seem, then that the structure of the DP is very close to that of a clause, as many have proposed. In the analysis just suggested, the parallelism goes further because coordination involves a functional projection both in the DP and in IP. The difference, however, is that the agreeing head in the IP case is a verb, here it is the adjective; IPs are extended verbal projections, but DPs are not generally taken to be extended adjectival projections.

Semantically Restricted Conjunction. I have argued that XP is an agreement projection where adjectives can trigger full agreement with both conjuncts. In this section I will explore the possibility that other elements may appear in this position. In particular, I will argue that certain operators linked to coordination may be in this position.

---

[98] This analysis does not capture in a natural way the fact that PP conjunction requires plural agreement. A stipulative solution is that the number features must be inserted above the DP, perhaps because inserting them low enough for partial agreement would prevent them from further movement out of the DP.

When two DPs are conjoined and there is an initial conjunction before the first conjunct, the range of semantic readings is often restricted. Thus, Larson (1985) notes the following contrast for English:

(100) a. John or Mary came.
       b. Either John or Mary came.

In (100)a, the disjunction is interpreted either as exclusive or as inclusive, but (100)b is only exclusive. The same observation has been made for Spanish disjunction (cf. Jiménez 1986):

(101) a. *O el presidente o el vicepresidente o los dos estarán ahí.
          or the president or the vicepresident or the two will-be there
          'Either the president or the vicepresident or both will be there.'
       b. El presidente o el vicepresidente o los dos estarán ahí.
          the president or the vicepresident or the two will-be there
          'The president or the vicepresident or both will be there.'

(101)a is ungrammatical because the first two conjuncts establish an exclusive disjunction, which is contradictory with the third conjunct. This is not the case in (101)b, because the first two conjuncts need not be interpreted exclusively.

What could be the structure for these cases? The minimal syntactic difference between (101)a and b is the presence of the first conjunction, so I will assume that this first conjunction bears the weight of the restricted (exclusive) semantic reading.

Suppose, following Larson's (1985) analysis, that exclusive readings involve an operator linked to the first conjunction. As we will see, this operator shows a similar distribution to cases of coordination with a distributive interpretation. This connection is not surprising: exclusive readings are semantically incompatible with collective interpretations: if *either Michael or Aaron drew a picture of Barry*, it is not possible that *Michael and Aaron drew a picture of Barry together*. What is the precise structure of these double conjunctions? A first clue comes from the fact that the structure with two conjunctions cannot appear inside a PP:

(102) a. Hablemos de cine   o de teatro.
          talk(SUBJ) of movies or of theater
          'Let's talk about movies or about theater.'
       b. ?Hablemos de cine   o teatro.
          talk(SUBJ) of movies or theater
       c. Hablemos o de cine   o de teatro.
          talk(SUBJ) or of movies or of theater
       d. *?Hablemos de o cine   o teatro.
          talk(SUBJ) or of movies or theater
       e. *Hablemos   o de cine o teatro.
          talk(SUBJ) or of movies or theater

In (102)a, we have a disjunction of two PPs with a *o* 'or'. A single disjunction is marginally acceptable if it joins DPs (cf. (102)b). The example becomes better if there is a list reading, where the options are not exhausted: 'let's talk about movies or theater or something...' In any case, the interpretation in (102)b cannot be exclusive. As I suggested earlier, coordination inside PPs tends to be collective. Given that distributivity is not generally available within PP, this suggests that exclusive disjunctive readings are linked to distributivity.

(102)c shows a disjunction of PPs with exclusive meaning. Once again, such a disjunction is impossible within the PP, as (102)d shows. (102)e gives us a clue about the structure of these cases: the conjuncts are not parallel. (102)e reflects a situation similar to the cases of temporal coordination reviewed in chapter 3. Recall that in those cases, it was not possible to conjoin different tenses (provided an adverb fixed the right level of coordination to the temporal/aspectual nodes). In the present case, the first conjunction seems to be doing exactly that: it determines that the level of coordination is the PP. However, the second conjunct is a DP, violating symmetry. Assuming the structure presented in the preceding section, the structure of (102)e would be the following:

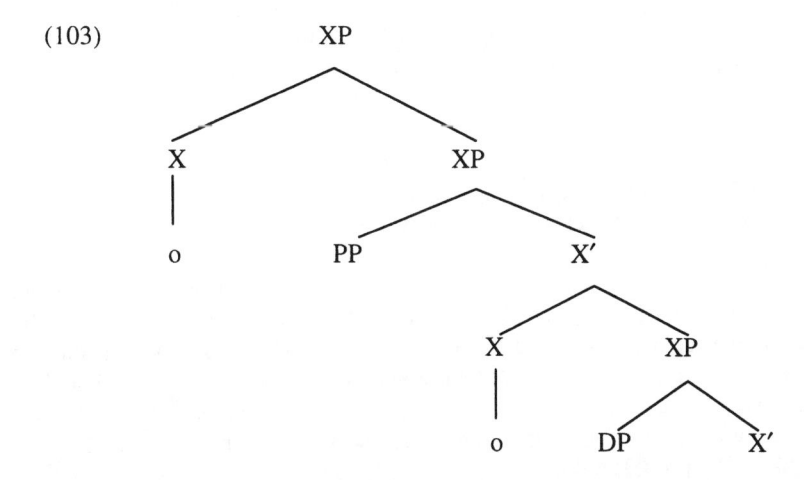

(103)

```
            XP
           /  \
          X    XP
          |   /  \
          o  PP   X'
                 /  \
                X    XP
                |   /  \
                o  DP   X'
```

In this structure, there is a mismatch between the feature specification of XP required to license PP in its higher spec position, and the specifications required to licensed the DP in the lower spec position. In the grammatical cases, the structure would be the following:

138   CHAPTER #4

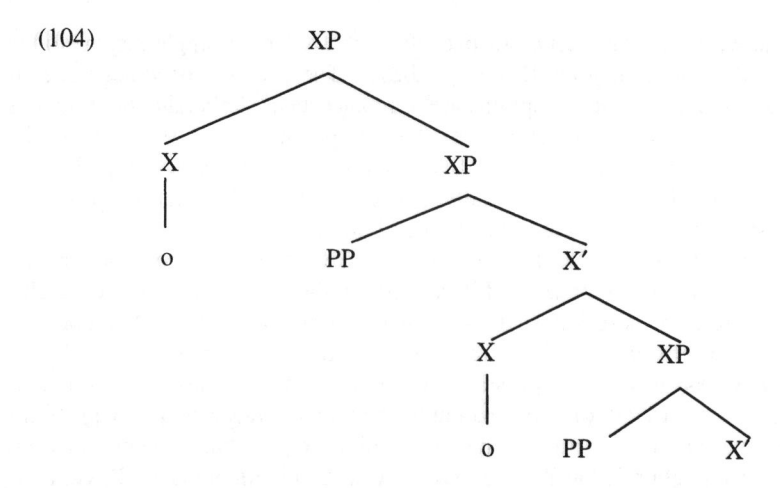

(104)

```
              XP
             /  \
            X    XP
            |   /  \
            o  PP   X'
                   /  \
                  X    XP
                  |   /  \
                  o  PP   X'
```

Arguably, the specifier of the higher XP is occupied by a distributive operator, which accounts for the exclusive reading.

A similar account can be given to cases of collective interpretation of repeated conjunctions, such as in the following examples from French. In this case, the specifier of XP would be occupied by a collective operator.

(105)   Et Jean et Pierre ont une maison.
        and Jean and Pierre have a   house
        'Both Jean and Pierre have a house.'

English confirms the analysis just presented for Spanish.[99] In English, interpretations inside a PP need not be collective, thus a sentence like (106) can be interpreted either collectively or distributively. As expected, an overt exclusive operator *either* can appear inside the PP coordination, as shown in (107)a. Note that, like in Spanish, unbalanced coordination is also marginal in English (cf. (107)b), for the same reasons that (102)e is ungrammatical: the structure involves coordination of a PP and a DP (cf. (103) below).

(106)   They went to San Francisco and San Diego (respectively)

(107)   a. Let's talk about either movies or theater
        b. ??Let's talk either about movies or theater

Negative Polarity Conjunction. Recall the generalizations about *ni*, the Negative Polarity conjunction from Bosque (1992) presented in chapter 3, repeated in (106), illustrated in (109) below:

(108)   i. *Ni* is a Negative Polarity Item which shows the characteristic

---
[99] Thanks to Roger Schwarzschild for judgements on the English data.

preverbal/postverbal asymmetries with respect to negation.
ii. Only object positions allow a single *ni*.

(109) a. Ni   Juan ni Pedro vinieron.
         neither Juan nor Pedro came
         'Neither Juan nor Pedro came.'
     b. No vi (ni)   a Juan ni a Pedro.
         not saw (neither) to Juan nor to Pedro
         'I didn't see neither Juan nor Pedro.'
     c. *Juan ni   Pedro vinieron.
         Juan nor Pedro came
         'Juan nor Pedro came.'
     d. *Juan ni   Pedro no vinieron.
         Juan nor Pedro not came
         'Juan nor Pedro didn't come.'

Bosque's analysis of these contrasts states that NPIs need to be licensed by movement to the specifier of NegP. Whenever this head is empty, it must be properly governed. This is why both instances of *ni* must appear preverbally, if only one appears, the null one will not be licensed because there is no proper governor.

Some other facts not noted by Bosque are relevant for this analysis. First, *ni* is necessarily distributive, even if only one of the conjunctions is present, as the ungrammaticality of (110)a, b shows: they cannot be direct objects of a verb that requires collective objects.

(110) a. *No reuní   ni   a Juan ni a Pedro.
         not got together neither to Juan nor to Pedro
     b. *No reuní   a Juan ni a Pedro.
         not got together to Juan nor to Pedro
     c. No reuní   a Juan y   a Pedro.
         not got together to Juan and to Pedro
         'I didn't get together Juan and Pedro.'

Second, some of the facts concerning the distribution of PP coordination do not readily follow from Bosque's analysis. Bosque predicts that a null *ni* cannot appear inside a PP, since prepositions are not proper governors in Spanish, as illustrated in (111)a. However, the ungrammaticality of (111)b is unexpected, since *ni* is overt in that example. N-words are not ungrammatical inside PPs, as (111)c shows, so this cannot be the reason. Finally, (111)d shows that *ni* can appear outside the PP.

(111) a. *No traje   el libro para Juan ni Pedro.
         not brought the book for   Juan nor Pedro
     b. *No traje el libro para ni Juan ni Pedro.
         not brought the book for neither Juan nor Pedro
     c. No traje   el libro para nadie.
         not brought the book for   nobody

'I didn't bring the book for nobody.'
d. No traje el libro ni para Juan ni para Pedro.
   not brought the book neither for Juan nor for Pedro
   'I didn't bring the book neither for Juan nor for Pedro.'

In chapter 3, I suggested that both instances of *ni* have to be licensed independently. This hypothesis squares with Bosque's intuition that the higher *ni* is an agreement marker. With this assumption, we can explain the unexpected grammaticality of (111)b: it follows from the distributive nature of *ni*. Since *ni* requires a distributive reading, it cannot appear inside the PP, which forces a collective interpretation. The proposed structure for a sentence like (111)b will be the following:

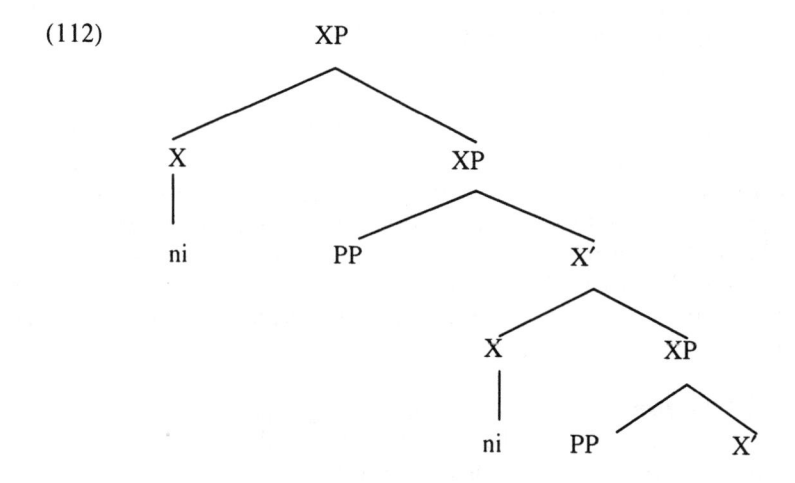

(112)

```
         XP
        /  \
       X    XP
       |   /  \
       ni PP   X'
              /  \
             X    XP
             |   /  \
             ni PP   X'
```

This structure is different from Bosque's in that it argues that *ni* is a head in both cases, not only in the case of the second *ni*.

There is another observation Bosque makes which also provides indication about the true nature of *ni*. An N-word can appear with only one *ni* in subject position, as seen below:

(113)   Nada   ni   nadie me obligaron.
        nothing nor noone CL forced
        'Nothing or nobody forced me.'

Bosque suggests that a negative element can license the null *ni* in (113). In the structure I am proposing, the lower NPI is licensed by the higher one (by head movement), which, in turn will be licensed in NegP.

To summarize, I have provided an analysis of semantically restricted coordination (both exclusive disjunction and NPI conjunction) which makes crucial use of the XP/AgrP projection proposed earlier.

Bare Nominals Licensed by Conjunction. I will now return to a topic I briefly presented in previous chapters. Singular bare nominals are ungrammatical in subject positions in standard varieties of Spanish, regardless of whether they are mass nouns, generics, etc.:

(114) a. *Hijo permaneció poco tiempo de visita.
          son remained little time of visit
     b. El hijo permaneció poco tiempo de visita.
          the son remained little time of visit
          'The son visited for a short time.'
     c. *Gente abre siempre esa puerta.
          people open always the door
     d. La gente abre siempre esa puerta.
          the people open always the door

In object position, the restriction is less severe: mass nouns can be bare, count nouns cannot (cf. Bosque (1996)):[100]

(115) a. Trajeron vino.
          brought wine
          'They brought wine.'
     b. *Trajeron lápiz.
          brought pencil
     c. Trajeron un lápiz.
          brought a pencil
          'They brought a pencil.'

However, bare nominals can appear both in subject and object position if they are conjoined, as in English (this observation for Spanish goes back to Bello [1847]1972, quoted by Contreras 1996. See Bosque 1996 and references cited there):

(116) a. Madre e hijo permanecieron poco tiempo de visita.
          Mother and son remained little time of visit
          'Mother and son visited for a short time.'

---

[100] An anonymous reviewer points out the contrast between (115)b and (i), which in turn contrasts with (ii). Clearly, other factors are involved in this distribution that are not relevant for he discussion (see Laca 1999):

(i.) No tengo lápiz.
      not have pencil
      'I don't have a pencil.'
(ii.) *Tengo lápiz.
      have pencil

142   CHAPTER #4

> b. Trajeron lápiz y   papel.
>   brought pencil and paper
>   'They brought pencil and paper.'

The conjoined elements in these cases are interpreted quantificationally, either as universal quantifiers or as indefinites. The first type of interpretation makes them ungrammatical in *there*-insertion contexts (examples from Bosque 1996, p. 38).[101]

> (117) a. Había mujeres en   la estación.
>   was   women in   the station
>   'There were women at the station.'
>   b. *Había todas las mujeres en la estación.
>   was   all   the women in the station
>   c. *Había mujer e   hijo en la   estación.
>   was   woman and son in the station

The second type of interpretation, as indefinites, allows them to appear in *there*-insertion contexts, and the reading is purely existential:

> (118) Había lápiz   y   papel en la mesa.
>   was   pencil and paper on the table
>   'There was pencil and paper on the table.'

Contreras (1996, p. 145) suggests that these structures can only appear with stage-level predicates:[102]

> (119) a. Mamá e   hijo estaban en la casa.
>   woman and son were   in the house
>   'The mother and the child were in the house.'
>   b. Tortillas y   café   abundaban   en los desayunos de los bares.
>   omelette and coffee were frequent   in the breakfast of the bars
>   'Coffee and omelette were frequent for breakfast in the bars.'
>   c. *Mamá e   hijo son altos.
>   mother and son are tall
>   d. *Tortillas y   café   son caros.
>   omelette and coffee are expensive(PL)

---

[101] It seems that (117)c contrasts with the corresponding sentence with *mother and son* in English, which is grammatical, as Barry Schein observes. I do not think they are in Spanish. However, these structures are not fully productive, and they have properties of semi-lexicalized compounds; to that extent, we expect them to be sensitive to the type of lexical item that can appear in them.

[102] But Benedicto (1998) gives examples such as (i) with an individual-level predicate.

> (i)   Esas cosas las han sabido mujeres jóvenes y viejas desde siempre.
>   those things CL have known women young and old since always
>   'Those things have been known by old and young women for a long time.'

(119)c becomes grammatical in the imperfect:

(120) Mamá e hijo eran altos.
mother and son were tall
'Mother and son were tall.'

The imperfect may serve to delimit the property, giving some kind of episodic reading. However, this is not the case with the typical contrasts between stage and individual level predicates.

Recall the analysis of these facts proposed in chapter 2, sec. 3.1. In particular, it was argued that the difference in distribution between bare plurals and conjoined NPs was related to the availability of a conjunction pro in the latter case, which could be licensed by the verb. The proposed structure is repeated below.

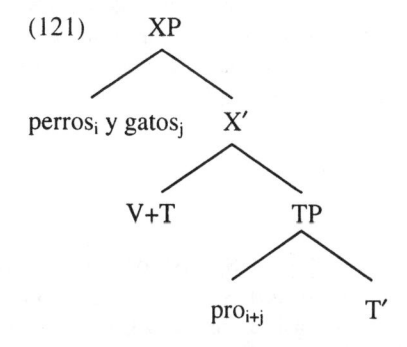

(121)
```
            XP
           /  \
   perros_i y gatos_j   X'
                       /  \
                    V+T    TP
                          /  \
                      pro_{i+j}  T'
```

This structure can also account for an important additional fact about the distribution of bare nominals in Spanish: bare mass nouns are better than bare count nouns, and count nouns need to be old information: for example, a sentence like (122)a is ungrammatical if out of the blue. However, if *viejo y niño* have been mentioned before in the discourse, then it becomes acceptable.

(122) a. *Viejo y niño escuchaban atentamente.
old(SG) and young(SG) listened attentively
b. De pronto, vi a un viejo y a un niño. Viejo y niño escuchaban atentamente.
'Suddenly, I saw an old man and a child. The old man and the child were listening attentively.'

The examples in (122) suggest that conjoined bare-NPs can be topics, whereas bare NPs cannot unless left-dislocated, as Casielles (1997) points out. For Casielles, and also for Benedicto (1998), the unavailability of bare-NPs as topics follows from the fact that they remain inside the VP. Supporting evidence for this comes from the observation that bare-NPs can never be interpreted as generics, as shown in the following contrast, from Casielles (p. 99):

(123) a. Juegan niños en la   calle.   (*generic)
         play   children in the street
         'Children play in the street.'
     b. *Juegan generalmente niños   en la calle.
         play   generally   children in the street
     c. Los niños   generalmente juegan en la   calle.
         the children generally   play in the street
         'Children generally play in the street.'

(123)a can be interpreted existentially: there are children playing in the streets. (123)b, on the other hand, cannot be interpreted generically, although it would be grammatical with an existential interpretation. The generic interpretation is only possible with the definite article, as in (123)c.

If bare-NPs must stay within VP, one can explain why the order must be VS. In the case of conjoined bare-NPs, they need not stay inside the VP because there is an additional category, conjunction pro, that is lower. This accounts for the possibility of having SV word order with coordination, and for the possibility of interpreting conjoined bare-NPs as topics (as shown in (122)).

2.6   Partial Dative Agreement

Recall from previous sections that datives in Dialect B of Spanish do not involve gapping (they do not require pauses or adverbs of any sort when partial agreement surfaces, as opposed to accusatives). In the following sections, I will explore the possibility that a difference in structure between dative and accusative clitics would account for their different distributional patterns. I will first review the evidence for the claim that datives involve more structure than accusatives.

2.6.1   The Clausal Structure of Ditransitive Verbs

It has been observed that datives behave like subjects in several ways. Aoun (1993), for example, suggests that "dative is a way to mark the occurrence of non-conventional subjects (p. 728, fn. 11)." In certain dialects of Spanish, datives and subjects also form a natural class with respect to some grammatical phenomena (cf. Camacho 1993). For example, imperatives with clitics have the following paradigm:

(124) a. De-n-me-lo.   (Standard Spanish)
         give-3P-CL(DAT)-CL(ACC)
     b. De-me-n-lo.   (Oral register, areas of Latin
         give-CL(DAT)-3P-CL(ACC)   American Spanish)
     c. *De-me-lo-n.   (Oral register, areas of Latin
         give-CL(DAT)-CL(ACC)-3P   American Spanish)

In Standard Spanish, the plural subject agreement morpheme -*n* follows the verbal root, followed by the dative and the accusative clitic. In a non-standard variety spoken in Bogotá, however, the dative clitic may precede subject agreement, but the accusative may not.[103]

Aside from these minor pieces of suggestive evidence, there is a clear data to support the following two generalizations, made by Demonte (1995): 1) sentences with dative clitics have a different structure than those without clitics and 2) in sentences with dative clitics the dative argument c-commands the accusative. Demonte suggests that the correct analysis of these generalizations is to say that doubled arguments are in a subject-like position. In the following paragraphs, I will summarize her analysis.

Demonte contends that Romance languages do have a dative alternation, contrary to standard assumptions. The apparent lack of dative alternation is seen in the English example ((125)a-b) versus the Spanish examples ((125)c-d):

(125) a. The teacher gave a book to the girl.
b. The teacher gave the girl a book.
c. La profesora le entregó un libro a la niña.
the teacher CL gave a book to the girl
'The teacher gave a book to the girl.'
d. *La profesora le entregó la niña un libro.
the teacher CL gave the girl a book
'The teacher gave the girl a book.'

Sentence (125)d is ungrammatical in any order. Demonte (1995) argues that the dative alternation surfaces in a slightly different form in Spanish: with the presence or absence of the dative clitic. For example, the configuration in (126)a is impossible. In this sentence, there is a bound possessive in the DO and a quantifier in the IO, and there is no clitic. If the quantifier is part of the DO and the pronoun part of the IO, then binding is possible (also without a clitic).[104]

(126) a. *La profesora entregó su dibujo a cada niño.
the teacher gave his/her drawing to each child
'The teacher gave his drawing to each child.'
b. ?La profesora entregó cada dibujo a su autor.
the teacher gave each drawing to its author
'The teacher gave each drawing to its author.'

It seems, then, that the grammatical configuration in (126)b shares the structural properties with the non-shifted version of English:

---

[103]Kany (1951) observes that the Southern Cone dialects do have the pattern V-DAT-ACC-AGR. Curiously, dialect A described earlier, which does not distinguish datives and accusatives in this way, belongs to this region.

[104]Although I share these judgements, there are some speakers who do allow binding in (126)a.

(127) a. I gave every book to its owner.
b. *I gave his book to every owner.

However, once the clitic is introduced, binding from a quantified IO into the DO becomes possible:

(128) a. La profesora le entregó su   dibujo a cada niño.
         The teacher CL gave his/her drawing to each child
         'The teacher gave his drawing to each child.'
      b. ?La profesora le entregó cada dibujo   a su autor.
         The teacher CL gave each drawing to its author
         'The teacher gave each drawing to its author.'

Although (128)b sounds reasonably acceptable, this is due to the distributive nature of the quantifier, which takes widest scope. As Demonte observes, if a non-distributive quantifier is tested, binding of the possessive is impossible:

(129) a. El presidente del   jurado no le entregó su premio a ningún
         the president of-the jury not CL gave his prize to no
         ganador.
         winner
         'The president of the jury gave no winner his prize.'
      b. *El presidente del   jurado no le entregó ningún premio a su
         the president of-the jury not CL gave no   prize to its
         ganador.
         winner
         'The president of the jury gave no prize to its winner.'

These contrasts indicate that the IO is structurally higher than the DO in ditransitive sentences with a dative clitic. The structure Demonte proposes, based on Larson (1988), is the following:

(130) LF structure for ditransitives with a dative

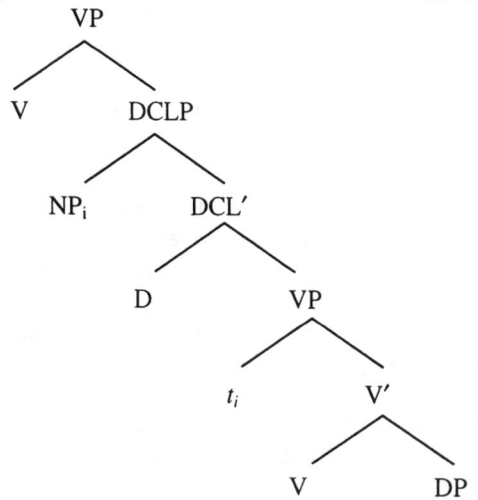

```
           VP
          /  \
         V    DCLP
             /    \
           NPᵢ    DCL'
                 /    \
                D      VP
                      /  \
                    tᵢ    V'
                         /  \
                        V    DP
```

This Larsonian VP shell has an additional Dative Clitic Phrase (DCLP). The doubled dative moves to the specifier of DCLP to check case. In a certain sense, the DatP is comparable to a predication projection where the Dative acts as the inflection but also has aspectual properties (affectedness). In any case, it is clear that the dative argument c-commands the accusative only when the clitic is present.

Further evidence for the subject-like nature of the dative comes from the surprising relative acceptability of the following sentences:

(131) a. Marta y   Julia le   fueron presentadas   a un
         Marta and Julia CL(SG.) were   introduced(FEM.PL.) to a
         carpintero.
         carpenter
         'Marta and Julia were introduced to a carpenter.'
      b. ?Marta y   Julia les   fueron presentadas   a un
         Marta and Julia CL(PL.) were   introduced(FEM.PL.) to a
         carpintero.
         carpenter
         'Marta and Julia were introduced to a carpenter.'

Sentence (131)a is a passive with a verb that takes two animate internal arguments, and with a conjoined subject. In this sentence, the clitic is singular, and it doubles the IO *un carpintero*. In (131)b, however, the clitic is plural, so it cannot be coindexed with the IO *un carpintero*, which is singular. Although somewhat marginal, this sentence shows a case of cliticization of a passive subject DO. This option is not available in the active counterpart, which indicates that passivization has triggered movement through the specifier of the clitic projection. This example clearly contrasts with the case of an accusative clitic, where the configuration just presented is impossible:

(132) *María y Marta las   fueron presented-a-s   a Pedro.
       Maria and Marta CL(PL) were introduced-FEM-PL to Pedro
       'Maria and Marta were introduced to Pedro.'

It is reasonable to blame this asymmetry between accusatives and datives on the idea that subjects and datives are part of the same syntactic natural class. One approach is that the features of these two categories are similar enough to allow the wrong checking under restricted circumstances such as raising.[105] Coming back to the structure of doubled datives, note that the agreement asymmetries do not change the structural properties of the arguments:

(133) a. La profesora le-s   entregó su   premio a cada niño y   a
         the teacher CL-PL gave   his/her prize to each boy and to
         cada niña.
         each girl
         'The teacher gave his prize to each boy and to each girl.'
      b. La profesora le   entregó su   premio a cada niño y   a
         the teacher CL(SG) gave   his/her prize to each boy and to
         cada niña.
         each girl
         'The teacher gave his/her prize to each boy and to each girl.'
      c. La presidenta le-s   entregó cada libro a su autor y   a
         the president CL(PL.) gave   each book to its author and to
         su editor.
         its editor
         'The teacher gave each book to its author and to its editor.'
      d. La profesora le   entregó cada libro a su autor   y   a su
         the teacher CL(SG) gave   each book to its author and to its
         editor.
         editor
         'The teacher gave each book to its author and to its editor.'

Suppose, following Demonte's intuition, that the dative clitic heads a functional projection. Note, however, that the number feature of the clitic does not strictly agree with the dative:

105This configuration is only available for third person clitics. Many people have pointed out asymmetries between third person clitics and first/second person clitics, see for example Uriagereka (1995) and Torrego (1996). In this particular case, the explanation for the asymmetry could be compatible with a theory that restricts mismatches to third person features. However, other evidence may suggest that the syntactic structure of first/second and third person is quite different, as both Uriagereka and Torrego have suggested.

(134) Le dije a los muchachos que se portaran bien.
CL(SG) told to the children(PL) that CL behave well
'I told the children to behave well.'

In this sense, the dative clitic in Spanish is like the cases in Arabic cases with an auxiliary and an aspectual verb where the auxiliary agrees with an expletive. However, Demonte's evidence suggests that when the clitic is present, the doubled NP c-commands the accusative. This means that the doubled DP must raise to the position of the clitic. Does the clitic have unspecified person features? The evidence suggests not. In particular, in clitic-left-dislocated structures (CLLD), the dative clitic must be plural if the dislocated DP is plural. Why should there be a contrast between CLLD cases and regular doubled dative cases?

Two possible analyses come to mind: first, CLLD elements are dislocated by movement from base-positions. Person marking on the clitic reflects movement through the clitic position. However, Cinque (1990) has argued that CLLD elements do not move, since they are not subject to certain island constraints. The second alternative is that CLLD elements are base-generated in their surface position. An element inside the sentence acts as a resumptive pronoun. This element can be either the clitic or an empty pro generated in the base position of the argument.

If the clitic is the resumptive element, this means that clitics have a dual nature: when they double DPs, they are agreement markers, in CLLD structures, they are pronouns. This dual nature unnecessarily complicates the picture. Additionally, there is no obvious reason why the clitic should have to be plural in the CLLD cases. On the other hand, if there is a null pronominal in the base position, the clitic will still be an agreement marker, the null element will need to be identified, and full identification of that element will require the clitic to be plural. Confirmation for this analysis comes from cases where the clitic does not double a DP:

(135) a. ¿Hablaste con ellos?
talked with them
'Did you talk to them?'
b. #Sí, le dije que vinieran.
yes, CL(SG) told that come
'Yes, I told (them) to come.'
c. Sí, le-s dije que vinieran.
yes, CL-PL told that come
'Yes, I told them to come.'

The question in (135) sets the background reference for a plural DP; only the answer with the plural clitic ((135)c) is a possible answer. If the clitic were simply unspecified for number, both answers should be equally possible. On the other hand, if the clitic identifies a null element, the contrast is expected.

The contrast paradigm in (135) is very similar to the one observed by Aoun and Benmamoun (1996) for Standard Arabic: what looks like partial agreement is not possible when null elements are present. Recall that their account involves postsyntactic merger, which can easily be extended to the cases at hand. The number features of the clitic do not surface overtly because the person features of the DP license them and block their appearance on the clitic.

An apparent problem for the postsyntactic merger analysis is that the clitic and the doubled element can be separated by the direct object in the cases at hand, so the postsyntactic merger cannot be a local operation. However, I already argued that the doubled element must end up in the specifier position of the dative phrase, since it c-commands the accusative. This movement must be covert, since the doubled element is to the right of the clitic. But at the same time, postsyntactic merger, by definition, cannot entail configurations that are reached after spell-out. With the theory of feature decomposition I am assuming, all these conditions can be satisfied: the relevant φ-features are already in the specifier of the clitic projection, allowing postsyntactic merger to take place.

3. SUMMARY

This chapter has explored the correlation between partial agreement and semantic interpretation. I have suggested that there are essentially two types of partial agreement: one with semantic effects, one without. The first one is straightforward: the φ-features of the agreeing conjunct determine agreement, an operation formalized as feature checking. The second case involves two different structures. Some languages, like Arabic and Irish, are subject either to a PF operation of restructuring or to gapping, or in some cases both; others involve a higher projection that hosts agreement. This projection was proposed for nominal projections in Spanish, and I have argued that it is reinforces the parallelism between DP and clausal structure. The data presented in this chapter provide substantial support for the theory of coordination developed in previous chapters in the following sense: on the one hand, partial agreement displays cases where one of the conjuncts seems to act independently of the other with elements outside the coordination. By assuming a structure in which each conjunct agrees separately with a head, these cases can be explained in a natural way.

CHAPTER #5

COORDINATION OF LARGER PHRASES

In the preceding chapters I have argued that conjunction joins predicational functional projections. In this chapter, I will return to the analysis of asymmetric coordination. Since I will argue that some of the asymmetric constructions involve gapping, I will also sketch an analysis of gapping. However, I will not propose a detailed analysis of gapping.

1. ASYMMETRIC COORDINATION

1.1 German Asymmetric Conjunction

As was mentioned in chapter 2, German has cases of coordination where conjuncts are not alike (cf. Höhle (1990) and Thiersch (1994). There are two subcases, a coordination of what looks like a VP and an IP; and a coordination of what looks like an IP and a CP. The following examples illustrate the second case (all the examples are from Höhle (1990)):

(1) a. Wenn jemand nach Hause kommt und da steht der
    If someone to house comes and there stands the
    Gerichtsvollzieher der Tür
    bailiff the door
    'If someone comes home and the bailiff is standing there in front of the door.'
  b. Wenn [jemand nach Hause kommt],...
  c. Wenn [da der Gerischtsvollzieher vor der Tür steht],...

(2) a. Wenn [[α jemand nach Hause kommt] und [β da steht der
    when someone to home comes and there stands the
    Gerichtsvollzieher vor der Tür]], ...
    bailiff at the door
    'When someone goes home and the bailiff is standing there at the door...'
  b. *Wenn [da steht der Gerichtsvollzieher vor der Tür steht]],...

(1)a involves two verb-final clauses, both of which can independently appear next to *wenn*, as (1)b, c show. However, (2)a is asymmetrical: it involves a verb-final clause and a verb-second clause. The second conjunct cannot independently appear after *wenn*, as shown in (2)b. Assuming that *wenn* selects for IP, α would be IP in (2)a and β, CP. Thus, the coordination involves asymmetric categories.

The second subcase of asymmetric coordination involves sentences with no subject in the second conjunct, which suggests that the conjoined categories are lower than those in the first subcase (IP and VP respectively), as illustrated in (3)-(4).

(3) a. Wenn [[jemand nach Hause kommt] und [den Gerichtsvollzieher sieht]],
   when someone to home comes and the bailiff sees
   'When someone goes home and sees the bailiff...'
   b. Wenn jemand [den Gerischtsvollzieher sieht],...

(4) a. Wenn jemand [[nach Hause kommt] und [sieht den
   when someone to home comes and sees the
   Gerichtsvollzieher]],...
   bailiff
   'When someone goes home and sees the bailiff...'
   b. *Wenn jemand [sieht der Gerichtsvollzieher],...

In (3)a, both conjuncts are verb final, the first one contains a subject, but the second one does not. As (3)b shows, the second conjunct can independently appear in the same position as the full coordination. In (4)a, on the other hand, the second conjunct is verb-initial, and cannot appear by itself in the same position as the whole coordination, as illustrated in (4)b. Since verb-final clauses and verb-second clauses are generally taken to be different projections, these two sets of cases raise a problem for the commonly held assumption that conjuncts must belong to like-categories (see Chomsky 1957 and Schachter's 1977 *Coordinate Constituent Constraint*). Thiersch's (1994) structure (presented in chapter 2) is repeated below:

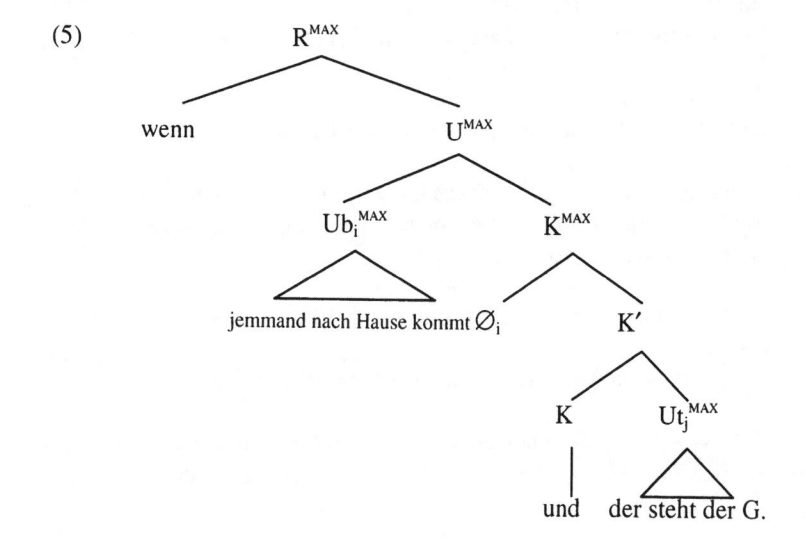

(5)

```
                    R^MAX
                   /      \
                 wenn      U^MAX
                          /      \
                     Ub_i^MAX    K^MAX
                     /    \      /    \
          jemmand nach Hause kommt Ø_i  K'
                                       /  \
                                      K    Ut_j^MAX
                                      |    /    \
                                     und  der steht der G.
```

Recall that in Thiersch's system, there are three types of COMP: argument COMP, labelled G (e.g. *dass*), a relative-like COMP, labelled R (e.g. Bavarian *wo* and *wenn* above), and an assertion COMP, labelled U, the landing site for the verb in V-2 clauses. The assertion COMP (U) appears in a basic word order (S-V), which Thiersch calls Ub, and in inverted word order (Ut). Both G and R can take U as a complement. The verb moves to U if and only if it is not governed by a lexical G. Finally, intermediate projections (X') only exist if licensed. Höhle's facts and Thiersch's analysis can be incorporated to the proposal developed in this book without too many changes, as illustrated below.

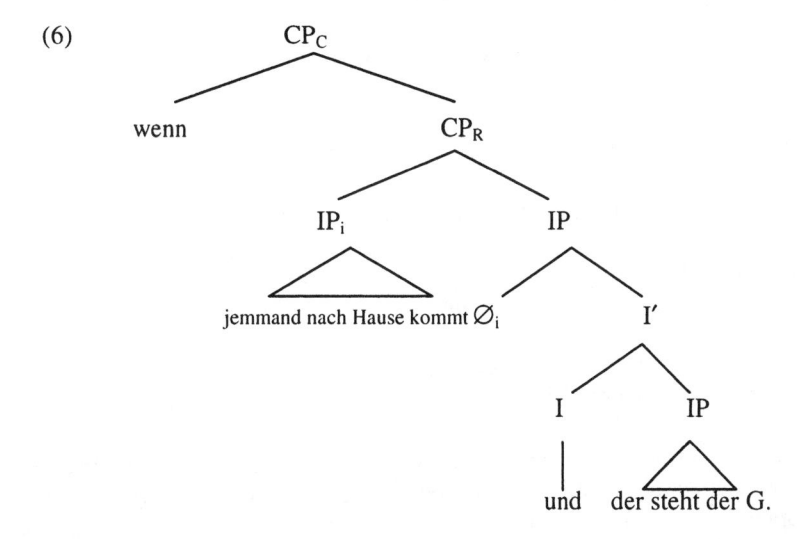

(6)

```
           CP_C
          /    \
       wenn    CP_R
              /    \
           IP_i     IP
           /\      /  \
  jemmand nach   I'
  Hause kommt Ø_i / \
                 I   IP
                 |   /\
                und der steht der G.
```

The standard analysis of German V2 vs. V-final clauses relies on the lexical/non-lexical nature of the complementizer: a non-lexical C forces movement of the verb to the C (the V2 position). Under this assumption, the reason why the second clause behaves as a V2 clause is that the governing C is too distant to license the second IP, forcing the verb to move to second position. As expected, further movement of the second V to C is ungrammatical as well. Restrictions on extraction from the second conjunct follow from the structural properties of coordination: extraction from the second conjunct will always yield a minimality effect when the extracted element crosses the higher specifier.[106]

2. GAPPING CONSTRUCTIONS

Ever since Ross's article on gapping (cf. Ross 1970), there has been a constant flow of studies on the various types of deletion constructions (a summary of the different

---

[106] Exceptions to the ban on extraction from a single conjunct are well-known, cf. Lakoff (1986), Postal (1995). I will not attempt to explain them here.

proposals can be found in Van Oirsouw 1987). Most of these proposals address one of two issues: first, what are the natural classes into which deletion phenomena fall? Can gapping and VP deletion be accounted for by using the same rule? The second area of research is the kind of constraints imposed on deletion structures. Thus, Jackendoff (1972), for example, proposes various restrictions on gapping: it is restricted to coordinated structures (cf. (7)), it only involves verbs, not nouns (cf. (8)), it requires identical auxiliaries (cf. (9)) and it does not allow unlike adverbs before the verb (cf. (10)):

(7) a. Sam played tuba and Max sax.
    b. *Sam played tuba whenever Max sax.

(8) *Dolores gave incriminating evidence about Harry to the FBI, and Frank sent to his mother-in-law.

(9) *John has written the words, and Paul will the music.

(10) *Simon quickly dropped the gold, and Jack suddenly the diamonds.

Finally, Jackendoff notes that if there is a negation on the auxiliary, the conjunction cannot be *and* but it must be *or*:

(11) a. *I didn't eat fish and Bill rice.
     b. I didn't eat fish nor Bill rice.

Most of these observations have been contradicted at some point or another. Levin (1978) and more recently Lasnik (1995), for example, have suggested that pseudogapping allows unlike auxiliaries. Likewise, Siegel (1984) quotes the following example that contradict the observation about (11):

(12) Ward can't eat caviar and Sue beans.

2.1 Recent Analyses of Gapping

A third line of research has recently focused on the actual structure of gapping constructions. Johnson (1994) and Zoerner (1995) for example, share the common idea that gapping is the product of across-the-board movement of material from within the VP. Johnson argues that the remnant of gapping is a constituent which has moved out of the VP before deletion. One of the main differences between Johnson and Zoerner is the structure they propose for coordination. Zoerner proposes one where each conjunct is a specifier of a &P, except the last one (see below), whereas Johnson assumes a ternary structure. Additionally, Zoerner tries to account for two correlations, the first one due to Ross (cf. Ross 1970): languages that gap forward are head initial, like English; languages that gap backward are head final, like Japanese. The second correlation, due to Koutsoudas (1971), is that languages that have V⁰ coordination and gapping also have right node raising. Zoerner's structure for coordination is the following:

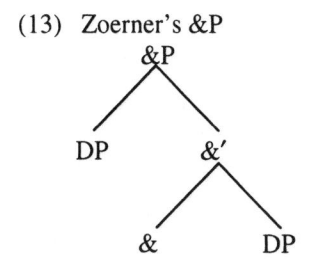

(13) Zoerner's &P

```
        &P
       /  \
      DP   &'
          /  \
         &    DP
```

For coordination involving deletions, Zoerner proposes an additional phrase, Relational Phrase, which is an arbitrary XP that differs from other XPs "only in that they do not inherently have a fully realized argument structure" (cf. Zoerner 1995, p. 179). The head only has the feature [-F(unctional)], and its contents have to be licensed by inheriting the features of another head. In the configuration of sisterhood, a lexical head X cannot license RP, since RP cannot satisfy the selectional requirements of that lexical head. Only when a &P intervenes can the head X transmit its features through &P to RP, which inherits them and satisfies X's selectional restrictions through its own arguments:

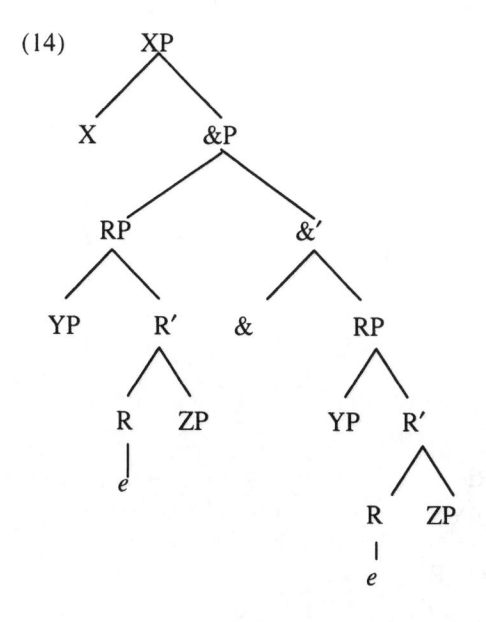

(14)

```
            XP
           /  \
          X    &P
              /  \
             RP   &'
            /  \  / \
           YP  R' &  RP
              / \   / \
             R  ZP YP  R'
             |       / \
             e      R   ZP
                    |
                    e
```

The specifiers of RP (YP) and its complements (ZP) satisfy the selectional restrictions of X because the R⁰ heads in a sense mirror X. Zoerner imposes an additional restriction on this representation: empty elements within RP are only licensed by the first c-commanding category outside &P. In (14) above, only X⁰ can license elements within RP. Furthermore, only heads license empty heads and only complements license empty complements. We thus have two configurations, the one in (14) for gapping, repeated below with details, and the one in (16) for Right-Node-Raising (RNR):

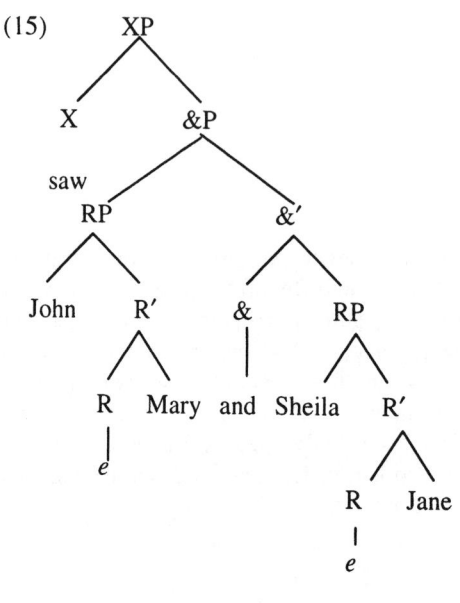

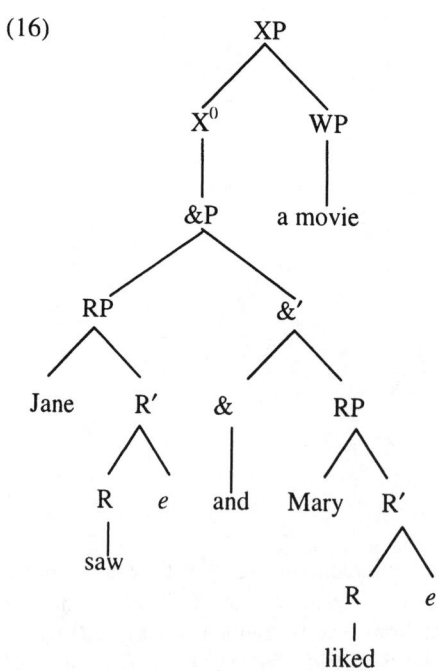

(15)

```
              XP
            /    \
           X     &P
          saw   /   \
              RP    &'
             /  \   / \
          John  R' &  RP
               / \ |  / \
              R Mary and Sheila R'
              |              / \
              e             R  Jane
                            |
                            e
```

(16)

```
                    XP
                  /    \
                 X⁰    WP
                 |      |
                &P   a movie
               /   \
              RP   &'
             /  \  / \
          Jane  R' & RP
               / \ |  / \
              R  e and Mary R'
              |             / \
             saw           R   e
                           |
                         liked
```

Note that a head X^0 dominates a maximal category &P, and the whole analysis hinges on this asymmetry between coordination of heads and coordination of complements.[107]

2.2 Some Revisions on Gapping and RNR

Upon closer inspection, Zoerner concludes that RP is quite similar to a predication projection that relates two arguments. If predication projections are sentential functional projections, as I am assuming, then, Zoerner's proposal would not be very different from the one proposed in previous chapters.

One point in which both analyses diverge is that in my analysis, heads are never conjoined, apparent head-coordination involves maximal phrases. Thus, in my analysis, V^0 coordination would have the following structure:

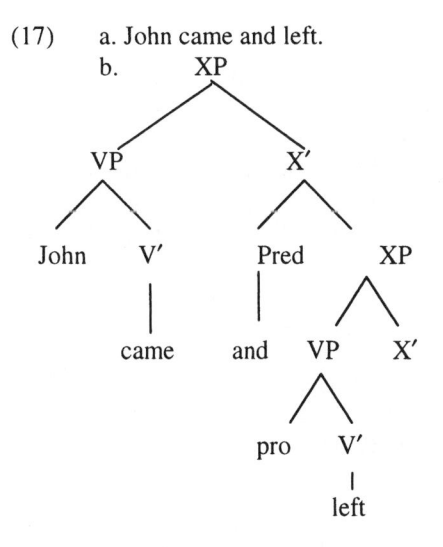

(17) a. John came and left.
      b.
```
                    XP
                   /  \
                 VP    X'
                /  \   / \
             John  V' Pred  XP
                   |   |   /  \
                 came and VP   X'
                         /  \
                       pro   V'
                             |
                            left
```

This structure raises a number of issues, particularly how the V-heads within the specifiers of XP move. One possibility is to say that they don't move. That is, they are licensed by the spec-head relation between the X head and the VP in its specifier, and it is the Pred head which actually moves. X0/Pred can be construed as an abstract inflectional head which does not contain actual morphemes but temporal/aspectual information. Agreement between X and each of the V-heads insures that the V-head receives a temporal/aspectual information. The subjects inside the lower VPs are licensed in one of two possible ways: either in situ by the verb, or the higher verb can move out of the VP to the higher TP specifier.

---

[107] In this system, as Zoerner points out, specifiers are never licensed as empty heads, and even if they were, the structure could not be distinguished from VP conjunction.

As for the lower subject, it is interpreted pronominally, as a null pro. This assumption, in turn, raises the issue of why there is a contrast between the following sentences:

(18) a. John came and Peter went.
 b. John came and went.

The first sentence tends to be interpreted as two separate events, the second one tends to be interpreted as a single event with two subevents. One could relate this observation with the level of coordination: in the first case, TP or CP, in the second case, a lower projection. In the case of the separate event interpretation, the semantic form will have to insure that the events are related in the appropriate way, although they need not overlap in time or in space. This mechanism of event cross-reference is presented in Schein (1997).

As for RNR, things are slightly different. Note the following contrasts in Spanish, from Fernández-Ramírez (1995):

(19) a. Desde aquel día fue y vino del Instituto.
 from that day went and came of-the Institute
 'From that day he/she went and came from the Institute.'
 b. Primero amedrentaron y luego dispararon contra los manifestantes.
 first harassed and then shot against the demonstrators
 'First they harassed, and then they shot at the demonstrators.'

(20) a. *Fue del Instituto.
 went of-the Institute
 'Went from the Institute.'
 b. *Amedrentaron contra los manifestantes.
 harassed against the demonstrators
 'They harassed against the demonstrators.'

(21) a. *Fue el Instituto.
 went the Institute
 'Went the Institute.'
 b. *Amedrentaron los manifestantes.
 harassed the demonstrators
 'They harassed the demonstrators.'

Ir 'go' requires the preposition *a* 'to'. It is ungrammatical with *de* 'from' as seen in (20)a and with nothing, as shown in (21)a. However, in (19)a *a* is absent, and yet the sentence is grammatical. The same reasoning holds for (19)b. The reverse order of the verbs is ungrammatical:

(22) a. *Desde aquel día vino y fue del Instituto.
 from that day came and went of-the Institute
 'From that day he/she came and went from the Institute.'

b. *Dispararon y   amedrentaron contra los manifestantes.
   shot   and harassed   against the demonstrators
   'They shot and harassed at the demonstrators.'

These paradigms raise the question of how the selectional restrictions of the first verb are satisfied. The configurations in (19)a and (19)b are very similar to the cases of partial agreement: the expected syntactic conditions are suspended for one of the conjuncts. In the case of partial agreement, the distant conjunct does not agree in the way it would if it were singleton, in the cases above, the distant conjunct does not have its proper selectional restrictions satisfied by the complement. The parallelism goes further: as in the case of partial agreement, "partial selection" is local.[108]

The contrasts in (19)-(22) indicate that the linearly last, structurally lower verb, imposes its selectional restrictions on the whole conjunction, an observation which is inconsistent with the classical RNR approach and also with Zoerner's analysis. In the classical analysis, RNR involves a conjunction of two full VPs with across-the-board raising of both complements to an adjoined position right of the coordinated constituent. Within this analysis, there is no reason why order should matter. This suggests that the shared object is not raised at all, but rather is the complement of the second verb, as in the following representation (see Schein 2001 for similar conclusions):[109,110]

---

[108] Not all verbs allow this configuration:

(i.) *?Conocen y hablan de Pedro.
      'They know and talk about Pedro.'
(ii.) *Hablan y conocen a Pedro.
      'They talk and know Pedro.'

The second sentence is much worse than the first one, as is the English translation. English has the option of preposition stranding, which Spanish lacks. At this point, it is not clear what the restrictions on asymmetric RNR are.

[109] As an anonymous reviewer points out, the heaviness effect associated with RNR is not captured under this analysis.

[110] It is not clear that all cases of RNR have this structure. In particular, it is conceivable that in some language the shared constituent will satisfy the requirements of both verbs. The mirror image situation is presented by Dalrymple and Kaplan (2000). In (i), the *wh*-phrase satisfies the case requirements of both verbs (accusative for *likes* and genitive for *hates*), although this is not RNR but wh-extraction.

(i.) kogo Janek lubi a   Jerzy nienawidzi?
      who Jane likes and Jerzy hates
      'Who does Janek like and Jerzy hate?'

(23)

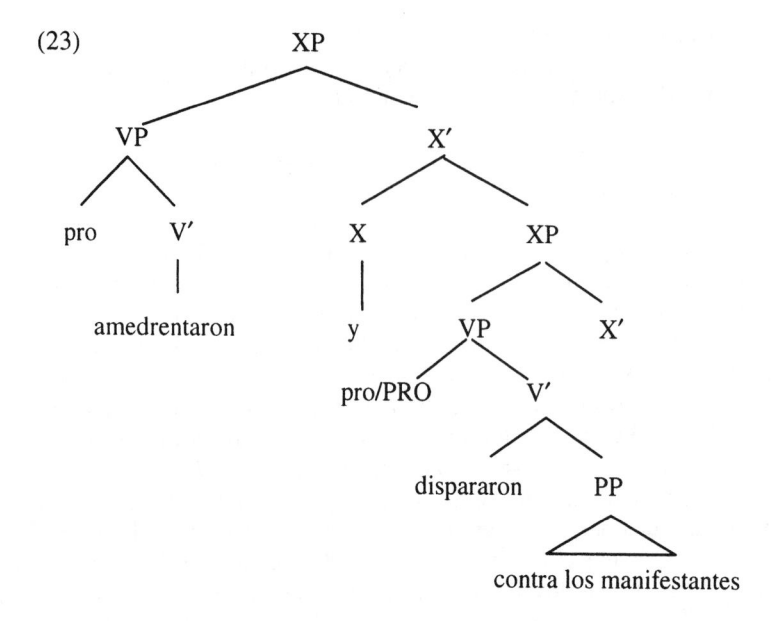

```
              XP
         /         \
       VP           X'
      /  \         /  \
   pro    V'      X    XP
          |       |   /   \
      amedrentaron y  VP    X'
                    /  \   /  \
                pro/PRO  V'
                        /  \
                  dispararon PP
                             /\
                    contra los manifestantes
```

In this light, let me review the Tümpisa Shoshone (TS) paradigm quoted by Zoerner. TS is essentially SOV, marks nominative with a zero morpheme, and objective with *-a, -i, -itta* and *-nna*:

(24) a. Nüü isapaippü-a punikkappühantü.
       I   coyote-OBJ saw
      'I saw a coyote'
   b. Tangummü nü tsitoohippühantü.
      man   me pushed
      'A man pushed me'

Subject coordinations follow the expected pattern:

(25) Wahattü nian püanümü ma'e nü namiangküppühantü sapettü
     Two   my   cousins and I were sent   there
     natiingwakkatu.
     to school
     'My two cousins and I were sent there to school.'

Object coordination, however, forces the order S-O-V-and-O:

(26) Nüü isapaippü-a punikkappühantü   tünga kammuttsi(-a).
     I   coyote-OBJ saw   and jackrabbit(-OBJ)
     'I saw a coyote and a jackrabbit.'

The second conjunct may or may not appear with the OBJ marking. Zoerner's analysis suggests that the &' constituent has right-adjoined to the VP.

Note that this is precisely the configuration that was missing in Arabic, according to Aoun, Benmamoun and Sportiche's (1994) analysis: one where the verb intervenes between the conjoined elements. Under the analysis presented earlier, this structure is actually predicted:

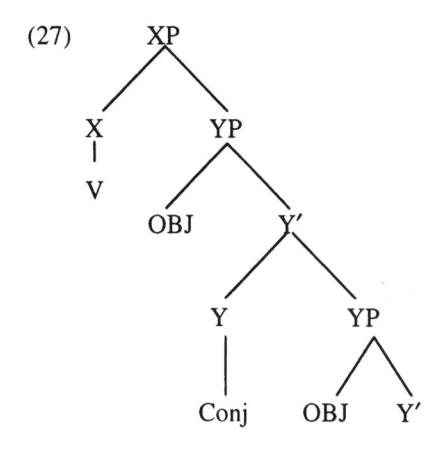

(27)

```
         XP
        /  \
       X    YP
       |   /  \
       V OBJ   Y'
             /   \
            Y     YP
            |    /  \
          Conj OBJ  Y'
```

(28) Derived Structure

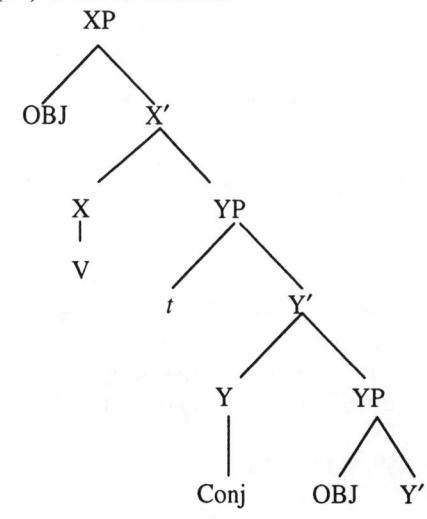

```
           XP
          /  \
        OBJ   X'
             /  \
            X    YP
            |   /  \
            V  t    Y'
                   /  \
                  Y    YP
                  |   /  \
                Conj OBJ  Y'
```

The optionality of case marking on the second object can be due to the nature of YP. If YP is the projection where object case is checked, then both objects will receive it, if case is checked lower, the higher object moves and checks it. These examples are somewhat parallel to instances of partial agreement, but with CASE. If this is correct, the reason why the first object moves higher than the verb must be independent. If this movement were related to CASE, then the optionality of marking on the second conjunct would remain mysterious.

According to the analysis presented, gapping differs from DP coordination in that the latter relates two DPs in specifier of the conjunction nodes; whereas gapping relates verbal projections in the specifier of conjunction nodes. With this difference in mind, let me return to the representation of accusative structures in Spanish, presented in the previous chapter.

2.3   Accusative Constructions in Spanish

Recall that the basic difference between datives and accusatives is that the latter do not appear with partial agreement when the doubled nominal is conjoined unless there is a strong pause and an adverb:

(29) a. Le   dije a Marta y   a Pedro que vinieran.   (Dative Clitic)
          CL(SG) told to Marta and to Pedro that come
          'I told Marta and Pedro that they should come.'
    b. *Lo   vi   a Juan y   a   Marta.   (Accusative Clitic)
          CL(SG.) saw to Juan and to   Marta
          'I saw Juan and Marta.'
    c. Lo   vi   a Juan, y   a Marta también.
          CL(SG.) saw to Juan, and to Marta also
          'I saw Juan and Marta also.'

The generalization we can draw from this contrast is that accusatives must gap, they cannot show number asymmetries if not gapped. This is a true case of gapping, and not another type of deletion, as the following test shows. Johnson (1994) points out, quoting Webber (1978), that gapping does not allow "split antecedents", unlike VP deletion:

(30) a. Wendy is eager to [sail *around the world*]₁ and Bruce is eager to [*climb Kilimanjaro*]₂, but neither of them can [vp 1+2] because money is too short.
    b. *Some [*sail around the world*]₁ in the summer, others [*climb Kilimanjaro*]₂ in the winter, and the rest [vp 1+2] in the Fall.

Accusatives in Spanish behave like (30)b, not like (30)a:

(31) *Unos [*lo llamaron a Pedro*]₁ a las 8,   otros [*lo llamaron a Juan*]₂ a las
       some   CL called   to Pedro at the 8, others CL called   to Juan   at the
       9 y   el resto [vp 1+2] a las 10 que vinieran.
       9 and the rest   at the 10 that came
       'Some called Pedro at 8, others called Juan at 9, and the rest called them at 10 so that they would come.'

Usually, however, gapping must leave at least two elements behind, as the following examples from Johnson (1994) show. However, clitic gapping does not (cf. (29)c). Thus, there is a minimal pair contrast between (29)c and (31), which may be due to the fact that the clitic forms some kind of unit with a verb, whereas in (31), both of the gapped constituents are separate constituents:

(32) a. *Sarah left and Betsy.
 b. *Sarah ate them and Betsy.

Johnson suggests this restriction might be due to the conditions on focus (remnants of gapping must be interpreted as contrastive focus, according to him). He observes that the above sentences become much better in the appropriate context and with the help of *too*:

(33) a. Who left?
 b. Sarah left, and Betsy too.

(34) a. Who ate them?
 b. Sarah ate them, and Betsy too.

This is precisely the type of adverb that we observe in the cases of accusative gapping in Spanish. If this is so, the structure would be similar to the ones we have already seen: two projections above the clitic are conjoined, with the gapped material in each specifier. The lower clitic is null:

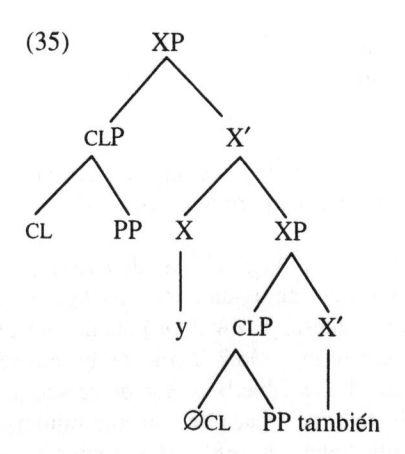

(35)
```
           XP
          /  \
        CLP   X'
       /  \  /  \
      CL  PP X   XP
             |  /  \
             y CLP  X'
               /  \  |
             ØCL  PP también
```

We will turn to the issue of the adverb and the identity of XP in the following section.

2.3.1 *The Nature of* también *'also'*

What is the role of the adverb? Note that not any adverb will license the structure:

(36) a. *Lo vi a Juan, y a Pedro esta mañana.
   CL(SG.) saw to Juan and to Pedro this morning
   'I saw Juan, and Pedro, this morning.'
   b. *Lo vi a Juan, y a Pedro siempre.
   CL(SG.) saw to Juan and to Pedro always
   'I saw Juan, and Pedro, always.'

También 'also' is a propositional, sentential adverb, a fact which fits in well with the analysis developed so far. However, the meaning of this adverb in gapping structures is different from its meaning in regular clauses, illustrated in (37)a.

(37) a. Marta también vino.
   Marta also came
   'Marta also came.'
   b. *Presupposition:* X came.

In (37)a, the adverb introduces the presupposition that someone came and the proposition states that Marta came, thus (37)a would be false if only Marta had come. Consider a gapping structure like (29)c repeated below. Suppose the presupposition introduced by *también* were the same as in a non-gapping sentence, as shown in (38)b.

(38) a. Lo vi a Juan, y a Marta también.
   CL(SG.) saw to Juan, and to Marta also
   'I saw Juan and Marta also.'
   b. *Predicted presuppositions:*
      1. For *lo vi a Juan*, {Juan} (due to clitic doubling, see Sánchez 2003)
      2. For *a Marta también*, {I saw X} (allegedly introduced by *también*)

By the time the second clause of the sentence is uttered, the first clause is contextually present in the discourse, so the speaker can assume it as background. However, the propositional content of that first clause (*I saw Juan*) should make redundant the presupposition introduced by *también* in (38)b.2 (*I saw X*), because *I saw Juan* entails *I saw X*. However, the use of the adverb is not perceived as redundant. Redundancy of the adverb may, in fact, be what rules out the minimal counterpart of (38)a without conjunction, illustrated in (38). This sentence is considerably more degraded.

(39) a. ??Lo vi a Juan. Y a Marta también.
   CL saw to Juan. And to Marta also
   'I saw Juan. And Marta also.'
   b. *Presuppositions:*
      1. For *lo vi a Juan*, {Juan} (due to clitic doubling)

2. For *y a Marta también*, {I saw X} (allegedly introduced by *también*)

This suggests that in gapping cases such as (38)a, the adverb does not introduce its usual presuppositional meaning. I believe that in those cases, *también* takes wider scope than in cases such as (37). In this sense, gapping *también* has the same scope as in (40).

(40) a. También llamó Juan.
    also   called Juan
    'Also, Juan called.'
   b. *Presuppositions:*
    1. {Something happened} (due clause-initial *también*)

In (40), the presupposition is that other things happened, not necessarily callings, aside from Juan's calling. Namely, it is simply asserting another proposition, not necessarily the same one (although it may be of the same type). Let us assume that in gapping cases, as well as in (40), *también* has higher scope than in (37). I will call it the *high scope interpretation* of *también*. For this interpretation to obtain, the adverb must be sentence initial. In non-gapping clauses, if *también* is sentence-final, or if it follows cltic left-dislocated elements, the high scope interpretation is not possible:

(41) a. A Marta, también la vimos.
    To Marta, also   CL saw
    'Marta, we also saw.'
   b. A Marta también se   lo   dijeron.
    To Marta also   CL(DAT) CL(ACC) told
    'Marta, they also told.'
   c. Juan vino también.
    Juan came also
    '(Several people came,) Juan came too.'

(41)a can only mean 'we saw someone in addition to seeing Marta', and (41)b 'they told someone else in addition to telling Marta.' Even sentences with a focused, preposed DP, can only have the lower scope reading:

(42) a. A MARTA, vimos también.
    To Marta, saw   also
    'MARTA, we also saw.'
   b. ?A MARTA, también vimos.
    To Marta, also   saw
    'MARTA, we also saw.'

Let us assume that gapping *también* also involves higher scope, as it does in (40). However, note that the preferred word order in gapping is remnant–adverb, which, as we have seen, usually does not allow for the high scope reading (cf. the discussion on (41)). The opposite order adverb–remnant is worse, but still marginally possible:

(43) ?Lo vi a Juan y también a Marta.
CL(SG.) saw to Juan and also to Marta
'I saw Juan and Marta also.'

We can draw some insights regarding the structure of gapping *también* from it a negative counterpart, *tampoco* 'either', which behaves as an NPI (cf. Bosque 1980 and also chapter 2). When this NPI appears in the second conjunct, it must be licensed by a negation in the first one, as the contrast in (44), from chapter 2 shows.

(44) a. Juan no vino y Miguel tampoco.
Juan not came and Miguel either
'Juan did not come and Miguel either.'
b. *Juan vino y Miguel tampoco.
Juan came and Miguel either
c. *Juan vino y Miguel no tampoco.
Juan came and Miguel not either

At the same time, the second clause in (44)a is interpreted as a negative clause: "Miguel did not come." This cannot be a consequence of the fact that negation in the first conjunct licenses the NPI in the second conjunct, since NPI licensing by negation in a separate clause does not necessarily entail a negative interpretation of the clause where the NPI is. This can be seen in (45), which means "I don't believe that anyone has come", not "I don't believe that anyone hasn't come."

(45) No creo que haya venido nadie.
not believe that has(SUBJ) come no one.
'I don't believe anyone has come.'

This suggests that the *tampoco*-clause in (44)a has a null negative. Assuming null negatives must be licensed because they are null elements, licensing can be done in one of two ways: by negation in the first conjunct, or by the NPI. The first option would raise the question why it is not possible to license negation in (45), in other words, why the embedded clause in this sentence cannot have a negative meaning. For this reason, we can assume that the NPI licenses negation by overt movement to NegP. This analysis would also explain why negation cannot be overt in the second conjunct, as shown in (46). If *tampoco* is preverbal, then negation cannot appear.[111]

---

[111] There is an alternative explanation: (46)b could be ungrammatical because, in general, negation must gap with the verb.

(46) *Juan no vino y Marta no tampoco.
    Juan not came and Marta not neither
    'Juan didn't come and Marta didn't come either.'

We can extend the reasoning to the case of *también*. In fact, *también* is a positive polarity item. If the first clause is negative, *también* is ungrammatical in the second clause, as seen in (47). This suggests that *también* is licensed by a SigmaP (cf. Laka 1990).

(47) *Yésica no vino y Meche también.
    Yesica not came and Meche also

The suggestion that *también* is a positive polarity item can explain the contrasts below. Laka (1990) noted that Spanish can have two negations, as in (48)b, a reply to (48)a. The same is true of two affirmations, as seen in (48)c:

(48) a. ¿Compraste leche?
        bought milk
        'Did you buy milk?'
    b. No, no compré.
        no, not bought
        'No, I didn't buy (milk).'
    c. Sí, sí compré.
        Yes, yes bought
        'Yes, I did buy (milk).'

Laka argues that the first negation is in SigmaP and the second one in NegP. Given this paradigm, note the contrasts in (49), also as replies to (48)a. The observation is that *también* can only coappear with the second affirmative word if postverbal.

(49) a. Sí, también compré.
        yes, also bought
        'Yes, I also bought.'
    b. *Sí, también sí compré.
        yes, also yes bought
        'Yes, I also bought.'
    c. ?Sí, sí compré también.
        yes, yes bought also
        'Yes, I also bought.'

The word order asymmetry is much like that of NPIs: if preverbal, it cannot coappear with the licensing head, if postverbal, it can. Unlike NPIs however, the licensing head is not obligatory if the polarity item is in postverbal position. In the case of negation, it seems that the PI can be licensed by it, but it does not force the head to disappear when the PI precedes the verb:

(50) a. ¿Compraste leche?
       bought   milk
      'Did you buy milk?'
   b. No, también no compré.
      no, also   not bought
      'No, I also did't buy.'

This exchange would be grammatical in the context where the second speaker has admitted to not buying several things. It shows that *también* does not head SigmaP in non-deletion contexts, since there are two negations, one of which has been assumed to be in Sigma. However, as we saw earlier, if the verb is missing, the presence of *también* becomes obligatory, and incompatible with negation. A final piece of the argument is that this incompatibility with negation is not a general property of NPIs as seen in the following examples:

(51) a. Marta no vio a ninguna amiga.
      Marta not saw to no   friend
      'Marta didn't see any friends.'
   b. Marta no vio a una amiga.
      Marta not saw to a friend
      'Marta didn't see a friend.'

All of these facts argue for the idea that *también* in gapping structures heads SigmaP. Despite appearances, then, high-scope *también* and *tampoco* are quite high in the structure of the sentence, and anything that precedes it is still higher, most likely because it must be focused. However, as we have seen, this is not possible in the case of non-gapped structures: in that case, anything that precedes the adverb forces the low-scope reading. How do we solve this paradox? Within the theory provided, the contrast comes out: if the conjoined node (XP in (35) above) is SigmaP, the adverb appears in the lowest Sigma head. The pre-adverb material actually appears within the specifier of the SigmaP:

(52) a. Lo vi a Juan y a Marta también.

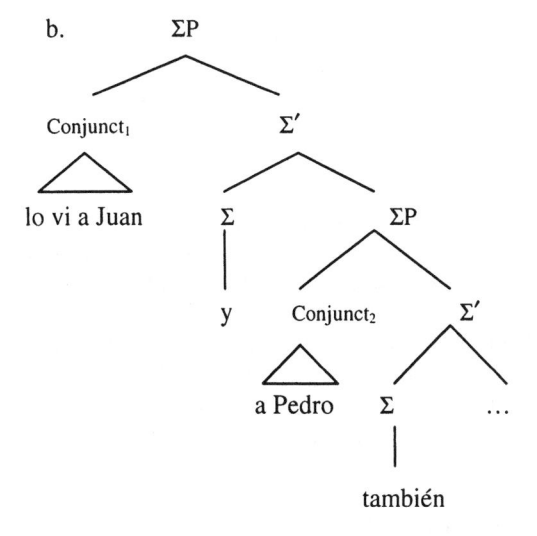

b.
```
        ΣP
       /  \
  Conjunct₁  Σ'
     /\    /  \
lo vi a Juan Σ   ΣP
             |  /  \
             y Conjunct₂ Σ'
                 /\     /  \
              a Pedro  Σ   ...
                       |
                    también
```

Notice, however, that there is still a symmetry requirement: the conjuncts must be parallel, which prevents overgeneration. The analysis manages to correlate the assertion reading of the adverb in an unexpected position with the fact that it appears in coordination.[112]

2.4 Agreement Asymmetries in Head-Final Languages

A subset of consistently head-final languages shows the following pattern for gapping:

(53) DP_{subj} DP_{obj} and DP_{subj} DP_{obj} V

In other words, the verb is sentence-final, and the conjoined DPs precede it. A group of those languages also have overt case marking with number distinctions on the verb, and several of them show the following pattern:[113]

(54) Naanu fish maththu John akki konkondo.   (Kannada)
     I   fish and   John rice bought(PL)
     'I bought fish and John rice.'

(55) Mein machchali aur John chaaval   kharidhey.   (Hindi)
     I   fish   and John rice   buy(PL)
     'I (bought) fish and John bought rice.'

---

[112] To the extent that conjunction heads a predication projection, this suggestion is related to Green's (1968, 1974) contention that *too* and *either* are conjunctions.

[113] These data were posted by Soren Wichman on The Linguist, vol 6:1687, the first two sentences are reported as personal communication from H. S. Gopal; the third one from Larry Trask.

170   CHAPTER #5

(56) Ni-k   ardo-a   eta Jone-k   sagardo-a edan
     I-ERG wine-DET and Jon-ERG cider-DET drink-PERF
     ditugu.   (Basque)
     PRES-PL-AUX-1.PL.ERG
     'I (drank) the wine and John drank the cider.'

These data illustrate the same paradox as Arabic: If these sentences involve two clauses one of which has gapped the verb or moved it across-the-board, why is the agreement on the verb plural? Note that Basque does not accept singular in those cases. These sentences reinforce the idea that coordination takes place lower than CP, and lower than the projection at which agreement takes place. However, given that they are interpreted as separate events, they must take place at least at the position where the main clausal event is located. Once we start looking at the Basque cases, things become more surprising, however.[114] The first observation is that object agreement on the verb must be singular[115]:

(57) a. Peru-k   ardoa   eta Mirene-k ura   eskatu
        Peru-ERG wine(SG) and Miren-ERG water(SG) order
        zuten.
        Obj(SG)-AUX-Sub(PL)-PAST
        'Peru ordered wine and Miren water.'
     b. *Peru-k   ardoa   eta Mirene-k ura   eskatu
        Peru-ERG wine(SG) and Miren-ERG water(SG) order
        zituzten.
        Obj(PL)-AUX-Sub(PL)
     c. *Pello-k   ardoa eta Mirene-k ura eskatu
        Pello-ERG wine and Miren-ERG water order
        zuen.
        Obj(SG)-AUX-Sub(SG)-PAST

For some speakers, even plural objects allow singular object agreement:

(58) a. Peru-k   babarrunak eta Mirene-k leka   patatak   jan
        Peru-ERG beans(PL.) and Miren-ERG green beans potatoes(PL.) eat
        dituzte.
        Obj(PL.)-AUX-Sub(PL.)
        'Peru eats beans and Miren potatoes with peas.'

---

[114] Thanks to Pablo Albizu, Arantzazu Elordieta and Gorka Elordieta for the data in this section.
[115] The judgement on (57)b contradicts (56). Since they come from different sources, there may be dialectal variation at stake.

b. Peruk babarrunak eta Mirenek leka patatak jan
Peru-ERG beans(PL.) and Miren-ERG green beans potatoes(PL.) eat
duzte.
Obj(SG.)-AUX-Sub(PL.)
'Peru eats beans and Miren potatoes with green beans.'

Even the speaker that disallows (58)b cannot have plural object agreement when the first object is singular and the second one is plural:

(59) a. Peru-k arroza eta Mirene-k babarrunak jan dute.
Peru-ERG rice(SG) and Miren-ERG beans(PL) eat Obj(SG.)-AUX-Sub(PL)
'Peru eats rice and Miren beans.'
b. ??Peru-k arroza eta Mirene-k babarrunak jan dituzte.
Peru-ERG rice(SG) and Miren-ERG beans(PL.) eat Obj(PL)-AUX-Sub(PL)
'Peru eats rice and Miren beans.'

To complete the paradigm, ditransitive verbs show the following pattern: dative agreement is plural, but object agreement is singular.

(60) a. *Pello-k Miren-i ardoa eta Jon-i ura
Pello-ERG Miren-DAT wine-ACC and Jon-DAT water-ACC
eskaini zion.
offer 3p(SG)ACC-AUX-3(SG)DAT-3P(SG)ERG
'Pello offered wine to Mary and water to Jon.'
b. *Pello-k Miren-i ardoa eta Jon-i ura
Pello-ERG Miren-DAT wine-ACC and Jon-DAT water-ACC
eskaini zizkion.
offer 3P(PL.)ACC-AUX-3(SG.)DAT-3P(SG.)ERG
'Pello offered wine to Mary and water to Jon.'
c. Pello-k Miren-i ardoa eta Jon-i ura
Pello-ERG Miren-DAT wine-ACC and Jon-DAT water-ACC
eskaini zien.
offer 3P(SG.)ACC-AUX-3(PL.)DAT-3P(SG.)ERG
'Pello offered wine to Mary and water to Jon.'
d. *Pello-k Miren-i ardoa eta Jon-i ura
Pello-ERG Miren-DAT wine-ACC and Jon-DAT water-ACC
eskaini zizkien.
offer 3P(S)ACC-AUX-3(SG.)DAT-3P(SG.)ERG
'Pello offered wine to Mary and water to Jon.'

If the second clause has a subject as well, the pattern is similar: subject agreement must be plural, indirect object agreement is also plural, but object agreement can be singular:

(61)   a. *Pello-k   Miren-i   ardoa   eta Gorka-k   Jon-i   ura
         Pello-ERG Miren-DAT wine-ACC and Gorka-ERG Jon-DAT water-ACC
         eskaini   zion.
         offer   3P(SG.)ACC-AUX-3(SG.)DAT-3P(SG.)ERG
         'Pello offered wine to Mary and Gorka water to Jon.'
      b. *Pello-k   Miren-i   ardoa   eta Gorka-k   Jon-i   ura
         Pello-ERG Miren-DAT wine-ACC and Gorka-ERG Jon-DAT water-ACC
         eskaini   zizkion.
         offer   3P(PL.)ACC-AUX-3(SG.)DAT-3P(SG.)ERG
         'Pello offered wine to Mary and Gorka water to Jon.'
      c. Pello-k   Miren-i   ardoa   eta Gorka-k   Jon-i   ura
         Pello-ERG Miren-DAT wine-ACC and Gorka-ERG Jon-DAT water-ACC
         eskaini   zien.
         offer   3P(SG.)ACC-AUX-3(PL.)DAT-3P(SG.)ERG
         'Pello offered wine to Mary and Gorka water to Jon.'
      d. *Pello-k   Miren-i   ardoa   eta Gorka-k   Jon-i   ura
         Pello-ERG Miren-DAT wine-ACC and Gorka-ERG Jon-DAT water-ACC
         eskaini   zizkien.
         offer   3P(SG.)ACC-AUX-3(SG.)DAT-3(SG.)ERG
         'Pello offered wine to Mary and Gorka water to Jon.'

It seems that Basque does not allow coordination lower than the projection where dative agreement takes place (for cases of gapping). Once again, this suggests that coordination involves projections fairly high in the tree.

3. SUMMARY

In this chapter, I have analyzed cases of coordination of higher projections, accusative constructions in Spanish, which I have analyzed as gapping, other general cases of gapping, including gapping in Basque, and right-node-raising. I have argued that the general structure for cases of gapping and RNR involves extra projections that have conjuncts in the specifier. For the case of RNR, I have argued that the right-node-raised element is, in fact, within the second conjunct, contrary to standard assumptions. The evidence relates to the subcategorization possibilities of the last verb conjunction as opposed to the first conjunct. In general, the idea that gapping and RNR involve a predication structure is expected if one assumes the overall analysis developed in this work. At the same time, if coordination always involves predicational projections located high in the functional structure of a sentence, one expects RNR and gapping structures to more much frequent across languages. In particular, many cases of apparent DP coordination will turn out to be gapping, as originally envisioned in the Conjunction Reduction analysis.

REFERENCES

Aoun, Joseph. "The syntax of Doubled Arguments." *Anuario del Seminario de Filología Vasca "Julio de Urquijo"*, 27(3): 709–730, 1993.

Aoun, Joseph. and Elabbas Benmamoun. "Agreement, Coordination and Gapping." Ms. USC and SOAS, 1996.

Aoun, Joseh., Elabbas Benmamoun and Domique Sportiche. "Agreement, Word Order and Conjunction." *Linguistic Inquiry* 25: 195–220, 1994.

Aoun, Joseph, Elabbas Benmamoun and Dominique Sportiche. "Further Remarks on First Conjunct Agreement." *Linguistic Inquiry* 30: 669–82, 1999.

Arnaiz, Alfredo. *N-Words and Wh-in-situ: Nature and Interactions*. Ph.D. thesis, USC, Los Angeles.

Arnaiz, Alfredo and José Camacho. "A Topic Auxiliary in Spanish" In *Advances in Hispanic Linguistics. Papers from the 2nd Hispanic Linguistics Symposium*, edited by J. Gutiérrez-Rexach and F. Martínez-Gil. Somerville, Mass.: Cascadilla Press, 1999.

Bahloul, Maher and Wayne Harbert. "Agreement Asymmetries in Arabic." In *Proceedings of the Eleventh West Coast Conference on Formal Linguistics*, edited by M. Kural and L. Moritz. Stanford: CSLI, 1992.

Baker, Mark *Incorporation: A Theory of Grammatical Function Changing*. Chicago: University of Chicago Press, 1988.

Beghelli, Filippo. and Tim Stowell. "Distributivity and Negation." In *Ways of Scope-Taking*, edited by A. Szabolcsi. Kluwer Academic Press, 1977.

Bello, Andrés. *Gramática de la lengua castellana para el uso de los americanos*. Caracas: Ministerio de Educación, 1972. Originally published in 1847.

Benedicto, Elena. "Verb Movement and Its Eeffects on Determinerless Plural Subjects." In *Romance Linguistics. Theoretical Perspectives*, edited by A. Schwegler, B. Tranel and M. Uribe-Etxebarria. Amsterdam: John Benjamins, 1998.

Benincà, Paola and Guglielmo Cinque On Certain Differences between Enclisis and Proclisis." Paper presented at the University of Geneva, 1990.

Benmamoun, Elabbas. *Functional and Inflectional Morphology: Problems of Projection, Representation and Derivation*. Ph.D. thesis, University of Southern California, 1992

Benmamoun, Elabbas. "Agreement Asymmetries and the PF Interface." In *Research in Afroasiatic Grammar*, edited by J. Lecarme, J. Lowenstamm, and U. Shlonsky, Ur. Amsterdam: Benjamins, 2000a.

Benmamoun, Elabbas. *The Feature Structure of Functional Categories*. Oxford: Oxford University Press, 2000b.

Bonet, Eulalia. *Morphology after Syntax: Pronominal Clitics in Romance*. Ph.D. thesis, MIT, Cambridge, Mass. Distributed by MITWPL, 1991.

Bonet, Eulalia. "Feature Structure of Romance Clitics." *Natural Language and Linguistic Theory* 13: 607–647, 1995.

Borsley, Robert. "In Defense of Coordinate Structures." *Linguistic Analysis* 24: 218–246, 1994.

Bosque, Ignacio. *Sobre la negación*. Madrid: Cátedra, 1980.

Bosque, Ignacio. "Constricciones Morfológicas sobre la Coordinación." *Lingüística española actual* 9: 83–100, 1987.

Bosque, Ignacio. "Sobre el Aspecto en los Adjetivos y en los Participios." In *Tiempo y aspecto en español*, edited by I. Bosque, pp. 177–204. Madrid: Cátedra, 1990.

Bosque, Ignacio. "Sobre las Diferencias entre los Adjetivos Relacionales y los Calificativos." *Revista Argentina de Lingüística* 9: 9–48, 1993.

References

Bosque, Ignacio. "La Negación y el Principio de las Categorías Vacías." In *Estudios de Gramática española*, edited by V. Demonte. México: Nueva Revista de Filología Española, 1993.

Bosque, Ignacio. "Por qué Determinados Sustantivos no son Sustantivos Determinados." In *El Sustantivo sin determinación. La ausencia de determinante en la lengua española*, edited by I. Bosque, pp. 13–120. Madrid: Visor Libros, 1996.

Bosque, Ignacio. "On Specificity and Adjective Position." In *Perspectives on Spanish Linguistic*, edited by J. Gutiérrez-Rexach and L. Silva, UCLA, 1996.

Bowers, John. "The Syntax of Predication." *Linguistic Inquiry* 24: 591–656, 1993.

Calvo Pérez, Julio. *Pragmática y gramática del quechua sureño*. Cuzco, Perú: Centro de Estudios Regionales Andinos Bartolomé de la Casas, 1993.

Camacho, José. "A mixed approach to Spanish clitics." Ms. University of Southern California. Los Angeles, 1993.

Camacho, José. *The Syntax of NP Conjunction*. Ph.D. thesis, University of Southern California, 1997.

Camacho, José. "How Similar are Conjuncts? Against Asymmetric Conjunction." In *Formal Approaches to Romance Syntax*, edited by J.-M. Authier, B. Bullock and L. Reed. Amsterdam: John Benjamins, 1999a.

Camacho, José. "La coordinación." In *Gramática Descriptiva de la Lengua Española*, edited by I. Bosque and V. Demonte. Madrid: Espasa-Calpe, 1999b.

Camacho, José. "On the Structure of Coordination." In *Ellipsis in Conjunction*, edited by K. Schwabe and N. Zhang. Tübingen: Niemeyer Verlag. 2000a.

Camacho, José. "Structural Restrictions on Comitative Coordination." *Linguistic Inquiry* 2: 366–75, 2000b.

Camacho, José. "On the Interpretation of Focus Features." In *Features and Interfaces*, edited by J. Herschenson, E. Mallén and K. Zagona. Philadelphia: Benjamins, 2001.

Camacho, José. and Liliana Sánchez. "Three Types of Conjunction." In *Proceedings of NELS 26*. University of Massachusetts at Amherst: GLSA, 1996.

Casielles, Eugenia. *Topic, Focus and Bare Nominals in Spanish* Ph.D. thesis, University of Massachusetts, 1997.

Chomsky, Noam. *Syntactic Structures*. The Hague: Mouton, 1957

Chomsky, Noam. "Remarks on Nominalization." In *Readings in English Transformational Grammar*, edited by A. Jacobs and P. Rosembaun, pp. 133–187. Waltham, Mass: Ginn and Co, 1970.

Chomsky, Noam. "Conditions on Transformations." In *A Festschrift for Morris Halle*, edited by S. Anderson and P. Kiparsky, pp. 323–86. New York: Holt, Rinehart and Winston, 1973.

Chomsky, Noam. *Knowledge of Language : Its Nature, Origins, and Use*. New York: Praeger, 1986.

Chomsky, Noam. *The Minimalist Program*. Cambridge, MA: MIT Press, 1995.

Cinque, Guglielmo. *Types of A-bar Dependencies*. Cambridge, Mass.: MIT Press, 1990.

Cinque, Guglielmo. *Adverbs and Functional Heads: A Cross-Linguistic Perspective*. Oxford: Oxford University Press, 1999.

Collins, Chris. (1988a): Part 1: "Conjunction Adverbs." Ms. MIT, 1988a.

Collins, Chris. (1988b): Part 2: "Alternative Analyses of Conjunction." Ms. MIT, 1988b.

Contreras, Heles. (1978): *El Orden de Palabras En Español*. Madrid: Cátedra, 1978.

Contreras, Heles. "Spanish Bare NPs and the ECP." In *Generative Studies in Spanish Syntax*, edited by I. Bordelois, H. Contreras and K. Zagona. Dordrecht: Foris, 1986.

Contreras, Heles. "Sobre la Distribución de los Sintagmas Nominales no Predicativos sin Determinante." In *El Sustantivo sin Determinación. La Ausencia de Determinante en la Lengua Española*, edited by I. Bosque, pp. 141–168. Madrid: Visor Libros, 1996.

Corbett, Greville. "Resolution Rules: Agreement in Person, Number, and Gender." In *Order, Concord and Constituency*, edited by E. K. Gerald Gazdar and G. Pullum, chapter 8, pp. 175–213. Dordrecht: Foris, 1983.

Cuervo, Rufino J. "Notas a la Gramática de la Lengua Castellana de D. Andrés Bello." in Bello, *Gramática de la lengua castellana para el uso de los americanos*. Originally published in 1881.

Cusihuamán, Antonio. *Gramática Quechua: Cuzco-Collao.*. Lima: Ministerio de Educación e Instituto de Estudios Peruanos, 1970.

Demonte, Violeta. "Dative Alternation in Spanish." *Probus*, 7: 5–30, 1995.

Everett, Daniel. *Why There are No Clitics. An alternative perspective on pronominal allomorphy*. Arlington, Texas: Summer Institute of Linguistics and University of Texas at Arlington, 1996.

REFERENCES

Fernández Ramírez, Salvador. *Archivo Gramatical de la Lengua Española*. Alcalá de Henares, Spain: Instituto Cervantes. Ed. by Ignacio Bosque, José Antonio Millán and Maria Teresa Rivero, 1995.

Finer, Daniel. *The Formal Grammar of Switch-Reference*. Garland Publishing, 1985.

Franco, Jon. *On Object Agreement in Spanish*. Ph.D. thesis, University of Southern California, Los Angeles, CA. Distributed by GSIL Publications, 1993.

Gazdar, Gerald., Ewan Klein, Geoffrey Pullum and Ivan. Sag. *Generalized Phrase Structure Grammar*. Cambridge, Mass.: Harvard University Press, 1985.

Gildersleeve, B. and G. Lodge *Gildersleeve's Latin Grammar*. London: Macmillan, 3rd edition, 1948.

Gleitmann, Lila. "Coordinating Conjunctions in English." *Language* 41: 260–293, 1965.

Godard, Danielle. "Empty Categories as Subjects of Tensed SS in English or French?" *Linguistic Inquiry* 20: 497–506, 1989.

Goodall, Grant. *Parallel Structures in Syntax*. Cambridge University Press, 1987.

Green, G. "On *Too* and *Either* and Not Just on *Too* and *Either*, Either." In *Papers from the 4th Regional Meeting of the Chicago Linguistic Society*, volume 4, pp. 75–88. Chicago, Ill.: Chicago Linguistic Society, 1968.

Green, G. "The Lexical Expression of Emphatic Conjunction. Theoretical Implications." *Foundations of Language* 10: 191–248, 1974.

Grimshaw, Jane. "The Best Clitic: Constraint Conflict in Morphosyntax." In *Elements of Grammar*, edited by L. Haegeman, pp. 165–196. Dordrecht: Kluwer, 1997.

Haiman, John. "On Some Origins of Switch Reference Marking." In *Switch-Reference and Universal Grammar*, edited by J. Haiman and P. Munro, pp. 105–128. Amsterdam: John Benjamins, 1983.

Hale, Kenneth and Laverne Jeanne. "Hopi workshop notes." Ms. University of Arizona, 1976.

Hernanz, María Lluisa. "Spanish Absolute Constructions and Aspect." In *Catalan Working Papers in Linguistics*, edited by A. Branchadell, B. Palmada, J. Quer, F. Roca and J. Solà, pp. 75–128. Barcelona: Universitat Autònoma de Barcelona, 1991.

Höhle, Tilman. "Assumptions about Asymmetric Coordination." In *GLOW Essays for Henk Van Riemsdijk*, edited by J. Mascaró and M. Nespor. Dordrecht: Foris, 1990.

Jackendoff, Ray. Gapping and Related Rules." *Linguistic Inquiry* 2: 21–35, 1972.

Jackendoff, Ray. *X' syntax: A Study of Phrase Structure*. Cambridge, MA: MIT Press, 1977.

Jaeggli, Osvaldo. *Topics in Romance Syntax*. Dordrecht: Foris, 1982.

Jelinek, Eloise. "Emtpy Categories, Case and Configurationality." *Natural Language and Linguistic Theory*, 2: 39–76, 1984.

Jiménez Juliá, Tomás. "Disyunción Exclusiva e Inclusiva en Español." *Verba* 13: 163–179, 1986.

Johannessen, Jane. *Coordination. A Minimalist Approach*. Ph.D. thesis, University of Oslo, 1993.

Johannessen, Jane. *Coordination*. Oxford: Oxford University Press, 1998.

Johannessen, Jane. "Partial Agreement and Coordination." *Linguistic Inquiry* 27: 661–676, 1996.

Johnson, Kyle. "Bridging the Gap." Ms. University of Massachusetts, Amherst, 1994.

Johnson, Kyle. Gapping Determiners." In *Ellipsis in Conjunction*, edited by K. Schwabe and N. Zhang. Tübingen: Niemeyer Verlag, 2000.

Kany, Charles. *American Spanish Syntax*. Chicago: University of Chicago Press, 1951.

Kayne, Richard. *Connectedness and Binary Binding*. Dordrecht: Foris, 1984.

Kayne, Richard. *The Antisymmetry of Syntax*. Cambridge, MA.: MIT Press, 1994.

Keyser, Samuel J. and Paul Postal. *Beginning English Grammar*. New York: Harper and Row, 1976.

Koutsoudas, Andreas. "Gapping, Conjunction Reduction, and Identity of Deletion." *Foundations of Language* 7: 337–386, 1971.

Laca, Brenda. "Presencia y ausencia de determinante" in *Gramática Descriptiva de la Lengua Española*, edited by I. Bosque and V. Demonte. Madrid: Espasa-Calpe, 1999

Laka, Itziar. *Negation in Syntax. On the Nature of Functional Categories and Projections*. Ph.D. thesis, MIT, Cambridge, Mass, 1990.

Lakoff, George. "Frame Semantic Control of the CSC." In *CLS 22 part 2. Papers from the Parasession on Pragmatics and Grammatical Relations*, edited by A. M. Farley. et al., volume 22. Chicago, Ill.: University of Chicago, 1986.

Larson, Richard. "On the Syntax of Disjunction Scope." *Natural Language and Linguistic Inquiry*, 3: 217–264, 1985.

Larson, Richard. "On the Double Object Construction." *Linguistic Inquiry* 19: 335–391, 1988.

Lasersohn, Peter. *Plurality, Conjunction and Events*. Dordrecht: Kluwer Academic Publishers, 1995.

Lasnik, Howard. "Pseudogapping." Presentation at the University of California, Irvine, 1991.

Levin, Nancy. "Some Identity-of-sense Deletions Puzzle me. Do They You?" In *Papers from the 14th Regional Meeting of the Chicago Linguistic Society*, volume 14, pp. 229–240. Chicago, Ill.: Chicago Linguistic Society, 1978.

Link, Godehart. "The Logical Analysis of Plurals and Mass Terms: A lattice-theoretical Approach." In *Meaning, Use and Interpretation of Language*, edited by R. Bäurerle, C. Schwartz and A. Von Stechow, pp. 302–23. Berlin: Walter de Gruyter, 1983.

Longobardi, Giuseppe. "Reference and Proper Names." *Linguistic Inquiry* 25: 609–666, 1994.

McCloskey, James. "Inflection and Conjunction in Modern Irish." *Natural Language and Linguistic Theory* 4: 245–281, 1986.

McCloskey, James and Kenneth Hale "On the Syntax of Person-number Inflection in Modern Irish." *Natural Language and Linguistic Theory* 1: 487–533, 1984.

McNally, Louise. Comitative Coordination: A Case Study in Group Formation." *Natural Language and Linguistic Theory* 11: 347–379, 1993.

Milner, Jean-Claude. "Interpretive Chains, Floating quantifiers and Exhaustive Interpretation." In *Studies in Romance Languages*, edited by C. Neidle and R. Nuñez-Cedeño, pp. 181–202. Dordrecht: Foris, 1987.

Mohammad, Mohammad. *The Sentence Structure of Arabic*. Ph.D. thesis, University of Southern California, 1989.

Montalbetti, Mario. *After Binding*. Ph.D. thesis, MIT, 1984.

Munn, Alan. "A Null Operator Analysis of ATB Gaps." *Linguistic Review* 9: 1–26, 1992.

Munn, Alan. *Topics in the Syntax and Semantics of Coordinate Structures*. Ph.D. thesis, University of Maryland, 1993.

Munn, Alan. First Conjunct Agreement: Against a Clausal Analysis." *Linguistic Inquiry* 4: 669–682. Michigan State University, 1999.

Munro, Pamela. "On the Syntactic Status of Switch-reference Clauses: The Special Case of Mojave Comitatives." In *Studies of Switch-Reference*, UCLA Papers in Syntax 8. Department of Linguistics, UCLA, 1980.

Munro, Pamela and John Haiman. *Switch-Reference and Universal Grammar*. John Benjamins, 1983.

Perlmutter, David. *Deep and Surface Structure Constraints in Syntax*. Holt, Rinehard and Winston, 1971.

Pesetsky, David. *Paths and Categories*. Ph.D. thesis, MIT, Cambridge, Mass, 1982.

Pesetsky, David. "Language-particular Processes and the Earliness Principle." Ms. MIT, 1989.

Pollock, Jean-Yves. "Verb Movement, Universal Grammar, and the Structure of IP." *Linguistic Inquiry*, 20: 365–424, 1989.

Postal, Paul. "The Status of the Coordinate Structure Constraint." Ms. New York University, 1995.

Progovac, Ljiljana. "Slavic and the Structure for Coordination." In *Formal Approaches to Slavic Linguistics*, edited by M. Lidseth and S. Franks, pp. 207–23. Ann Arbor: Michigan Slavic Publications, 1997.

Pullum, Geoffrey and Arnold Zwicky. "Phonological Resolution of Syntactic Feature Conflict." *Language* 62: 751–773, 1986.

Pustejovsky, James. "The Syntax of Event Structure." In *Lexical and Conceptual Semantics*, edited by B. Levin and S. Pinker. Cambridge, Blackwell, 1991.

Rigau, Gemma. "Predication Holistique et Sujet Nul." *Révue des Langues Romanes* 6: 201–221, 1989.

Rigau, Gemma. The Semantic Nature of Some Romance Prepositions." In *Grammar in progress: GLOW essays in honour of Henk van Riemsdijk*, edited by J. Mascaró and M. Nespor, pp. 363–373. Dordrecht: Foris, 1990.

Ross, John R. *Constraints on Variables in Syntax*. Ph.D. thesis, MIT, 1967.

Ross, John R. "Gapping and the order of constituents." In *Progress in Linguistics*, edited by K. Heidolph. The Hague: Mouton, 1970.

Sag, Ivan, Gerald Gazdar, Thomas Wasow and Steven Weisler. "Coordination and How to Distinguish Categories." *Natural Language and Linguistic Theory*, 3: 117–171, 1985.

Sánchez, Liliana. *Syntactic Structures in Nominals: A Comparative Study of Spanish and Southern Quechua*. Ph.D. thesis, University of Southern California, 1995.

Sánchez, Liliana. "Clitic Doubling and the Checking of Exhaustive Focus." Ms. Rutgers University, 2003.

Schachter, Paul. "Constraints on Coordination." *Language* 53: 86–103, 1977.

Schein, Barry. "Conjunction reduction redux." Ms. University of Southern California, 1992.

REFERENCES

Schein, Barry. "DP and DP." Chapt. 2 of "Conjunction Reduction Redux". University of Southern California, 2001.
Schmitt, Cristina. "Lack of Iteration: Accusative Clitic Doubling, Participial Absolutes and *have*+agreeing Participles." *Probus* 10, 243-300, 1998.
Siegel, Muffy. "Gapping and Interpretation." *Linguistic Inquiry* 15: 523–30, 1984.
Silva-Corvalán, Carmen. The Difussion of Object-verb Agreement in Spanish." In *Proceedings of the Tenth Anniversary Symposium on Romance Linguistics: Papers in Romance*, edited by H. Contreras and J. Klausenburger, pp. 163–176. Seattle: University of Washington, 1981.
Sportiche, Dominique. "Clitic Constructions." In *Phrase Structure and the Lexicon*, edited by J. Rooryck and L. Zaring. Dordrecht: Kluwer, 1996.
Stirling, Lesley. *Switch-Reference and Discourse Representation*. Cambridge: Cambridge University Press, 1993.
Stockwell, Robert, Paul Schachter and Barbara Partee (1977): *Major Syntactic Categories of English*. New York: Holt, Rinehart and Winston, 1977.
Suñer, Avel.lina. *La Predicación Secundaria en Español*. Ph.D. thesis, Universitat Autònoma de Barcelona, 1990.
Thiersch, Craig. "Asymmetrical Coordination as Adjunction." Ms. Revised version of a GLOW talk, 1994.
Toporisic, J. *Slovenski Knjizýni jezik*, volume 3. Maribor: Zalozỳba Obzorja, 1972.
Torrego, Esther. "On Quantifier Float in Control Clauses." *Linguistic Inquiry* 27: 111–126, 1996.
Uriagereka, Juan. "Aspects of the Syntax of Clitic Placement in Western Romance." *Linguistic Inquiry* 26: 79–124, 1995.
van Oirsouw, Robert. *The Syntax of Coordination*. London: Croom Helm, 1987.
Webber, Bonnie. *A Formal Approach to Discourse Anaphora*. Ph.D. thesis, Harvard University, Cambridge, MA, 1978.
Williams, Edwin. "Across-the-board Rule Application." *Linguistic Inquiry* 9: 31–43, 1978
Woolford, Ellen. "An ECP Account of Constraints on Across-The-Board Extraction." *Linguistic Inquiry* 18, 1987.
Zagona, Karen. *The Syntax of Spanish* Cambridge University Press, 2002.
Zoerner, Edward. *Coordination: The Syntax of &P*. Ph.D. thesis, University of California, Irvine, Irvine, CA, 1995.

INDEX

across-the-board movement 4, 64, 70, 72, 74, 106, 156, 161, 172
adjectives
    extensional 28, 29, 30, 133
    intensional 28, 29, 133
    relational 29
adverbs
    propositional 25
agreement
    feminine 95
    full adjectival 135
    full, number 134
    gender 95–99, 98
    LF 93, 94, 104, 113, 117
    masculine 95
    partial 2, 10, 70, 91–102, 96, 104–31, 135, 136, 145, 150, 151, 161, 163, 164
    partial, and word order 91
    partial, gender 134
    partial, number 134
    PF 93, 94, 98, 104, 115, 116, 117, 125, 130
    referential nouns vs. abstract nouns 131
    semantically plural 107
    singular 25, 93, 99, 102, 107, 113, 118, 130
anaphor 88, 89, 93, 94, 104, 108
antecedents. 89
Aoun, Benmamoun and Sportiche 10, 21, 70, 91, 93, 100, 104, 107, 114, 115, 163
Arabic 11, 25, 70, 91, 100, 104, 105, 109, 110, 111, 113, 114–19, 120, 124, 125–26, 128, 150, 151, 163, 172
    Lebanese 93, 105
    Morrocan 91, 105
    number 125

pronominal binding 21
Artstein 66

Bantu 87
bare nouns 72, 142
bare plurals 144
Basque 36, 172, 174
    gapping 174
Benincá and Cinque 63
binders 89
Binding Theory 16, 18, 62
Boolean Phrase 16
Bosque 62–65, 66–68
Brazilian Portuguese 91, 104, 108, 109–14, 117, 124, 125, 129

Camacho iii, 1, 4, 5, 10, 11, 12, 13, 19, 21, 22, 24, 27, 33, 42, 45, 57, 58, 145, 175
case 80, 81, 84
    checking 87
Catalan
    comitatives 15
categorial matrix 90
c-command
    asymmetries in 1, 16, 18, 22
    pragmatics and 17–18
Chomsky 1, 6, 19, 22, 39, 51, 55, 62, 64, 78, 154
clitic
    feature underspecification 79
Clitic Left Dislocation 101
clitics
    coordination and \r 63
    dative 146, 147, 149, 150
CLLD 101, 102, 150
comitatives 21, 46, 47, 48, 49
    collectivity and 21, 58
conjunction
    group forming operator 22
    phrase 5, 17, 22, 88, 89, 114
    Reduction 1, 6, 22, 39, 43, 44, 49
    transformation 1
coordination
    anaphors and 7, 30, 69, 70, 71, 88, 94, 105, 107, 109, 114, 115, 124
    anaphors and 122
    asymmetric 10, 69, 153, 154
    balanced See coordination, symmetric
    constituency effects of 70
    internal structure of 1
    plurals and 17, 25
    propositional interpretation of 22

INDEX

symmetric 1, 5, 86
tridimensional structure for 6
unbalanced 1, 10, 69, 114, 139. See also coordination, asymmetric
Czech 93, 104

Dalrymple and Kaplan 4, 87, 161
Dative Clitic Phrase 148
determiners 97, 129, 130, 131, 133
disjunction 137, 138, 141
    exclusive 137, 138, 139, 141
    inclusive 137
distributive operator 139

ellipsis 1, 70, 71
English v, 4, 7, 10, 25, 33, 34, 37, 42, 49, 51, 54, 75, 82, 92, 119, 125, 129, 132, 137, 139, 142, 143, 146, 156, 161

feature
    formal 85
    indeterminacy 11
    resolution 11, 13, 16, 87
    underspecification 59, 78
feminine 96, 97, 108, 123, 135
focus 18, 30, 165
French 64, 65, 134, 139
fusion 84, 85

gapping 2, 21, 27, 31, 41, 43, 99, 100, 101, 115, 116, 119, 145, 151, 153, 155, 156, 158, 164–68, 170, 171, 174
Gazdar 37
gender 13, 16, 95, 97, 98, 104, 105, 109, 116, 129, 134, 136
German 92, 109, 115, 117, 124, 125
    asymmetric coordination 14–15, 153–55
Goodall 5, 6–7, 9, 16, 22, 31, 34, 39

Haiman 40, 41, 42, 177, 178
Haiman and Munro 40
Hale and Jeanne 41, 42, 43, 46
head-initial languages 10
heads
    coordination of 62
Hopi 42, 44, 46, 49, 128
    switch reference 43

interpretation
    collective 23, 77, 139
    distributive 21, 23, 58, 76, 77, 100, 104, 106, 137, 140, 141, 147

group-like See interpretation, collective
Irish 93, 94, 114, 117, 125, 126–28, 151
    analytic form 126, 127, 128
    salient unaccusatives 127
    synthetic form 126, 127, 128
Italian 23, 63, 131

Johannessen 1, 5, 6, 7, 10, 23, 33, 34, 88, 92, 93, 104, 114, 115

Kany 146
Kaplan and Maxwell 5, 6, 7, 8, 9
Kayne 16, 34, 59, 60, 67, 68, 99, 131, 133
Kayne \r 63

Lakoff 155
Lasnik 156
Latin 79, 122, 136, 145
Law of Coordination of Likes See Wasow's generalization
Leftness Condition 19, 20
Lexical-Functional Grammar 7
licensing symmetry 1, 3, 4, 5, 6, 7, 9, 14, 16, 39, 89
Longobardi 23, 130, 131

masculine 95, 97, 98, 109, 135
matrix
    categorial 78–82
    nominal 86
McCloskey 93, 94, 126, 127, 128
McCloskey and Hale 94
McNally 21
Mojave 40, 46, 47, 48, 49, 50, 51, 128
Munn 1, 5, 10, 16, 17, 19, 22, 23, 27, 88, 89, 104, 107, 109, 110, 111, 113, 114, 129
Munro 40, 41, 46, 47, 48, 49, 177

Negation 12, 35
Norwegian 7, 10, 33
NPI 20, 21, 22, 35, 36, 141, 168

Ono 41, 42

Pesetsky 75, 82
plurals 22, 23, 24, 25, 27, 30, 31, 88, 107, 128
postsyntactic merger 116, 117, 125, 127, 128, 150, 151
predicate
    collective 23, 31, 94, 105
    individual-level 94, 109, 111, 124, 143
    stage-level 94, 109

Progovac 5, 16, 17, 18, 19, 20, 21, 22
Pullum and Zwicky 4, 5, 176, 177

quantifer binding 19
Quechua
    Southern 57, 58

referential nouns 132
resolution rules 88
Rigau 15
Right Node Raising 26, 131, 157–61, 174
Ross 69, 120, 155, 156

salient unaccusatives 127
Sánchez iii, 28, 29, 37, 57, 58, 99, 133, 166, 176
Schachter 154
Schein iii, 2, 20, 22, 25, 27, 54, 108, 109, 143, 160, 161
Schmitt 111
Siegel 156
Spanish v, 4, 11, 13, 17, 20, 22, 25, 26, 29, 33, 34, 35, 36, 37, 42, 51, 54, 60, 66, 68, 69, 72, 73, 75, 81, 91, 99, 104, 108, 111, 113, 117, 124, 125, 129, 131, 132, 135, 137, 139, 140, 142, 143, 144, 145, 146, 150, 151, 160, 161, 164, 165, 169, 174
    adjectival agreement 125, 129, 135
    adjectives 95–99
    adverbs 26
    Clitic coordination 62–65
    comitatives 15
    coordination of temporal categories 12
    Latin American 79
    plurals 23
    right-node-raising 26
spec-head configuration 5, 114, 117
SR See switch-reference
Stirling 40, 41
switch-reference 40, 43, 44, 45, 47
    coordination and 42, 46, 47
    different subject 40, 42, 43, 45, 48, 49
    gapping 41–42
    Hopi 43
    Mojave 46
    same subject 40, 41, 42, 48, 49

tense 8, 9, 12, 13, 82, 83, 116, 126
Thiersch 5, 14–15, 153–55, 154

Uriagereka 149

Wasow's generalization 4, 5, 12, 13, 16, 26
wh-words
   coordination and 75, 78
   D-linked 75, 76
Williams 4, 70, 72, 89, 106

Xhosa 87

Zoerner 1, 5, 31, 34, 51, 75, 87, 119, 156, 157, 159, 161, 162, 163

φ-features 16, 78, 80, 81, 83, 88, 122, 125, 127, 128, 136, 151

Studies in Natural Language and Linguistic Theory

Managing Editors
Liliane Haegeman, *University of Geneva*
Joan Maling, *Brandeis University*
James McCloskey, *University of California, Santa Cruz*

Publications
1. L. Burzio: *Italian Syntax.* A Government-binding Approach. 1986.
   ISBN Hb 90-277-2014-2; Pb 90-277-2015-0
2. W.D. Davies: *Choctaw Verb Agreement and Universal Grammar.* 1986.
   ISBN Hb 90-277-2065-7; Pb 90-277-2142-4
3. K. É. Kiss: *Configurationality in Hungarian.* 1987.
   ISBN Hb 90-277-1907-1; Pb 90-277-2456-3
4. D. Pulleyblank: *Tone in Lexical Phonology.* 1986.
   ISBN Hb 90-277-2123-8; Pb 90-277-2124-6
5. L. Hellan and K. K. Christensen: *Topics in Scandinavian Syntax.* 1986.
   ISBN Hb 90-277-2166-1; Pb 90-277-2167-X
6. K. P. Mohanan: *The Theory of Lexical Phonology.* 1986.
   ISBN Hb 90-277-2226-9; Pb 90-277-2227-7
7. J. L. Aissen: *Tzotzil Clause Structure.* 1987.
   ISBN Hb 90-277-2365-6; Pb 90-277-2441-5
8. T. Gunji: *Japanese Phrase Structure Grammar.* A Unification-based Approach. 1987.　　ISBN 1-55608-020-4
9. W. U. Wurzel: *Inflectional Morphology and Naturalness.* 1989
   ISBN Hb 1-55608-025-5; Pb 1-55608-026-3
10. C. Neidle: *The Role of Case in Russian Syntax.* 1988　　ISBN 1-55608-042-5
11. C. Lefebvre and P. Muysken: *Mixed Categories.* Nominalizations in Quechua. 1988.　　ISBN Hb 1-55608-050-6; Pb 1-55608-051-4
12. K. Michelson: *A Comparative Study of Lake-Iroquoian Accent.* 1988
    ISBN 1-55608-054-9
13. K. Zagona: *Verb Phrase Syntax.* A Parametric Study of English and Spanish. 1988　　ISBN Hb 1-55608-064-6; Pb 1-55608-065-4
14. R. Hendrick: *Anaphora in Celtic and Universal Grammar.* 1988
    ISBN 1-55608-066-2
15. O. Jaeggli and K.J. Safir (eds.): *The Null Subject Parameter.* 1989
    ISBN Hb 1-55608-086-7; Pb 1-55608-087-5
16. H. Lasnik: *Essays on Anaphora.* 1989
    ISBN Hb 1-55608-090-5; Pb 1-55608-091-3
17. S. Steele: *Agreement and Anti-Agreement.* A Syntax of Luiseño. 1990
    ISBN 0-7923-0260-5
18. E. Pearce: *Parameters in Old French Syntax.* Infinitival Complements. 1990
    ISBN Hb 0-7923-0432-2; Pb 0-7923-0433-0
19. Y.A. Li: *Order and Constituency in Mandarin Chinese.* 1990
    ISBN 0-7923-0500-0

Studies in Natural Language and Linguistic Theory

20. H. Lasnik: *Essays on Restrictiveness and Learnability.* 1990
    ISBN 0-7923-0628-7; Pb 0-7923-0629-5
21. M.J. Speas: *Phrase Structure in Natural Language.* 1990
    ISBN 0-7923-0755-0; Pb 0-7923-0866-2
22. H. Haider and K. Netter (eds.): *Representation and Derivation in the Theory of Grammar.* 1991 ISBN 0-7923-1150-7
23. J. Simpson: *Warlpiri Morpho-Syntax.* A Lexicalist Approach. 1991
    ISBN 0-7923-1292-9
24. C. Georgopoulos: *Syntactic Variables.* Resumptive Pronouns and A' Binding in Palauan. 1991 ISBN 0-7923-1293-7
25. K. Leffel and D. Bouchard (eds.): *Views on Phrase Structure.* 1991
    ISBN 0-7923-1295-3
26. C. Tellier: *Licensing Theory and French Parasitic Gaps.* 1991
    ISBN 0-7923-1311-9; Pb 0-7923-1323-2
27. S.-Y. Kuroda: *Japanese Syntax and Semantics.* Collected Papers. 1992
    ISBN 0-7923-1390-9; Pb 0-7923-1391-7
28. I. Roberts: *Verbs and Diachronic Syntax.* A Comparative History of English and French. 1992 ISBN 0-7923-1705-X
29. A. Fassi Fehri: *Issues in the Structure of Arabic Clauses and Words.* 1993
    ISBN 0-7923-2082-4
30. M. Bittner: *Case, Scope, and Binding.* 1994 ISBN 0-7923-2649-0
31. H. Haider, S. Olsen and S. Vikner (eds.): *Studies in Comparative Germanic Syntax.* 1995 ISBN 0-7923-3280-6
32. N. Duffield: *Particles and Projections in Irish Syntax.* 1995
    ISBN 0-7923-3550-3; Pb 0-7923-3674-7
33. J. Rooryck and L. Zaring (eds.): *Phrase Structure and the Lexicon.* 1996
    ISBN 0-7923-3745-X
34. J. Bayer: *Directionality and Logical Form.* On the Scope of Focusing Particles and Wh-in-situ. 1996 ISBN 0-7923-3752-2
35. R. Freidin (ed.): *Current Issues in Comparative Grammar.* 1996
    ISBN 0-7923-3778-6; Pb 0-7923-3779-4
36. C.-T.J. Huang and Y.-H.A. Li (eds.): *New Horizons in Chinese Linguistics.* 1996 ISBN 0-7923-3867-7; Pb 0-7923-3868-5
37. A. Watanabe: *Case Absorption and WH-Agreement.* 1996
    ISBN 0-7923-4203-8
38. H. Thráinsson, S.D. Epstein and S. Peter (eds.): *Studies in Comparative Germanic Syntax.* Volume II. 1996 ISBN 0-7923-4215-1
39. C.J.W. Zwart: *Morphosyntax of Verb Movement.* A Minimalist Approach to the Syntax of Dutch. 1997 ISBN 0-7923-4263-1; Pb 0-7923-4264-X
40. T. Siloni: *Noun Phrases and Nominalizations.* The Syntax of DPs. 1997
    ISBN 0-7923-4608-4
41. B.S. Vance: *Syntactic Change in Medieval French.* 1997 ISBN 0-7923-4669-6
42. G. Müller: *Incomplete Category Fronting.* A Derivational Approach to Remnant Movement in German. 1998 ISBN 0-7923-4837-0

Studies in Natural Language and Linguistic Theory

43. A. Alexiadou, G. Horrocks and M. Stavrou (eds.): *Studies in Greek Syntax.* 1998 ISBN 0-7923-5290-4
44. R. Sybesma: *The Mandarin VP.* 1999 ISBN 0-7923-5462-1
45. K. Johnson and I. Roberts (eds.): *Beyond Principles and Parameters.* Essays in Memory of Osvaldo Jaeggli. 1999 ISBN 0-7923-5501-6
46. R.M. Bhatt: *Verb Movement and the Syntax of Kashmiri.* 1999
 ISBN 0-7923-6033-8
47. A. Neeleman and F. Weerman: *Flexible Syntax.* A Theory of Case and Arguments. 1999 ISBN 0-7923-6058-3
48. C. Gerfen: *Phonology and Phonetics in Coatzospan Mixtec.* 1999
 ISBN 0-7923-6034-6
49. I. Paul, V. Phillips and L. Travis (eds.): *Formal Issues in Austronesian Linguistics.* 2000 ISBN 0-7923-6068-0
50. M. Frascarelli: *The Syntax-Phonology Interface in Focus and Topic Constructions in Italian.* 2000 ISBN 0-7923-6240-3
51. I. Landau: *Elements of Control.* Structure and Meaning in Infinitival Constructions. 2000 ISBN 0-7923-6620-4
52. W.D. Davies and S. Dubinsky (eds.): *Objects and other Subjects.* Grammatical Functions, Functional Categories and Configurationality. 2001
 ISBN 1-4020-0064-2; Pb 1-4020-0065-0
53. J. Ouhalla and U. Shlonsky (eds.): *Themes in Arabic and Hebrew Syntax.* 2002
 ISBN 1-4020-0536-9; Pb 1-4020-0537-7
54. E. Haeberli: *Features, Categories and the Syntax of A-Positions.* Cross-Linguistic Variation in the Germanic Languages. 2002
 ISBN 1-4020-0854-6; Pb 1-4020-0855-4
55. J. McDonough: *The Navajo Sound System.* 2003
 ISBN 1-4020-1351-5; Pb 1-4020-1352-3
56. D.E. Holt: *Optimality Theory and Language Change.* 2003
 ISBN 1-4020-1469-4; Pb 1-4020-1470-8
57. J. Camacho: *The Structure of Coordination.* Conjunction and Agreement Phenomena in Spanish and Other Languages. 2003
 ISBN 1-4020-1510-0; Pb 1-4020-1511-9

Kluwer Academic Publishers – Dordrecht / Boston / London